MYTHS AND REALITIES OF EXECUTIVE PAY

The executive pay model used widely in the United States is essential both to the continued success of companies and to the U.S. economy itself. The successful application of this model, which is built on the foundation of pay-for-performance, has helped create an economic juggernaut, resulting in trillions of dollars of wealth for shareholders and substantial income and net worth for millions of corporate employees and their families. High executive pay simply reflects the strong demand for top talent and can be evaluated with consideration of the performance that leads to high pay. Yet, myths of a failed model still abound, perpetuated by occasional excesses, recent corporate scandals, and controversy over the use of stock options. This book documents the realities of executive compensation by investigating the extent to which the pay-for-performance model governs executive pay levels. It also assesses the relative success of this model in creating value for shareholders and robust job growth for U.S. employees and provides detailed, real-world guidance for designing and executing effective executive compensation plans. Based on extensive empirical research and decades of direct experience in the field, *Myths and Realities of Executive Pay* settles the debate about executive compensation and the role it plays in the broader U.S. economy.

Ira T. Kay, Ph.D., global practice director of executive compensation consulting at Watson Wyatt Worldwide, headquartered in Washington, DC, is a nationally recognized expert on executive compensation. He has helped U.S. public, private, and international companies develop annual and long-term incentive plans to increase shareholder value. Dr. Kay has written and spoken extensively on executive compensation issues and conducted research on executive pay, stock ownership, and stock options. He is coauthor of the book *The Human Capital Edge* and is the author of *CEO Pay and Shareholder Value: Helping the U.S. Win the Global Economic War* and *Value at the Top: Solutions to the Executive Compensation Crisis.* Dr. Kay has published articles in the *Harvard Business Review*, *McKinsey Quarterly, Journal of Deferred Compensation*, and *Across the Board.* He has also presented analysis of executive compensation issues before the Federal Reserve Board, the Securities and Exchange Commission, the Financial Accounting Standards Board, and a U.S. Senate subcommittee. He is frequently quoted in the major business press and speaks globally on executive compensation issues.

Steven Van Putten is the East region practice leader of Watson Wyatt's executive compensation consulting practice. He focuses primarily on advising compensation committees and senior management on executive and director compensation matters. Mr. Van Putten has spoken and written on executive and incentive compensation and specializes in the design and development of annual and long-term incentive programs that drive business strategy and support organizational objectives. He is also an expert on FAS 123(R) and its implications for stock-based incentives.

MYTHS AND REALITIES OF EXECUTIVE PAY

Ira T. Kay, Ph.D.

Watson Wyatt Worldwide

Steven Van Putten

Watson Wyatt Worldwide

CAMBRIDGE
UNIVERSITY PRESS

CAMBRIDGE UNIVERSITY PRESS
Cambridge, New York, Melbourne, Madrid, Cape Town, Singapore, São Paulo, Delhi

Cambridge University Press
32 Avenue of the Americas, New York, NY 10013-2473, USA

www.cambridge.org
Information on this title: www.cambridge.org/9780521871952

First published 2007

Printed in the United States of America

A catalog record for this publication is available from the British Library.

Library of Congress Cataloging in Publication Data

Kay, Ira T.
Myths and realities of executive pay / Ira T. Kay, Steven Van Putten.
    p.   cm.
Includes bibliographical references and index.
ISBN 978-0-521-87195-2 (hardback)
1. Chief executive officers – Salaries, etc. – United States.   2. Executive ability –
United States.   3. Competition, International.   I. Van Putten, Steven.   II. Title.
HD4965.5.U6K389   2007
331.2′8165800973–dc22   2007000721

ISBN   978-0-521-87195-2 hardback

Contents

Acknowledgments   *page* xi
Prologue: The Compensation Committee Meets   xiii

Introduction: The Battle over Executive Compensation **1**

Executive Compensation in the U.S. Corporate Model   3
The Goals of Executive Compensation   4
Our Approach   6
    Our Views, 6

1 The Myths and Realities of Pay-for-Performance **8**

The Realities of Pay-for-Performance   9
Other Issues   22
Case Studies of Pay-for-Performance   23

2 Managerial Power **28**

Academic Response to Bebchuk and Fried   30
The Realities of Managerial Power   33
Camouflaged Compensation   35
At-the-Money Strike Prices   36
Repricings and Reloads   38
Diversifying, Hedging, and Timing   38
Peer Group Data and Upward Bias   39
Other Factors in Setting Pay   40
Fixed Shares versus Constant-Dollar Techniques   42
Conflicts of Interest   44
Conclusion   45

3 External Pressures: The New Context for Executive Compensation **47**

Characteristics of External Forces   47
Cyclical Reforms and Unintended Consequences   49

The Genesis of the Current Environment   50
The Regulators   52

    Securities and Exchange Commission, 52 • Financial
    Accounting Standards Board, 54 • Internal Revenue
    Service, 54 • NYSE and NASDAQ, 55 • Congress, 57

The Reformers   58

    Institutional Investor Perspectives, 60

Concerns with Lack of Pay-for-Performance   60

    Stock Incentives, 61 • Performance Metrics, 62 • Severance
    and Change-in-Control Agreements, 62

The Financial Activists   64
LBO Impact   64

    Impact of Change-in-Control Protection, 66 • Hedge
    Funds, 67

Media Critics and Public Figures   68
What We Can Learn   69

4 End of an Era: The Decline of the Stock Option 71

The 1990s: The Decade of the Stock Option   72
2000–2002: A Turning Point   75
The Decline of the Stock Option   76
The Realities of Expensing   77
Perceived Value   79
The Case for Stock Options   81

    Growth Companies, 82 • Situational Cases, 82

Costs and Stock Prices   83
Reducing the Expense   85

5 The Future of Long-Term Incentives 87

Factors Influencing LTI Design   89
Designing an LTI Program   89

    Setting Performance Goals and Metrics, 95

Basis for Measurement   98

    Internal Goals, 99 • External Goals/Indexing, 99 • Hybrid
    Goals, 100

Goal Setting   101
Determining Share Award Sizes   103
A Look to the Future   105

**6 Executive Stock Ownership: The Solution to the Executive
Compensation Crisis 107**

Agency Theory and Costs   107

Moral Hazard   109
Driving Superior Returns   110
    Stock Incentive Levels and Structures Are in
    Transition, 114
Stock Ownership Guidelines   114
Stock Holding Requirements   115
Net Share Retention Requirements   116
Other Mechanisms for Creating Ownership   118
Management Stock Purchase Plans   119
    Tax Implications, 120 • FAS 123(R), 121
Finding the Right Solutions   121

7 Director Compensation in the New Environment **123**
The Evolution of Director Compensation   125
Move Away from Stock Options   126
Activity-Based Compensation   128
Compensating Committee Chairs and Members   128
General Electric as a Reference Point   130
Director Compensation Levels and Mix   131
Director Share Ownership   132
Stock Ownership Guidelines   133
Net Share Holding Requirements   134
Ownership Effectiveness   135
Structuring the Optimal Director Compensation Package   137
The Future of Director Compensation   139

8 The Compensation Committee: Creating a Balance between
Shareholders and Executives **141**
Legal Context   142
Right from Wrong?   144
    Are Stock Options Performance-Based? 144 • Are
    Performance Shares the Perfect Solution? 145 • Should
    Directors Be Required to Own Company Stock? 145 •
    Should Peer Groups Be Used to Set Executive Pay? 145 •
    What Constitutes a Good Board Member? 145
Foundations for Best Practices   146
Creating Excellence in Corporate Governance   147
Institutional and Regulatory Governance Recommendations
    and Mandates   148
Consultant Independence   150
Setting the CEO's Pay as Rigorously as Possible   151
Case Study of an Internal Promotion   152
Creating a Pay-for-Performance Environment   154

Rule 10b5–1 Plans – Preannounced Purchases or Sales of
Stock   159
Best Governance Practices in Designing Annual and
Long-Term Incentives   161

9 Aligning All Employee Pay to Improve Corporate Performance 162

Elements of Alignment   163
    Aligning Architecture and Performance Measures, 163
Untenable Forms of Alignment   164
Performance-Pay Solutions   165
    Merit Increases, 167 • Short-Term Incentives, 168 •
    Stock-Based Incentives, 169
Employee Stock Ownership   169
The Role of Stock Options   170
Moving Beyond Options   172
Converting to Restricted Stock   174
Adjusting Stock-Based Incentives   176
Alignment in Practice   177
Building Better Alignment   178

10 International Executive Pay Comparisons 180

U.S. Competitive Advantage   181
The International Executive Pay Gap   183
United Kingdom   185
France   189
Canada   192
Asia   194
    Japan, 197 • Singapore, 197 • China, 197 • Hong Kong,
    199
Summary   202

Conclusion: The Future of Executive Compensation 204

Epilogue: Back in the Boardroom 209

**Appendix A. Legal and Regulatory Requirements for Executive
Compensation Plans 215**

Nonqualified Stock Options   215
Incentive Stock Options   218
Stock Appreciation Rights   219
Restricted Stock Units   222
Restricted Stock   226

Appendix B. Summary of the Regulatory and Institutional Mandates and Recommendations **229**

CalPERS   229
TIAA–CREF   230
Fidelity   231
Vanguard   232
Union-Sponsored Funds   232
Other Organizations   234

    The Council of Institutional Investors, 234 • Institutional Shareholder Services, 236 • Glass, Lewis & Company, 238 • National Association of Corporate Directors, 239 • The Conference Board, 240

Appendix C. Academic Articles on Pay-for-Performance and the Effectiveness of the Executive Labor Market **243**

Notes   247
Index   253

Acknowledgments

The myths of ever-rising executive pay, unchecked management power, and a failed pay-for-performance model, perpetuated by the media, have reached a visceral crescendo. We have reached a critical juncture in the future of executive pay. We present a different and successful reality of executive pay comprising pay-for-performance, an efficient labor market, and an effective corporate governance model. This reality is based on extensive primary and secondary research combined with dozens of years of experience consulting to successful corporations. In our effort to separate fact from fiction and thus dispel the myths surrounding executive compensation, we are greatly indebted to our colleagues and clients, who have allowed us to test many of our hypotheses in real-world situations.

Our colleagues at Watson Wyatt Worldwide contributed greatly, both directly and indirectly, to the contents of this book. In particular, we would like to thank Steve Seelig for his contributions to Appendixes A and B, Chris Hamilton for his contributions to Chapter 8, and Michael Marino for his contributions to Chapter 5. We also greatly appreciate the contributions of our international colleagues who contributed significantly to Chapter 10 on international executive pay, specifically Stéphane Lebeau from Canada, Dominique Paris from France, Hans Kothius from the Asia-Pacific region, and John Ball from the United Kingdom.

This book would not have been written without the efforts of Fay Hansen, who was able to seamlessly mesh our styles and viewpoints. We also thank Dave Simmons, Richard Luss, Bob McKee, David Popper, Dana Finkelstein, Emily Rieger, Jacqueline Coles, and Renee Mailhoit, who were instrumental in helping us get this book ready for publication.

We also extend our appreciation to the critics of executive pay, including Lucian Bebchuk, Jesse Fried, Bud Crystal, and others who conduct important research that elevates the debate on executive pay. We hope that this book serves to further a constructive dialogue on the important issues of executive pay and performance.

Steven Van Putten would also like to acknowledge Paul Platten and Bruce Hanson, both of whom were critical to his development as an executive pay consultant during the formative years of his career.

Finally, and most importantly, we thank our wives and children for their constant support and understanding: Carol, Sarah, Ben, Jon, Sam, William, and Jacob Kay; and Carolyn, Luke, Kelley Rose, and Sarah Van Putten.

The Compensation Committee Meets

May 23, 2006

The chair of the compensation committee scans next week's committee meeting agenda. The first several items are perfunctory – approval of minutes from the prior meeting, new-hire and promotional stock option awards, and an update on a succession-planning project. No surprises there. But the last two agenda items leap off the page: *status of employee stock purchase plan (ESPP) and broad-based option awards*, and *CEO employment agreement renewal*.

These are not unexpected. Several months ago, one of the outside directors called the chair to discuss the ESPP and broad-based option awards, raising a concern that the company was not getting much bang for its buck; that it was incurring significant expense and dilution for these stock-based awards that appeared to have little perceived value among employees.

In effect, the outside director was asking the committee to revisit the preceding year's decision to continue providing broad-based stock option awards and an ESPP – a decision that was agreed to by both management and the committee. That stay-the-course decision had been made in the face of mandatory stock option and ESPP expensing that would go into effect in January 2006. At the time, the decision made sense. The company's stock was trading near an all-time high, employee morale was strong, and the company was having little difficulty attracting and retaining top talent. With the company's broad-based equity programs apparently a key contributor to its success, the committee and senior management were disinclined to make any rash changes.

But during the year, events had occurred that, in retrospect, called into question the appropriateness of the strategy. The company's stock price had languished as a result of macroeconomic factors that adversely affected the company's industry. The fact that the company's flat stock price reflected better performance than that of its peers offered little solace to employees whose stock options were now just treading water.

The situation for option holders was compounded by the company's decision to institute a fairly healthy dividend, which gave shareholders a tax-effective return but provided option holders with no extra value. In addition, at the board of directors' annual off-site meeting, the CEO had described a short-term strategy that would necessitate several capital investments, the benefits of which would likely not be reflected in the stock price in the near term.

At the same time, through its outside compensation consultant, the committee learned that the competitive landscape was indeed changing. In a recent presentation to the committee, the consultant had noted that many peer companies had begun to deemphasize stock options by introducing alternative programs for senior levels of management and by reducing participation and/or shifting to vehicles offering a greater line of sight between actions and rewards at lower employee levels.

The chair understands that these factors merit a reappraisal. But she is concerned that dramatic changes could subvert several key objectives: fostering a culture of share ownership, promoting long-term retention and perspective, and maintaining alignment with shareholders. She also worries that a transition away from stock options to full-value shares could negatively affect the company's emphasis on pay-for-performance.

On top of that, and even more visible, is the ironic juxtaposition with the last agenda item – the renewal of the CEO's employment agreement.

Three years ago, to lure the CEO to the then-underperforming company, the board of directors had constructed an impressive pay package. In addition to competitive cash and equity compensation arrangements, the three-year employment agreement provided a large sign-on restricted-stock award, credited years of service under the company's supplemental executive retirement plan (SERP), and provided a severance benefit equal to three times the combined base salary and annual bonus.

In the event the CEO was let go in connection with a change in control and his severance and related benefits constituted an excess parachute payment (as defined under sections 4999 and 280G of the Internal Revenue Code), he would be entitled to a gross-up payment to reimburse him for any excise taxes incurred. After reviewing detailed peer practices, the compensation committee was comfortable that the package was appropriately competitive.

Three years later, the board thinks the CEO has earned every penny of his compensation package and that shareholders, in turn, have earned an above-market return on their investment in the new CEO. The CEO's unrelenting focus on controlling costs and realizing growth through new distribution channels has spurred the company to its best performance on record, despite a recently sluggish stock price.

Not surprisingly, rumors have been circulating that several companies in need of a well-regarded turnaround expert have placed this CEO at the top of their lists. For his part, the CEO enjoys working for the company, and he and his family want to stay in the area. He has communicated his wish to remain with the company and is interested in entering into a new agreement that would secure his services for the duration of his career. The board wants the same thing, but external pressures are constricting its ability to craft a new, attractive employment deal.

First, the company was recently sued by two separate shareholders who claim that the CEO received excessive compensation. The chair knows that the lawsuit is frivolous and thinks it stemmed from the committee's efforts to improve the transparency of executive compensation disclosure a year before being required to do so by the Securities and Exchange Commission. In the company's recently filed proxy statement, the compensation committee included a table showing the CEO's total remuneration, including the annualized value of benefits and perquisites. Because the CEO was a mid-career hire, the annualized SERP value, including the credited years of service, was an eye-popping number. The lawsuit specifically notes the elements of compensation, including the SERP and the sign-on restricted-stock award, that are not directly related to performance.

To compound matters, in the same proxy statement, two large institutional shareholders submitted separate executive pay resolutions, the first to limit severance benefits to no more than one times the combined salary and bonus and the second to require shareholder approval of the SERP. While the chair knows that these proposals are nonbinding, she is sensitive to the scrutiny the company will receive if they pass and the company subsequently files a Form 8-K disclosing the terms of a new CEO employment agreement.

It is apparent to the chair that there are multiple stakeholder perspectives on these issues and that most are in conflict. Therefore, she has asked that the final two agenda items be structured as review and discussion items rather than approval items. She has also asked the head of human resources to survey a cross section of employees about the current equity programs compared with other forms of remuneration. And she has asked the compensation consultant to collect and interpret data on peer practices.

A week before the meeting, the chair and the committee members receive the requested materials and the agenda. The challenge for the chair will be to channel the discussion toward achieving an outcome that benefits all stakeholders and, at the same time, reflects good corporate governance practices that will withstand public scrutiny.

May 30, 2006

At the meeting, the chair quickly dispenses with the initial items on the agenda. Diving right into the item on the employee stock option awards and ESPP, she asks the senior vice president of human resources to discuss the results of the employee survey. The SVP notes several pervasive themes: that the ESPP is viewed as an attractive benefit and that most employees value options for the recognition – and the affinity to the company – they provide. Like shares acquired through the ESPP, options are generally cashed in as soon as they vest.

One finding from the survey that concerns, but does not surprise, the SVP is the wide disparity in views based on demographics and employee level. Older employees in general prefer the security of restricted stock or cash to the upside potential of options more than younger employees do. However, the more senior the position, the greater the value the individual places on stock options. The SVP is concerned that changes to the current programs could create internal strife.

The compensation consultant then provides an overview of the changing competitive landscape. An increasing number of peer companies are shifting away from stock options, as evidenced by declining annual share usage rates and award sizes. At the executive level, companies are making up for reduced option award levels by introducing long-term performance plans, denominated in cash or shares. Although less clear from publicly disclosed data, it appears that companies are limiting stock option award eligibility for lower-level employees and that several are shifting to restricted stock with award levels that are differentiated on the basis of individual performance.

The chair asks the consultant to work with the SVP and his team to develop alternative approaches and evaluate long-term incentives (LTIs). She says that the committee expects a specific recommendation with supporting LTI rationale.

At this point, the chair excuses senior management, and the committee goes into executive session to discuss the CEO's employment agreement. She tells the committee members that the CEO has said he is looking for more security that will in effect lock him in with the company for the rest of his career. He has mentioned the possibility of an additional restricted-stock award and an enhancement to his supplemental retirement benefit.

One of the committee members objects, saying that maintaining links to performance is the key objective and that the prior restricted-stock and SERP credits were used as part of an employment inducement strategy.

The chair asks the consultant to develop alternative approaches and to work with her directly on the issue. With the meeting adjourned, she turns to the consultant and asks how executive compensation became so complicated so fast. "It's an interesting story," he says, "and the myths often overshadow the realities."

The Battle over Executive Compensation

Two perceptions of corporate executive pay now compete for acceptance in the United States. The first views executive compensation as a reasonably well-executed pay-for-performance model, characterized by high pay for high performance and less pay for lower performance. The successful application of this model has helped create an economic juggernaut, resulting in trillions of dollars of wealth for shareholders and substantial income and net worth for millions of corporate employees and their families. Consistent with basic microeconomic theory, high executive pay simply reflects the strong demand for top talent.

The other perception sees a failed pay-for-performance model with immorally high and rising executive pay, unrelated to corporate performance, and enormous wealth for executives who benefit from a "rising tide" in the stock market. Executives essentially set their own pay by wielding power over boards of directors that have not fulfilled their duty to balance the interests of executives with those of stakeholders. Executive pay – which has enriched management at the expense of shareholders, employees, customers, and their communities – is an embarrassment to our country and has done more economic harm than good, leading to business scandals, the demoralization of employees, and unacceptable levels of income inequality.

This second view broadly challenges the credibility of the entire corporate community. Fed most notably by a series of financial scandals, the popular press, the business press, and a group of powerful public organizations have whipped the perception of a failed pay model into a full-blown mythology of a corporate America ruled by executive greed.

For years, headlines have seized on anecdotal accounts of outrageous amounts earned by executives at failing companies and the financial tragedy that strikes shareholders and employees when executives line their own pockets at the expense of the organization. Images of lavish executive lifestyles are now engraved in the popular consciousness and propel public support for political responses that include new regulatory measures and demands for greater shareholder control over executive compensation. Fresh accusations of executives paid for nonperformance appear regularly.

One of the focal points for these attacks is stock options – once the cornerstone of the executive pay-for-performance model. Interestingly and ironically, stock options were part of the redesign of executive pay programs that occurred more than a decade ago in response to claims that executive pay should be more closely linked to corporate performance.

We are the first to acknowledge that a poorly constructed and executed pay-for-performance model can damage productivity, employee morale, and social objectives. But, like most mythologies, the current conception of executive compensation distorts or exaggerates actual events. The mythology has too easily found larger-than-life examples of personal gain and sumptuous lifestyles with no link to superior corporate performance.

Unfortunately, outliers exist – companies where executive pay is high and where severance arrangements or supplemental pensions create large payouts for mediocre or poor performance. Within the workings of the free market that broadly characterize the U.S. economy, these outliers are called out in the press, and their executives are ousted for poor performance.

But our research, stated throughout this book, shows that most companies have substantial amounts of pay-for-performance, with realized executive pay fluctuating with company performance. To the extent that the current mythology leads to a rejection of the pay-for-performance model and restrictions on the risk-and-reward structure for setting executive compensation, U.S. corporate performance will suffer. If boards are pressured into reducing executive pay, we will see more turnover and less talent in the executive suite as the top job candidates move on to other professions.

In fact, the most prominent proponents of the current mythology – institutional shareholders and unions – will be among those that suffer most as executive talent declines, earnings shrink, share prices drop, and jobs are destroyed. Worse yet, companies may attempt to circumvent plans that engage shareholders. For example, they may move away from stock options to cash incentives to avoid the need for shareholder approval. This may reduce the alignment between management and shareholders and subvert the principal–agent relationship, which critics say is poorly executed.

While we readily join those who criticize boards that reward executives who do not produce, we know that this is not the case at the vast majority of U.S. corporations. Our experience has demonstrated clearly that the pay-for-performance model is not only viable but essential to the continued success of U.S. companies and the U.S. economy.

Executive Compensation in the U.S. Corporate Model

The stakes involved in the outcome of the argument are huge. The debate about executive compensation must take place in the broader context of the U.S. corporate model, which generates wealth for shareholders, a good income for millions of Americans, and retirement benefits and health care protections for employees and their dependents.

The U.S. corporate model also protects the economy from devastating cyclical swings. The U.S. economy is volatile, but stock market corrections and economic recessions are far shallower than they were in the past because the corporate model rewards flexibility and efficiency. Executives are paid to keep their companies lean and survive the downturns. Because companies are well managed going into a recession, they are able to pull out quickly and with less long-term job loss than we see abroad.

There are many reasons for the strength of the U.S. corporate model – its organizational flexibility and creativity, high levels of research and development, and technological prowess – but its success is closely connected to its unique approach to human capital, an approach based on relatively unregulated labor markets, high labor mobility, and a century-long reliance on various forms of incentive pay.

Executive compensation is determined by the labor market for managerial talent and by a pay-for-performance system that extends from the executive suite down to the factory floor and has contributed to high productivity rates in the United States for more than a century. Some argue that the labor market for executives is no longer efficient and that the pay-for-performance model no longer applies to CEOs, but this is not the case. CEOs are routinely dismissed or subjected to sharp pay cuts when they fail to produce.

Running a corporation involves making major decisions about expansions and divestitures, job creation and layoffs. Although some people consider it unseemly to reward executives who cause others to lose their jobs, the resulting efficiencies create growth and employment and secure the long-term survival and success of the whole system. When executives are not rewarded for making the tough decisions, companies do not perform as well.

Those who argue that we should abandon these executive pay practices deny the dynamic nature of the corporate model and the economy it supports. It is not a coincidence that the Dow Jones Industrial Average, which stood at 5,000 in 1996, is now well above 13,000. While U.S. executive pay practices do not entirely explain this rise, there is little doubt that it would not have occurred without them – and no evidence that the rise would have been even larger if the sums paid to executives had instead been paid to shareholders or reinvested.

The U.S. corporate model and the executive pay practices that drive it have created investment returns for millions of shareholders and funded pension and retirement savings plans now worth trillions of dollars. Over their careers, the top five executives at U.S. companies receive, on average, 2 percent to 3 percent of the value generated by the corporations they manage. The small savings that might occur by reducing executive pay would be swamped by the resulting decline in productivity, profitability, stock market returns, and the overall value of the corporation. Whether corporate success is measured in stock price performance, productivity, or employment, it starts at the top of the corporate structure.

U.S. executives are universally recognized as the best in the world. While there are few examples of U.S. companies importing international executives to boost corporate performance, many foreign companies have hired U.S. executives to improve earnings and efficiency. In fact, we have never encountered a case where a U.S. board has imported a CEO from abroad to cut compensation costs at the executive level. Such a move would run counter to board members' primary responsibilities: to ensure continuity of management and financial success. Compensation committees, for good reason, are unwilling to take such a risk.

The Goals of Executive Compensation

The debate about executive pay comes down to one's view of the executive labor market. Is it working properly – with risks and rewards, intense negotiations, and executives fired for failure – or is it a rigged system in which executives stack boards with their cronies and get paid huge amounts of money regardless of whether they succeed or fail?

A long list of pressures, including resistance from institutional investors, accounting and tax changes, enhanced proxy disclosure requirements, federal legislation, and media scrutiny, are forcing companies to rethink the design and delivery of their executive compensation programs, especially their stock-based incentives. But these pressures are having a decided, and many would argue adverse, impact on other employees. The current storm over executive pay is more likely to damage the far larger world of nonexecutive employees, who could lose their stock-based plans, now under attack.

The key is a proper mix of risks and rewards. Base pay provides a stable, competitive income. Benefits attract and retain talent in a tight labor market. Annual incentives motivate short-term behaviors and actions that drive long-term value creation. Long-term incentives (LTIs), in the form of equity, encourage employees to maximize long-term shareholder value. Pensions, SERPs, and deferred compensation plans promote long-term retention and company affiliation and long-term capital accumulation. Severance plans allow executives to take the risks necessary to seek maximum shareholder value, even if it means jeopardizing their own jobs. The compensation package must address both the need for income and security and the opportunity to accumulate assets.

Executive pay programs must also be aligned with employee pay programs so that efforts are synchronized throughout the organization. They must send signals about the company's strategic imperatives to other stakeholders – especially shareholders – and ensure the implementation of those imperatives. If a company is losing market share or operating in a stagnant industry, for example, the pay program should reward executives for profitability but also, perhaps more important, for revenue growth.

Pay programs must motivate executives to make the capital investments and business decisions that earn a greater return than the cost of that capital. They must motivate executives to divest units that are not earning more than they cost, even if that means shrinking an organization that the executive has helped build. Shareholders, too, must earn a return in excess of the cost of human capital. Investing in a top executive involves up-front costs, and the return on that investment can be evaluated only over time.

Although we contend that the basic executive pay model is sound, specific improvements will allow it to continue to succeed: real stock ownership among executives, the right mix of long-term incentives, more modest severance and perquisites, and compensation committee practices and procedures that reflect good corporate governance.

Our Approach

By looking at the recent history of U.S. executive pay, investigating the extent to which the pay-for-performance model has governed executive pay levels, and assessing the success of this model in creating value for shareholders and robust job growth for U.S. workers, we hope to initiate a thoughtful discussion of what is working well in executive compensation and what could be improved.

OUR VIEWS

Although we demonstrate that executive compensation is closely tied to corporate performance, some aspects of executive pay are deeply flawed. We agree with the critics, for example, that the excessive use of stock options may negatively affect corporate performance. We also agree that more disclosure – especially with respect to supplemental retirement plans, deferred compensation, and severance payouts – is necessary. With the recent introduction of new proxy disclosure rules, the SEC has taken a substantial step in improving the disclosure of these elements.

Institutional investors, a potentially powerful influence on executive compensation, have serious criticisms of the current executive compensation model. Their concerns must be addressed where appropriate. Our goal is to provide solutions to specific problems and examine the best techniques for sustaining an effective pay-for-performance model.

The prologue shows the challenges facing a compensation committee chair. We begin in Chapter 1 with a detailed review of the myths surrounding executive pay and the evidence that refutes those myths. Chapter 2 discusses managerial power, which critics claim has undermined the pay-for-performance model, and the various aspects of executive compensation that critics see as manifestations of that power. Chapter 3 focuses on the external pressures that now surround executive pay. Chapter 4 traces the decline of the stock option as the primary vehicle for performance-based rewards.

Chapter 5 looks at new directions in stock-based incentives and long-term incentive programs. Chapter 6 discusses executive stock ownership as a solution to the executive compensation crisis. Chapter 7 covers director compensation in the context of increased director responsibilities and liability. Chapter 8 sets forth best practices for compensation committees and governance issues related to executive pay. Chapter 9 looks at stock programs designed for the broader employee population, the fate of those programs in the new regulatory environment, and alternative incentive plan designs. Chapter 10 compares executive compensation plans abroad with plans in the United States.

We close with an epilogue that returns the reader to the compensation committee meeting described in the prologue and reviews the committee's work to resolve the problems raised there. Appendix A describes the legal and regulatory requirements for executive compensation plans. Appendix B outlines the regulatory and institutional mandates that now affect executive compensation. Appendix C lists a number of academic studies relevant to the pay-for-performance model discussed here.

As always, we welcome any criticisms that contribute to the attempt to distinguish myth from reality in executive compensation and create the conditions for a constructive discussion of its future.

1 The Myths and Realities of Pay-for-Performance

The work of those who criticize CEO pay, although appealing, simply does not "prove" that any particular CEO is overpaid, much less that an entire class of CEOs is overpaid. What is lacking in such work is some indication of what the CEOs would earn if the market for their services were more efficient. In the absence of evidence that the "overpaid" individuals would have been willing to accept less for their services, or that CEOs occupy some sort of monopoly position regarding executive services, it is difficult to accept the proposition as proven.

Mark J. Loewenstein, professor, University of Colorado School of Law

The perception among reporters and other [critics] that the corner suite is a sinecure with huge rewards and little accountability bears no resemblance to present reality. Fully half of the Fortune 1,000 companies have replaced their man at the top since 2000.

"Off with Their Heads," editorial, *Wall Street Journal*, August 1, 2006

The full-blown mythology of a corporate America ruled by executive greed and excess consists of two related components: a failed pay-for-performance model and managerial power. The myth of the failed pay model hinges on the idea that the link between executive compensation and corporate performance never truly existed and therefore does not determine executive pay levels. The myth of excessive managerial power accepts the idea of a failed model and puts in its service the image of unchecked executives dominating subservient boards as the explanation for decisions resulting in excessive executive pay.

Our findings indicate that pay levels are highly sensitive to fluctuations in corporate performance. The research also shows that the U.S.

executive labor market is dynamic and sensitive to changes in the economy and in corporate performance. These sensitivities play a role in the U.S. economy's overall health.

The myth of the failed pay-for-performance model finds its touchstones in real examples of companies where executives have collected huge sums in cash compensation and stock options while shareholder returns declined. In some instances, CEOs have been richly rewarded for mediocre or even poor performance. But instances where CEOs became wealthy and the company shareholders made tens of billions of dollars have also been lumped into the failed model.

The myth of managerial power satisfies the need for a simple explanation for the failed pay-for-performance model and meshes with recent reports of corrupt governance practices and ineffective boards. Cases of overstated profits – or outright fraud – have fueled the idea that performance measures can be manipulated to justify higher pay while boards remain silent. The perceived ability of executives to time the grant or exercise of their stock options and collect additional pay through covert means has made the situation even worse.

The powerful combination of these two myths appears in statements from institutional investors, trade unions, and the media. The California Public Employees' Retirement System (CalPERS, the nation's largest public pension fund) provides a typical example in its November 15, 2004, press release announcing its new campaign "to reign [sic] in abusive compensation practices in corporate America and hold directors and compensation committees more accountable for their actions."

The AFL-CIO's Web site embraces the same myths:

Each year, shocking new examples of CEO pay greed are made public. Investors are concerned not just about the growing size of executive compensation packages, but the fact that CEO pay levels show little apparent relationship to corporate profits, stock prices or executive performance. How do CEOs do it? For years, executives have relied on their shareholders to be passive absentee owners. CEOs have rigged their own compensation packages by packing their boards with conflicted or negligent directors.[1]

The Realities of Pay-for-Performance

Even if the critics are somewhat correct about some of the flaws in executive pay – too high, too many stock options, too much managerial influence and manipulation, too little disclosure, too generous pensions and severance – they are wrong about pay-for-performance, which trumps the other concerns. As explained in this book, high levels of pay opportunity have turned out to be a great investment for shareholders as well as for the executives. In the worst case, enormous shareholder wealth has been created despite those problems. In the best case, some of those factors allowed U.S. corporations to attract and motivate perhaps the greatest managerial generation in economic history.

The myth that executive pay is not tied to corporate performance includes several components: CEOs receive high pay even at companies with lackluster returns to shareholders; CEO pay rises when performance is strong but does not fall when performance declines; and stock options are ineffective rewards and a poor investment for the company.

Watson Wyatt conducts extensive research on the impact of executive pay and stock options on executive, corporate, and overall economic behavior. In evaluating thousands of companies annually for 10 to 15 years – yielding nearly 20,000 "company-years" of data – not only Watson Wyatt but dozens of economists have come to the same conclusion. For most companies, there is substantial pay-for-performance sensitivity. Simply put, high performance generates high pay, and low performance generates low pay.

MYTH 1: Executives are paid far more than they are worth in relation to the value they create for their companies.

REALITY 1: Executives generally receive only a small portion of the substantial value they help create for their companies and their shareholders.

There is no doubt that U.S. CEOs are well paid. As Figure 1.1 shows, the median CEO at the 1,500 largest U.S. companies had total direct compensation (TDC) opportunity (TDC = salary + bonus + present value of new long-term incentives) of approximately $3.2 million in 2005. As Figure 1.2 shows, CEOs' total pay opportunity increased by only 2.9 percent, a reduced growth rate from prior years. The amount these CEOs actually receive depends on stock performance plus other financial metrics that underlie their incentive programs. But as media and other pay critics often note, CEOs' actual pay is also high relative to that of other employees. A 2005 *BusinessWeek* article, "A Payday for Performance," lists 12 executives with more than $160 million in unexercised stock option profits.[2]

In reality, CEO pay is a very small part of a company's overall cost structure. Total CEO pay in 2004 was less than 0.09 percent of sales,

FIGURE 1.1
S&P 1500 CEO Pay Opportunity, 2005 Median

	($000)	2005 SIZE	($BILLION) (MEDIAN)
Salary	$697	Market cap	$2.2
Bonus	$625	Sales	$1.5
Total cash	$1,330	Assets	$2.1
Restricted stock	$1,128*		
LTIP target	$1,400*		
Stock options (grant value)	$1,672*		
Total LTI	$1,726		
TDC	$3,207		

*For those who received a grant.

Note: Data from 1,313 CEOs who were in the job 2004–2005.

Source: Watson Wyatt.

0.06 percent of market capitalization, and 1.3 percent of net income for the Standard & Poor's 500 (see Figure 1.3).

These findings are consistent with a study by Brian J. Hall and Jeffrey B. Liebman, who found that "the dramatic increases in CEO pay over the past 15 years [1980s–1990s] are not very large relative to the market value of the firm."[3]

Peter Drucker, the late management guru, argued in the *Wall Street Journal* that "the American CEO is . . . fast becoming a major U.S. export"

FIGURE 1.2
S&P 1500 CEO Compensation Opportunity, 2004–2005 (Percentage Change)

	CHANGE (MEDIAN)	PERFORMANCE	MEDIAN
Salary	3.3%	TRS	8.0%
Bonus	2.3%	Change in EPS	15.0%
Total cash	4.2%		
Restricted stock*	0%		
Target LTIP*	12.0%		
Stock options (grant value)	−4.0%		
Total LTI	1.5%		
TDC	2.9%		

*For those who received grants in the fiscal year.

Note: Covers same 1,313 CEOs who were in job 2004–2005 and whose proxies were filed by June 1, 2005.

Source: Watson Wyatt.

FIGURE 1.3
CEO Pay and Corporate Costs

	2004 CEO PAY*	SALES	MARKET CAPITALIZATION	NET INCOME	CEO PAY AS PERCENTAGE OF SALES	MARKET CAP	NET INCOME
Total	$6.9 billion	$8.1 trillion	$12.0 trillion	$552 billion	0.09%	0.06%	1.26%
Average	$5.0 million	$5.8 billion	$5.8 billion	$395 million	0.09%	0.06%	1.26%

*Salary + bonus + stock options exercised + long–term incentive payouts.

Note: Sample size = 1,398 companies.

Source: Watson Wyatt.

and is being adopted all over the world to help drive superior organizational performance.[4]

It is extremely difficult to be an effective CEO, but an effective CEO can make a huge difference in the performance of a company. The scramble to fill vacant CEO spots at major companies – recent examples include Hewlett Packard, Morgan Stanley, Boeing, 3M, Tyco, and Starwood Hotels – indicates the importance of this position as well as those of other senior executives.

Chief executive officers, while well paid, are not unique. Consider the pay of other professionals, including musicians, actors, athletes, venture capitalists, and investment bankers. The CEO job is as difficult as any of these. It also is fraught with risk, helps create millions of jobs, and creates terrific investment opportunities for the average investor.

Ultimately, the level of CEO pay is a fairly efficient labor market outcome. In a January 2006 working paper titled "Why Has CEO Pay Increased So Much?"[5] economists Xavier Gabaix and Augustin Landier empirically demonstrate that "the six-fold increase of CEO pay between 1980 and 2003 can be fully attributed to the six-fold increase in market capitalization of large US companies." In a fully competitive labor market, top CEO talent aspires to run larger, more complex companies. As company size and complexity increase, so, too, does CEO pay.

MYTH 2: There is no pay for performance.

REALITY 2: High executive pay correlates with and contributes to high company performance.

While there are certainly instances of pay without performance, to test the idea that at the vast majority of companies actual pay is highly aligned with company performance, we studied the relationship between pay and performance at more than 1,000 U.S. companies. But before getting to the results, it is important to note that even if we can prove a statistical correlation between pay and performance and not causality, it is essential from a corporate governance policy perspective that compensation committee members understand and believe that their pay policies motivate and, consequently, cause the higher level of performance. The correlation does not prove causality; it merely demonstrates that there is a statistical relationship. High pay could cause high performance, or high performance could cause high pay. We evaluate both possibilities.

An essential part of the U.S. corporate model involves changing pay and other human resources policies – for example, modifying bonuses, moving away from stock options, or shifting recruiting strategies – to raise the likelihood of improved company performance. There is an explicit assumption that changes in pay policies can affect the behavior of employees, including executives, and consequently the performance of the company.

However, it is extremely difficult to test for causality, even though a correlation has been established. In some of our analyses, we looked at a pay policy in a given year – for example, 2000 – and evaluated the performance in subsequent years, for example, 2000 to 2005. While this technique does not prove that higher pay opportunity causes the higher performance, the timing of the variables makes it impossible to conclude that the higher performance caused the higher pay.

With this as background, we tried to answer the following questions through our research:

- Do higher-paid CEOs, in terms of realized pay, work at better-performing companies than lower-paid CEOs?
- Do high-performing companies have CEOs with greater stock option profits than lower-performing companies?
- Does CEO pay move up and down?
- Do companies whose CEOs have higher stock ownership show superior performance in the subsequent five years than companies whose CEOs have lower stock ownership?

Our study of nearly 1,000 companies verifies that performance is dramatically better at companies with high actual CEO pay (salary + bonus + profit from stock options exercised + long-term incentive payouts). As shown in Figure 1.4, CEOs who had higher total actual pay in 2004

FIGURE 1.4

High CEO Realized Pay Correlates with High Corporate Performance

	TOTAL ACTUAL CEO PAY** (MMS)*	ONE-YEAR ANNUALIZED TRS*	THREE-YEAR ANNUALIZED TRS*	FIVE-YEAR ANNUALIZED TRS*	ROE*	ROA*	ONE-YEAR EPS GROWTH*	TOBIN'S Q*
High	$4.7	20.7%	14.4%	12.9%	14.3%	5.4%	26.6%	1.33
Low	$1.0	11.8%	7.7%	6.8%	8.3%	3.1%	16.3%	1.23
All	$2.1	16.8%	10.7%	10.0%	11.8%	4.1%	22.1%	1.28

**Total Actual Pay = 2004 Salary + Bonus + Profit from stock options exercised + Long-term incentive plan payout.
*Significant at 0.05 level.

Note: Financial information as of December 31, 2004; Sample size = 1,398 companies.

Source: Watson Wyatt.

worked at companies that had higher five-year total returns to shareholders (TRS).

In Figure 1.4, we divided our database into companies whose CEOs received higher-than-median realized total compensation in 2004 and those whose CEOs received below-median compensation. Because most companies deliver CEO pay through stock options, we conclude that companies are directly linking executive and shareholder interests. While it is impossible to say that the opportunity for higher pay caused better performance, the results indicate a causal relationship. In comparing Figures 1.1 and 1.4, note that the median realized pay ($2.1 million) was slightly lower than the median pay opportunity. While the numbers are not entirely comparable, they indicate that executives are earning what the board intended.

The data also indicate that CEOs at companies performing above the median had larger increases in actual pay – a 47 percent increase for firms with a median TRS of 34.3 percent (see Figure 1.5). On the other hand, CEOs at low-performing firms, with a median TRS of 1.2 percent, had only a 10 percent increase in realized pay.

In the late 1980s and early 1990s, critics argued that executives' pay was not linked to the performance of their companies' stock. During the expansion of the 1990s, executive pay opportunity increased at 15 percent to 20 percent annual compound growth rates at the typical billion-dollar company. Most of that increase was in the form of stock-based compensation, primarily stock options. Those stock options had value only if the stock price rose.

Harvard economist Martin Feldstein has studied the following two questions: Why has U.S. productivity growth improved dramatically in the last 10 years, and why is U.S. productivity so much higher than that

FIGURE 1.5
Corporate Performance and CEO Actual Pay

	ONE-YEAR ANNUALIZED TRS*	TOTAL ACTUAL CEO PAY (MM$)		
		2003	2004*	% CHANGE 2003–2004*
High	34.3%	$1.52	$2.60	47.1%
Low	1.2%	$1.47	$1.73	10.4%
All	17.1%	$1.50	$2.17	29.2%

*Significant at 0.05 level.

Note: Sample size = 1,222 companies.

Source: Watson Wyatt.

in Japan and Europe? He concludes that U.S. growth is stronger because of cash and stock-based incentives.

"The increase in incentive compensation, tied to individual and company performance, also caused executives and lower-level managers to take risks, to work harder and to engage in the unpleasant tasks that raised productivity," Feldstein wrote in a working paper for the National Bureau of Economic Research in 2003. Some economists believe that the way the United States pays its executives is a major source of competitive advantage and that we reject it at our peril.

Appendix C provides a list of some recent academic studies of executive pay and corporate performance that conclude that the pay-for-performance model is intact and appropriately determining pay levels for top executives.

MYTH 3: Executive pay only rises.

REALITY 3: Executive pay rises and falls in tandem with stock prices and the financial performance of the company.

Critics claim that executive pay rises when performance improves but does not decline when performance drops. However, our data demonstrate that this is not the case. For both 1999 to 2000 and 2000 to 2001, total pay decreased with the decline in corporate profits and stock prices. At the largest 1,200 companies, total pay fell by nearly 30 percent, with 72 percent of the CEOs experiencing a decline.

This research is supported by the noted economist Alan Reynolds: "The incomes of the top 100–500 CEOs rose unexpectedly with the stock market boom of 1997–2000, then fell by an estimated 48–53 percent through 2003. Such ups and downs of CEO pay cannot be explained by the theory that managers dominate their boards."[6]

FIGURE 1.6
CEO Long-Term Incentive Compensation
Opportunity Rises and Falls

YEARS	% CHANGE TOTAL LTI*
2001–2002	−21%
2002–2003	−10%
2003–2004	+17%

*Includes new stock option grants, restricted stock, and other LTIs.

Note: Data from 914 companies for 2001–2002; 1,047 companies for other years.

Source: Watson Wyatt.

It is possible to find examples of companies where executive pay rose while profit and stock prices declined, but these are the exceptions – and institutional investors and the media quickly call out these inconsistencies.

As shown in Figure 1.6, CEO pay and LTI opportunity clearly rise and fall with the stock market. These data also show large declines in stock option values – 24 percent from 2001 to 2003 – and increases in restricted-stock and performance plans. We estimate that the total economic value of stock options granted by the S&P 1500 fell from $120 billion in 2001 to $50 billion in 2004. This is explained by pressure from institutional investors and new accounting rules.

Executives' stock option profits also rise and fall. Figure 1.7 shows a five-year history of changes in option profits and how they move with total returns to shareholders. The large increase from 2002 to 2003 is explained by the stock option grants in 2000, 2001, and 2002 at low strike prices combined with the resurgence of the stock market in 2003.

Figure 1.8 shows the results of a Watson Wyatt study of 95 companies. From 2004 to 2005, the higher-TRS companies had an increase in

FIGURE 1.7
In-the-Money Value of Stock Options

YEAR	% CHANGE	TRS
2000–2001	−9.2	0.8
2001–2002	1.4	−10.5
2002–2003	192.0	30.8
2003–2004	33.0	17.1
2004–2005	12.3	7.7

Source: Watson Wyatt.

FIGURE 1.8
In-the-Money Value of Stock Options, 2004–2005

TRS PERFORMANCE	MEDIAN TRS	% CHANGE IN IMV
High	24.5	47.3
Low	-3.2	-51.6

Note: Number = 95; Watson Wyatt estimates.

Source: Watson Wyatt.

potential stock option profits of more than 47 percent, up more than $1 billion. The lower-TRS companies saw declines of more than 50 percent, a decline of nearly $500 million.

Academic research also shows that pay rises and falls with performance. Academics have found that actual CEO pay is highly sensitive to stock price changes because of the high and rising amounts of stock-based wealth owned by executives.

Hall and Liebman's seminal 1998 article found that CEOs' pay-for-performance sensitivity increased dramatically from 1980 to the mid-1990s. This was almost exclusively due to stock option profits and stock ownership. They note that in 1994, a stagnant year for the stock market, about 24 percent of the CEOs in their sample lost money. The average loss was $13 million for the more than 100 CEOs. Watson Wyatt research found that from 2004 to 2005, 34 CEOs at 95 of the largest companies saw their unrealized stock option profits decline by 42 percent – more than $400 million in total – while their shareholders experienced a 6 percent decline. The top half of this group saw their unrealized option profits rise by 50 percent, while their shareholders had a 25 percent return.

In a study published in 2003, Brian J. Hall and Kevin J. Murphy showed that option grants in the last three decades have closely tracked general stock market indices. They found that "CEO cash compensation is weakly correlated with the Dow Jones average but CEO total compensation is strongly correlated with the stock market." They go on to say that "the increase in options coupled with the renewed focus on shareholder value creation may help explain the overall growth in the stock market since the early 1990s."[7]

MYTH 4: The labor market for top executives does not function properly because of managerial power and does not justify high levels of executive compensation.

REALITY 4: The labor market for top executive talent is highly competitive and compels companies to offer attractive pay packages to recruit the talent they need.

Critics argue that the labor market for CEOs does not function as a free market but as a rigged market in which CEOs stack boards with their cronies, who set pay as high as possible. The compensation committee – comprised mostly of directors who are under the control of the CEO – approves egregious compensation programs that are not approved by the shareholders.

Our research, as detailed in what follows, shows that the CEO labor market meets all the criteria of any free market, including independent supply and demand, transparency, and liquidity. In the thousands of board and compensation committee meetings we have attended, we have observed that board members are generally thoughtful and independent and take their responsibilities seriously. They often vote down or modify management's proposals on pay matters.

The managerial power myth states that executives collect "rents" that they do not deserve but obtain via sociological "power." One piece of evidence cited by the "power" advocates is that as a result of the rent, most CEOs are paid the same, irrespective of performance. They confuse pay opportunity with realized pay. We acknowledge that pay opportunities, which are mostly comprised of new stock incentive plans, especially stock options, may not be highly correlated with historical performance. This occurs because pay opportunity in the form of stock options has no real value to employees until the vesting period is over and the stock price rises. On the other hand, realized pay – which includes the in-the-money value of stock options and the amount of bonuses and performance shares that are actually earned – has a very high correlation with historical performance, as we showed in Figure 1.4.

But in a free labor market, there are substantial differences in realized pay for individuals. The executive labor market has tremendous variations in pay, which is consistent with an efficient market. Some of our studies have shown differences of 1,000 percent or more from the lowest paid to the highest, mostly due to stock options granted in a given year.

Various factors determine compensation at the top levels: the executive's pay and performance history, whether the executive was promoted from within or recruited from outside, and even net worth; it may take more pay to attract an ideal candidate who happens to be wealthy. The industry itself is relevant. The executive pay structure of a particular industry, in terms of both pay levels and compensation mix, can take on its own anthropological and historical momentum. Fundamentally, if investors want to be in a specific industry, they must pay the freight of compensation levels for that industry. The history of Wall Street, for example, is littered with failures of great companies that tried to enter that dominion. American Express and General Electric bought Wall Street firms in the 1980s that they eventually sold under duress.

Executives, like other employees, generally are paid commensurate with their skills. Their pay levels reflect marketplace supply and demand and are also in line with compensation levels for top people in other sectors – investment, entertainment, or athletics – who reach rarefied levels of achievement.

In the last 10 to 15 years, executive pay opportunity has risen faster in percentage terms than inflation and faster than average employee pay. It has not risen faster than the broad stock market and individual company share prices. It is also true that executives who own a large amount of stock receive above-average grants of new stock options and other stock. Critics may consider this unnecessary, but it is a reality of the labor market.

Top executives are recruited to become CEOs at other companies. Top executives at Motorola, NCR, BellSouth, and General Electric were recruited in the early 2000s to become CEOs at Tyco, Hewlett Packard, Sprint, 3M, and Boeing. The recruiting packages – $30 million or more in some instances – reflected the executives' success and their large amounts of unvested restricted stock and stock options for which they had to be compensated. In addition, the companies needed to offer them upside opportunities in the new company. These new-hire packages have a significant impact on the pay packages for internal promotions as well.

Apart from the specific short-term risk of losing a CEO to another company, the broader long-term risk of underpaying corporate executives is that top talent from colleges and business schools will enter other more lucrative, and arguably more interesting, professions, such as investment banking, venture capital, and management consulting.

Private equity firms also recruit corporate executives for very lucrative pay packages. This puts upward pressure on corporate and CEO packages and demonstrates that private companies can pay as high as public companies.

For example, *Fortune* reported in February 2006 that "Top talent has never been more valuable, nor the competition for it more fierce." The shortage of top executive talent will only grow worse in the coming years:

"The allure of being a corporate executive may be fading. Hedge fund managers can make far more money. And people who like running businesses rather than stock portfolios may decide they'd rather avoid the hassles of publicly traded companies."[8] The *Fortune* article cites John Joyce of IBM, Vivek Paul of Wipro, and Richard Bressler of Viacom as examples of top executives who left public companies to work for private equity firms.

Steven A. Cohen, hedge fund manager at SAC Capital, earned more than $500 million in cash in 2005; Steven A. Schwarzman of the Blackstone Group earned more than $300 million.[9] Cohen takes up to 50 percent of his hedge fund's profits before investors are paid; Schwarzman and his team take 20 percent.

A February 27, 2006, *BusinessWeek* cover story[10] lists dozens of executives who have bolted from the realm of short-term pressures and endless scrutiny to the greater rewards and more satisfying work of private equity firms. "The attractions are two-fold: money and freedom," the article notes. Top executive talent now lost to private firms includes former Paine Webber Group CEO Donald B. Marron and former Target Corp. vice chairman Gerald Storch.

An August 24, 2006, article in the *Wall Street Journal*[11] provides another example of the growing power of private equity. General Electric Co. vice chairman David Calhoun was offered at least $100 million to join Dutch media firm VNU.

Executives, especially CEOs, experience high levels of both voluntary and involuntary turnover. The demands of compliance with the Sarbanes-Oxley Act and the inherent job risk of being held responsible for poor performance – fairly or unfairly – have created a situation where many top executives do not necessarily want to become CEOs. According to a Booz Allen Hamilton report on the world's 2,500 largest companies, more than 14 percent of their CEOs left office in 2004, and nearly one-third of them were terminated because of inadequate performance.[12] Comparable numbers apply to the United States as well. A Russell Reynolds Associates study of CFOs found that 16 percent of Fortune 500 companies changed CFOs in 2004, up from 13 percent in 2003. About one-fifth of this turnover was from resignations.[13]

MYTH 5: High levels of executive compensation take money out of the pockets of shareholders and employees and act as a drag on the U.S. economy.

REALITY 5: High levels of executive compensation generated by effective performance-pay practices contribute to successful companies that yield high returns for their shareholders, generate millions of jobs, and drive U.S. economic growth.

The U.S. economy has performed extremely well in the last 10 to 15 years, despite large trade and budget deficits, outsourcing, a weakening dollar, soaring health care costs, and rising oil prices. This stellar performance has coincided with and can be linked to the explosion in stock-based compensation and rising executive compensation levels.

The World Economic Forum's 2005 competitiveness ranking shows the United States as the second most competitive country in the world, the same position as in 2004.[14] No other major industrialized country ranks in the top 10. Finland holds the first position, and Japan ranks twelfth. This stunning accomplishment speaks volumes about corporate America, the engine of the U.S. economy.

Although executive pay remains controversial, investors should consider the behavior of the typical company and not the most extreme examples. In the last 10 years, we have asked institutional investors whether they would prefer to invest in the executive pay model, corporate governance, and total returns of companies in Japan or the United States. In other words, would they prefer the low pay, "perfect governance," and terrible stock market returns of Japan, or would they rather rely on the U.S. system? We have also asked the TIAA–CREF staff whether they would rather have had U.S. stocks or Japanese stocks in their fund in the last 15 years. The answers are obvious.

MYTH 6: Out-of-control executive pay is one item in a long list of poor U.S. corporate governance practices.

REALITY 6: Many experts consider U.S. corporate governance to be among the best and most successful in the world. The model reflects the unique institutional factors in the United States, particularly highly dispersed shareholders.

Critics say that excessive executive pay is emblematic of the overall problems with how corporations are governed. There are several responses to this:

- The U.S. corporate governance model is very effective.
- U.S. corporate governance has improved dramatically over the past 10 years, a time of explosive executive pay increases.
- There are legitimate economic and institutional reasons why U.S. executives have so much economic bargaining power, including both

an abundance of employment alternatives and a more dispersed shareholder base relative to Europe and Japan.

- To the extent that there is statistically solid pay for performance, any criticisms of corporate governance are either wrong or irrelevant.

Other Issues

Critics claim that options are frequently repriced when the stock price declines. Repricing occurs when the "strike," or exercise, price is lowered sometime after the original stock option grant is made, thereby creating a huge advantage that benefits executives and employees more than shareholders, certainly over the short term. While some companies have repriced their stock options in the last several years, our research shows that of the more than 10,000 publicly traded companies, no more than a few hundred have done so.

The critics also argue that executives' inside information allows them to time their sales of stock and their stock option grants and exercises. Because executives have more information than outside investors, many companies have blackout periods on the sale of stock. However, companies could police this area better by, for example, requiring executives to announce via Securities and Exchange Commission 10b5–1 plans that they are going to sell. Stock option grant timing should follow a fixed, preestablished schedule.

An article by David Yermack, professor of finance at New York University, claims that executives time their stock option grants based on earnings releases.[15] In all the meetings we have attended, we have never seen evidence of this. Because a careful reading of the article shows that only a handful of the companies could be called into question, the study yielded statistical but not economic significance.

In 2006, some companies were accused of "backdating" their stock option grants to pick up low historic strike prices. This of course is extremely shareholder-unfriendly. We believe only a tiny minority of companies (less than 1 percent) have done this. Unfortunately, the search for companies that have backdated stock options threatens to include, and therefore tarnish, companies that have done nothing wrong. This could unintentionally result in companies playing it safe when it comes to implementing business strategies or the hiring and motivating of executives. But, despite some well-publicized stories about companies that have admittedly backdated their options, we believe this is not a widespread problem. As far as we can tell, all of the companies that have ever backdated a stock option completely eliminated the practice several years ago.

Critics also claim that executives commonly receive massive amounts of "stealth" compensation, with executives being paid under the table when they do not earn money on their bonuses and stock options. Although there are examples of CEOs getting special perquisites, ranging from use of the corporate jet to consulting contracts, we estimate that these perks represent substantially less than 1 percent of total pay. In general, Watson Wyatt's research shows that hierarchical companies with many status distinctions perform more poorly than those with fewer perks, so we typically advise companies to minimize these programs.

We agree that several key areas in the noncash arena need improvement. Until 2004, competitive studies created for compensation committees did not generally include a supplemental executive retirement plan comparison with their competitors' SERPs. Now it is standard to include a SERP calculation. The new Securities and Exchange Commission disclosure rules will rectify many of the disclosure problems created by the widespread use of SERPs and other noncash forms of compensation.

Case Studies of Pay-for-Performance

We have presented thus far the theories and facts about pay-for-performance in corporate America. But, in the real world, we at Watson Wyatt evaluate pay-for-performance for companies both before and after the fact.

After the fact, we look at the CEO's realized pay and the company's performance and evaluate the overall fairness of the compensation – to the employee and to the shareholders. Before the fact, we incorporate the company's predicted performance and link it to the executive compensation that will be delivered for that performance. The future levels of executive pay and company performance should match to a large degree. To the extent that companies fail to match performance and compensation, the analysis will not show pay-for-performance.

Some organizations with challenging performance goals may underpay their executives in light of the excellent results reported by the company. Although there are statistically as many of these companies as there are in the first group, they attract little attention. Although our research, as detailed in this book, shows a tight relationship between executive realized pay and corporate performance, some companies overpay their executives relative to the company's poor performance – or its good but not outstanding performance.

The most common explanation for overpayment is that the company is in a turnaround. A turnaround might require bringing in an outside executive, which itself requires guaranteed compensation, or paying retention bonuses to ensure management continuity. Sometimes the board retains the existing management team for the turnaround. Cynics wonder why a company would retain a management team that has underperformed. Unfortunately, it can be difficult to recruit an executive to a damaged company, so the current management team may be the only team available. Additionally, the performance could have been worse under a different management team.

One of the board's primary roles – to ensure management continuity – can go a long way toward explaining some of the difficult decisions that boards make, including setting relatively competitive compensation opportunity levels for what has been poor historical performance. The key issue for the board is whether the existing management team is the right one or whether a new team should be brought in. But once the board decides that it is going to rely on these executives, it must motivate and retain them. This always should take the form of more pay-for-performance types of programs (incentives, stock options, and performance shares, for example) rather than fixed pay (salaries and pensions).

To determine the success of a client company's compensation programs and gauge what it needs to do going forward, we develop a peer group of companies and compare our client's performance against this peer group on important financial metrics, normally those that are used in its short- and long-term incentive plans. For example, if a client uses return on net assets and revenue growth as short-term incentive performance metrics, we analyze its performance on those two indicators. The long-term performance analysis assesses relative TRS as well as any long-term performance metrics that are employed in a long-term performance plan. For example, if the client's performance is in the 60th percentile, the company outperforms 60 percent of the peer companies and underperforms 40 percent.

We then do the same exercise for compensation. For short-term pay, we compare the actual paid bonuses for the CEO and other named executive officers with those of the peer group. For long-term pay, we look at the in-the-money value of stock options awarded in the last three years, current value of restricted stock awards made in the last three years, and any long-term performance plan payouts attributable to that three-year

FIGURE 1.9
Short-Term Pay-for-Performance Assessment

SHORT-TERM PERFORMANCE (2003)				SHORT-TERM INCENTIVES (2003)		
PEER GROUP	OPERATING PROFIT	OPERATING CASH FLOW	SALES GROWTH	PEER GROUP	CEO	NEOs
75th percentile	6.0%	5.1%	12.9%	75th percentile	$2,525	$611
Median	4.0%	−4.8%	11.6%	Median	$1,833	$489
25th percentile	−2.3%	−15.1%	−2.9%	25th percentile	$996	$358
[Client]	−10.0%	3.0%	8.0%	[Client]	$1,050	$425
Percentile	10th	60th	33rd	Percentile	32th	33rd

Composite performance relative to peers:
34th percentile

Composite pay relative to peers:
33rd percentile

Source: Watson Wyatt.

period. This allows us to create a nearly perfect comparison of executive pay and corporate performance during the same period. Figures 1.9 and 1.10 are examples of short-term and long-term pay-for-performance assessments where there is fairly close correlation between pay and performance.

Not only do the comparisons correlate pay and performance, they also provide insight into the degree of difficulty of the goals. If the company is paying incentives in the upper quartile and performance is in the lower quartile, the performance goals may be too easy. If pay is in the bottom

FIGURE 1.10
Long-Term Pay-for-Performance Assessment

LONG-TERM PERFORMANCE (2001–2003)				LONG-TERM REALIZABLE GAINS		
PEER GROUP	THREE-YEAR EPS CAGR	THREE-YEAR EPS GROWTH	THREE-YEAR FCF GROWTH	PEER GROUP	CEO	NEOs
75th percentile	10.4%	76.9%	227.7%	75th percentile	$20,827	$5,915
Median	3.2%	22.0%	110.6%	Median	$12,725	$3,499
25th percentile	−9.8%	−13.8%	−160.1%	25th percentile	$8,879	$2,115
[Client]	−2.0%	−5.0%	80.0%	[Client]	$7,000	$1,800
Percentile	34th	30th	46th	Percentile	18th	18th

Composite performance relative to peers:
37th percentile

Composite pay relative to peers:
18th percentile

Source: Watson Wyatt.

FIGURE 1.11
Total Value of In-the-Money Stock Options

The total in-the-money value of SAMPLE 2 executive stock options are generally between the 50th and 75th market percentile for peer companies, except for the CEO, which is below the 50th percentile.

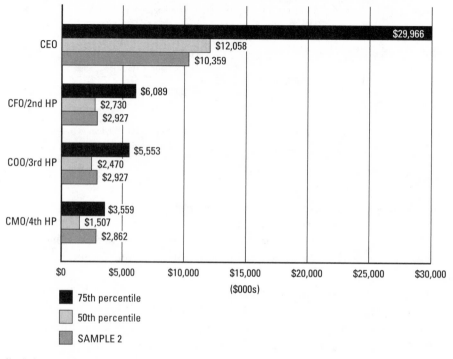

Note: In-the-money values of stock options for SAMPLE 2 and the peer group likely increased during 2004 due to rising stock prices.
Source: Watson Wyatt.

quartile of the peer group and performance is at or above the median, the goals may be too difficult.

In addition to the short- and long-term comparisons, we often look at other analyses to determine the relationship between value delivery and company performance. A "carried interest" analysis (total shares + stock incentives held), for example, looks at CEO and senior executive equity ownership and opportunity relative to the peer group. Figures 1.11 and 1.12 illustrate these comparisons for in-the-money stock option values and outright stock ownership, respectively. Compensation committees find this type of analysis useful in determining the effectiveness of the executive compensation program.

FIGURE 1.12
Outright Stock Ownership

Outright ownership is calculated as the difference between the total beneficial shares owned (as shown in the 2003 proxy) and the number of stock options that are vested or will become vested within 60 days.

Analysis of FY2003 Results:

- The CEO and CFO total outright ownership levels are between the 50th and 75th percentiles of the peer group.

- In contrast, the COO and CMO total outright ownership levels are significantly above the 75th percentile of the peer group.

- Current SAMPLE 2 ownership guidelines require: CEO – 50,000 shares; NEO – 15,000 shares.

CEO	VALUE OF OUTRIGHT OWNERSHIP	CFO	VALUE OF OUTRIGHT OWNERSHIP
SAMPLE 2	$14.664M (620,035 shares)	SAMPLE 2	$3.928M (166,087 shares)
Peer group: 50th percentile	$6.982M	Peer group: 50th percentile	$3.158M
Peer group: 75th percentile	$17.743M	Peer group: 75th percentile	$4.519M
COO	VALUE OF OUTRIGHT OWNERSHIP	CMO	VALUE OF OUTRIGHT OWNERSHIP
SAMPLE 2	$4.554M (192,568 shares)	SAMPLE 2	$4.913M (207,748 shares)
Peer group: 50th percentile	$1.224M	Peer group: 50th percentile	$1.407M
Peer group: 75th percentile	$3.095M	Peer group: 75th percentile	$2.319M

Source: Watson Wyatt.

The overall myth about U.S. executive pay is false. But the elements that are true – that shares should be handled more carefully, SERPs should be better disclosed, and stock sales should be preannounced – are being addressed. Corporate America needs to fix what it can and keep doing what it does best: create enormous wealth for shareholders.

2 Managerial Power

Ultimately, though, [Bebchuk and Fried's] managerial power view is both problematic as a theoretical matter, and too simplistic to explain executive pay practices.[1]

Kevin J. Murphy, Marshall School of Business,
University of Southern California

Managerial power describes a corporate governance structure in which executives hold sway over a capitulating board of directors, usurping its decision-making power for their own benefit. Many executive pay critics now cast managerial power as the dominant force in determining executive pay. Those who argue that the pay-for-performance model is broken or nonexistent frequently turn to the concept of managerial power as the cause of the breakdown and the best explanation for the excessive levels of executive compensation that they believe must be corrected.

The corporate scandals of recent years fueled the mythology of corrupt CEOs and passive boards, with shareholders and employees left powerless in the face of widespread abuse. These scandals are terrible for the surviving corporations, the economy, and the morale of the investing public. But there is no evidence that they are the tip of an iceberg of out-of-control CEOs setting their own pay. A number of factors, mostly economic, influence the CEO pay market; managerial power is only one of them. In rare cases, it is the most important.

The most persuasive argument for the myth appears in Lucien Bebchuk and Jesse Fried's *Pay without Performance: The Unfulfilled Promise of Executive Compensation*, published in 2004.[2] According to Bebchuk and Fried, the managerial power of CEOs over their "captive" boards is a major problem in corporate governance and especially in executive pay practices. They claim that CEOs essentially set their own pay by hiring, influencing, and firing board members, which yields exorbitant and rising pay levels that bear little relationship to company performance.

Bebchuk and Fried collect both standard and obscure criticisms of executive pay to support their thesis. They acknowledge that U.S. corporate performance has been strong and that management has played a role in that performance. Nevertheless, they argue that the executives were overpaid and that shareholder value creation would have been even higher had the executives been paid less.

Their criticisms include the following:

- CEOs have too much power over their boards. CEOs who have less power and are paid less include CEOs who are not chairman of the board; CEOs at companies with a major shareholder; and CEOs who are not heavily involved in the board nominating process.
- CEOs in other countries, who have less power over their boards, are paid less than U.S. CEOs.
- CEOs secretly hedge sales of their stock to reduce their economic exposure.
- Companies hire compensation consultants to help ratchet up executive pay; internal human resources staff is complicit in this.
- Executives receive excessive supplemental retirement plans to camouflage their pay from shareholders.
- Executives receive at-the-money stock options, which confer excessive benefits.
- Executives have their stock options repriced when the stock price falls so that they can recoup their losses.
- Companies backdate their stock option grants to give the executive an unfair advantage.

Bebchuk and Fried cite academic articles that support their point of view, including studies of companies with weak corporate governance that overpay their CEOs and companies that grant stock options before good news and after bad news to create favorable strike prices. They also cite reports that calculate the number of stock option repricings that have occurred. Some in fact find that companies with more independent boards pay their CEOs less than those with less independent boards and that their financial performance does not necessarily suffer.

But it is a major leap of faith to conclude that if all companies had ideal practices and policies, the average or median performance would improve accordingly. As Bengt Holmström and Steven Kaplan point out in "The State of U.S. Corporate Governance: What's Right and What's Wrong?" U.S. corporate governance practices have improved dramatically in the last 20 years.[3] This is at the same time that CEO pay, especially stock option grants, skyrocketed and U.S. corporate performance improved both relative to its own historical performance and in comparison with Europe and Japan, its main economic competitors.

Bebchuk and Fried also support the argument put forward by some economists that companies use at-the-money stock options, where small stock price increases yield large gains to the executive, when other forms of stock options would be better. At-the-money options can provide substantial payments for below-average performance. The authors argue that these options are an outcome of CEOs' domination of their boards. But the crucial question that these critics fail to ask is whether the below-average performance would have been even lower without the at-the-money options. Our research, as detailed throughout this chapter, indicates that in the majority of cases, performance would indeed have been worse.

Academic Response to Bebchuk and Fried

Pay without Performance and the concept of managerial power have sparked academic research, but the articles generally criticize Bebchuk and Fried's model and reject its policy implications. All of the studies agree that while there is a great amount of managerial power inside the corporation, it is trumped by pay-for-performance, balanced bargaining power, and other attributes of the CEO labor market.

The core issues revolve around two questions: First, are boards creating optimal arm's-length contracts with their executives, or does managerial power prevent that from happening, thereby yielding excessive payments to management? Second, are Bebchuk and Fried correct in their contention that there is little pay-for-performance in the pay packages of top executives as a result of managerial power?

John E. Core, Wayne R. Guay, and Randall S. Thomas's article "Is U.S. CEO Compensation Inefficient Pay without Performance?" criticizes Bebchuk and Fried on both fronts. They state that "when we argue ... that many [executive compensation] contracts with managers may in fact be optimal, we are not claiming that U.S. corporate governance is perfect. ... What we mean is that U.S. corporate governance [regarding executive pay] may in fact be extremely good given the existence of information costs, transaction costs, and the existing U.S. legal and regulatory system."[4]

Core et al. then present research to support that the U.S. executive pay model is arguably the best in the world. Their argument can be summarized as follows: Bebchuk and Fried's analysis focuses on whether CEO annual pay opportunity varies with firm performance but ignores the main source of CEO incentives: the large holdings of stock and options that provide powerful incentives and ensure that the wealth of most CEOs varies with their firm's stock price. This is consistent with the data shown in Chapter 1. When one considers this source of CEO incentives, Bebchuk and Fried's claim that CEO compensation is "pay without performance" falls apart.

In another challenge to Bebchuk and Fried, Randall S. Thomas refutes the managerial power, or "board capture," theory and proposes four explanations of why U.S. CEOs are paid more than their international counterparts:[5]

1. U.S. CEOs contribute more to their firms' value.
2. U.S. CEOs contribute more to their companies because U.S. boards are smaller and the labor market for these CEOs is part of an individualistic, winner-take-all culture.
3. The opportunity costs for U.S. CEOs are higher. Established companies must compete for managerial talent with the numerous opportunities available to U.S. executives, such as leveraged buy-out (LBO) and private equity firms.
4. The role of U.S. CEOs in vetoing hostile takeovers beginning in the 1980s greatly increased the bargaining power of U.S. CEOs.

With respect to the theory of managerial power, Thomas concludes:

> In my view, economic forces are the most important factors in the determination of the market pay rate for CEOs and other top executives. The CEO's contribution to her firm's value, or the top executive's best alternative job opportunities, are powerful explanations of her relative pay scale. It seems unlikely that these values are fixed through some massive secret conspiracy to keep managerial pay levels high.[6]

Other experts also criticize the managerial power thesis. For example, Iman Anabtawi, in "Alternatives in the Pay without Performance Debate"

(2004), says that "there is limited evidence to suggest that managers exert influence over boards of directors to decouple their pay from their performance."[7]

Stephen Bainbridge, in "Executive Compensation: Who Decides?" (2004), argues that Bebchuk and Fried overstate the extent to which management controls the compensation process and says "they have not made a convincing case for the reforms to corporate governance they propose." He also questions why large shareholders tolerate the same type of executive compensation programs as those in companies that have a more dispersed, and presumably weaker, shareholder base, supposedly dominated by management.[8]

Kevin Murphy, in "Explaining Executive Compensation: Managerial Power versus the Perceived Cost of Stock Options" (2002), raises questions about the managerial power thesis.[9] For example, why do newly hired CEOs have higher compensation than internally promoted CEOs when the latter supposedly have more power over their boards? And why did executive compensation rise so dramatically at a time of increased proxy disclosure and improved corporate governance initiatives – the exact opposite of what the managerial power theory would have predicted?

Holmström and Kaplan, in "The State of Corporate Governance" (2003), argue that the U.S. governance model, including executive compensation, is at least as good as other models in the industrialized world, and arguably better.[10] They also note that the U.S. stock market and economy have performed extremely well, possibly because of those compensation strategies, not despite them.

Martin Conyon and Lerong He, in "Compensation Committees and CEO Compensation Incentives in US Entrepreneurial Firms" (2004), conclude that initial public offering (IPO) firms do not support the managerial power model and that a compensation committee will act in its own self-interest rather than be co-opted by the CEO.[11]

Franklin Snyder, in "More Pieces of the CEO Compensation Puzzle" (2003), says that "most of the results that [Bebchuk and Fried] see as requiring us to postulate managerial dominance turn out to be consistent with a less sinister explanation." For example, what they call "undue influence" might more properly be called "dominant bargaining power." Snyder explains that the paucity – or perceived paucity – of CEOs gives these executives a great deal of legitimate economic power relative to the board:

Even an average CEO of a large firm is in a very powerful bargaining position. Leadership transitions are a huge distraction to a firm that is trying to focus on its business and the selection process itself is long, intense, and often extremely expensive.... This is not the sort of process that a firm wants to go through often. Therefore, the board is not in a particularly powerful position to resist the CEO's compensation demands if they are backed by a credible threat of departure or retirement.[12]

In two studies, Tod Perry and Marc Zenner concluded that there is significant pay-for-performance in large-company CEO pay packages. "Overall... pay for performance sensitivity increased throughout the 1990s, resulting in increased alignment between the CEO and shareholders."[13]

Most academics, board members, and compensation consultants, and certainly all large-company executives, think that Bebchuk and Fried's theory is deeply flawed. In fact, the academics – the most independent and scientific commentators in this whole matter – have found that the U.S. executive compensation model benefits the U.S. economy. See Appendix C for a list of academic articles supporting the pay-for-performance approach and other aspects of the efficiencies of the U.S. executive labor market.

But Bebchuk and Fried's theory has received a warm response from the media, including the *New York Times* and *The Economist;* selected executive compensation critics, such as Arthur Levitt, former SEC chairman; and some institutional investors – especially those representing unionized employees and state employees. And even though the larger institutional funds have criticisms of executive pay, they are generally satisfied with the outcome: the returns to them as shareholders. If they could achieve the same returns for less executive pay, they would certainly install that model. Their shareholding and proxy voting behavior suggests, however, that they doubt a different model would produce the same results.

The Realities of Managerial Power

Support for the myth of managerial power has come primarily from investor groups, media reports, and a small minority of the academic community. These academics may gain direct information from a limited number of companies. Institutional shareholders may obtain information from a small number of companies in which they have a specific interest. Members of the media may occasionally interview directors or executives. But we have never encountered one of these professors or a member of the press in a compensation committee or board meeting. The myth of managerial power is based on speculation rather than observation.

As Murphy and other experts note, the managerial power hypothesis is inconsistent with two recent phenomena: major improvements in corporate governance and the extremely high pay for CEOs who are hired from outside the organization.[14] It is also interesting to note that the governance improvements in the last 5 to 10 years, which came about as a response to pressures from institutional investors, the SEC, and Congress, happened at the same time as the explosion in executive compensation, which was primarily driven by large stock option grants and an improving stock market.

The position of critics such as Bebchuk and Fried was made even more dubious by changes in economic conditions and recent corporate governance reforms. In the last few years, corporate performance was marked first by a decline and then a subsequent rise – and executive pay levels followed accordingly.

Furthermore, recent individual examples of a lack of pay-for-performance – ranging from high pay for poor performance to big bonuses linked to accounting fraud – have been handled quite efficiently by boards (who reduced pay or terminated executives) and the courts (through civil suits and criminal actions). In essence, managerial power becomes limited when U.S. corporations aggressively step up their governance standards and wayward executives are sent packing or slapped with lawsuits.

The controversy about managerial power in executive pay is nothing new. More than 70 years ago, Adolf Berle and Gardiner Means set the framework in *The Modern Corporation and Private Property* (1932), in which they outlined the ineffectiveness of boards in checking managerial power in the interests of shareholders.[15] As they drafted their hugely influential book, shareholders and the media expressed outrage at the board of directors of Bethlehem Steel Corporation, where executives received bonuses worth 6.3 percent of net earnings in 1929 and president Eugene G. Grace received a bonus of $1.6 million.

"Opinions in Wall Street vary sharply as to the desirability of large bonuses," the *New York Times* reported. "It is pointed out by some that Bethlehem's high prosperity last year was the result of aggressive and intelligent management and that, therefore, the principal officials are entitled to large compensation."[16] Two years later, the Bethlehem board installed a new bonus plan designed to end shareholder litigation and the debate over the executive bonus payments. But the board, mindful of the motivational effects of the bonuses, included in the new plan provisions for a maximum of 8 percent of net profit in bonuses to sustain performance incentives.[17]

The current controversy cites developments in executive pay practices that presumably demonstrate the impact of managerial power. We analyze each of these developments and note where our research does and does not support the associated claims about managerial power.

Camouflaged Compensation

Proponents of the view that managerial power is having an undue influence on executive pay claim that CEOs worry about the outrage their cash compensation may spark among various groups – the media, employees, shareholders, and policymakers. Therefore, executives go to great lengths to camouflage it through the use of stock options, deferred compensation, perquisites, supplemental pensions, and other noncash payments. The critics fail to note, however, that executive pay practices at U.S. companies have historically been the most fully disclosed in the world. Ironically, this transparency, combined with a robust labor market, played a major role in ratcheting up executive pay.

If CEOs have attempted to camouflage their pay, they have not succeeded in avoiding anger. Despite the fact that the United States has always required more detailed disclosure of executive pay than other countries, the subject of executive pay has drawn outrage for the better part of two decades. As a result, Congress and the various regulatory agencies crafted new rules on disclosure and the relationship between pay and performance. In 1992, the SEC improved disclosure significantly. In 1994, the IRS put much more emphasis on pay-for-performance, especially with respect to stock options. In the post-Enron corporate environment, the government and stakeholder groups have pushed for fairness in executive pay and even more disclosure.

It is another irony that the outrage-fueled pressures played a role in the most recent boosts in executive pay. The use of stock options – a result of efforts to link pay to performance – motivated CEOs to increase company performance, and the resulting stock market rise pushed up executive pay levels in the late 1990s and early 2000s.

Although there is little evidence of "camouflage," there could be closer monitoring, management, and disclosure of supplemental executive retirement pensions and deferred compensation. Newly recruited CEOs frequently receive service credit when they join a new company because they are being bought out of their old SERP. This drives up the value of SERPs for internally promoted CEOs as well. SERPs can be expensive, and presumably are worth it, but they are expensed over the career, so the expense has already been factored into (subtracted from) today's market capitalization (the current share price times the number of shares outstanding). While that may not justify a very expensive plan, critics will have to demonstrate that if the SERP were lower, the market cap would be higher. In 2006, the SEC improved the proxy disclosure rules, including how SERPs are presented. As a result, it is very likely that many companies will reduce their use of SERPs.

At-the-Money Strike Prices

Critics of executive pay levels use the managerial power myth to explain why almost all stock options have a strike price that is equal to the stock price – the fair market value on the date of grant. This type of stock option, commonly referred to as an at-the-money stock option, benefits executives because they have to increase the stock price only a small amount to generate significant wealth for themselves.

According to the critics, if power were more evenly balanced, boards would experiment with different types of stock options, including indexed, premium, or performance-vested ones. Critics often recommend using indexed stock options, with the strike price pegged to a stock index, to reduce windfall profits and answer the rising tide of criticism of executive pay. They also say that premium-priced options – or stock options that are out-of-the-money from the initial grant date, with a strike price higher than the fair market value on the date of grant – would be more shareholder-friendly than at-the-money stock options.

Many corporate experts claim that most companies have not used indexed stock options because of the APB 25 accounting rule, which was in effect until 2006. Under this rule, indexed stock options were very expensive, whereas at-the-money stock options had no accounting expense. Bebchuk and Fried argue that because efficient markets look through accounting expense to incorporate all true economic information into stock prices, managerial power – not accounting – causes the strong preference for at-the-money stock options. Most executives prefer them because it's more difficult to earn high pay with indexed or premium stocks. But if directors thought that indexed or premium options were superior in other ways, more companies would use them.

The primary reason why companies grant at-the-money options, however, is that boards think the best motivation and retention will come from a high probability that the incentive plans will pay out for the executive. Boards emphasize management continuity because of the tremendous economic damage that can be done from CEO or other executive turnover. They prefer to err on the side of overpayment. Boards also believe that it is difficult to increase the stock price at most companies, so a premium price is too difficult to achieve and more options need to be granted.

Employees and even executives discount the value of stock options to themselves relative to their cost to the company. Any option plan that makes it more difficult to earn a payout will be even further discounted. In addition, a truly symmetrical indexed stock option would have its strike price rise and fall with proportionate movements of the index. Based on numerous conversations with board members, it is apparent that most boards would be uncomfortable lowering a strike price, especially in today's corporate governance environment.

If the strike price could only be adjusted upward, Murphy estimates that much less than 50 percent of options would pay out under that model, which means they would have little retention or motivational value. In fact, some experts have argued that indexed or premium stock options could motivate executives to undertake too much risk, relative to what the shareholders want, in trying to beat the index.

Bebchuk and Fried are technically correct about the market's reaction to accounting issues and indexed stock options, but they are wrong about the perceptions and motives of management and boards, grossly underestimating how much emphasis they place on accounting-based earnings. Our experience is that management and boards think that accounting expense matters a great deal and simply regard indexed stock options as too expensive. This expense – not managerial power – explains the unpopularity and limited use of indexed options.

With stock option expensing now required under the new accounting rules, companies have begun to experiment with various types of plans that were previously considered too expensive. However, companies have rapidly moved away from stock options of all types, with few trying indexed options, performance vesting, or premium-priced options, and only under certain circumstances. The likely migration to other performance-based equity plans, if properly implemented, will be good for corporations and the economy.

Repricings and Reloads

In a repricing, the strike price of "underwater" (out-of-the-money) stock options is lowered to the current fair market value. In a reload, employees automatically receive a new grant of stock options each time they exercise an option using a "stock for stock" exercise. Both techniques provide downside protection to the employee at the expense of shareholders. Repricings – heavily used by the technology sector in the mid-1990s to retain its employees – reward poor performance or, more accurately, absolve the employee of accountability. Critics claim that these designs are a manifestation of managerial power.

Changes in the accounting rules have made repricings and reloads effectively obsolete. However, even at their peak, they were used by only 2 percent of all companies and 10 percent of large companies – never the crisis or symptom that Bebchuk and Fried and other critics imply but a focused strategy by particular companies with particular circumstances and exactly the type of policy variation that diversified, highly competitive companies would explore.

Diversifying, Hedging, and Timing

Those who claim there is an overuse of managerial power also argue that diversifying, hedging, and specifically timing stock option grants stem from the power that CEOs have over their boards. They claim that these strategies reduce the incentive power of stock options and increase the value of the shares to the executive.

Executive stock ownership has risen dramatically in the last two decades. High ownership motivates executives to make better decisions about acquisitions, divestitures, layoffs, stock buybacks, research and development, pricing, product development, and other critical business issues.

But having so much invested in the company may also create risk-averse executives who will diversify at any opportunity unless specific policies prevent them from doing so. More than 50 percent of the typical executive's net worth may be tied up in company assets, including both stock and nonqualified pensions. If human capital components – career development and reputation, for example – are included, the percentage of true net worth tied up is likely well above 50 percent for most executives.

Stock ownership guidelines, and the increased use of net share holding requirements, have resolved much of the problem of executive stock sales and diversification. The idea is that if employees meet ownership guidelines, they can exercise their options and sell their shares for diversification or current income reasons.

Many critics of executive pay cite hedging as a major flaw in executive behavior. Although there are limited data on this, we estimate that of the tens of billions of dollars in stock and options sold each year by employees, only 1 percent to 2 percent were hedged.

Executives' timing of both stock option grants and exercising stock options and selling shares is a problem. Fueled by a few egregious examples, the issue contributes to negative perceptions of executive pay practices. Policy solutions may be appropriate. Even though very few companies move their grant dates or backdate, and fewer still change them to pick up favorable strike prices, companies should avoid the practice and use a common date each year for granting.

Peer Group Data and Upward Bias

Critics argue that managerial power pushes up all forms of CEO compensation. They claim that directors approve excessive pay packages to curry favor with the CEO in exchange for high fees, reappointment, and even contributions to their favorite charities. But according to the myth, the complicity does not stop there. Chief executive officers also co-opt their human resources staffs and the compensation consultants who are charged with benchmarking the company's executive pay against 10 to 30 peer companies.

Selecting the peer group is a self-serving process, the critics say. The human resources staff and the consultants choose companies that are larger, higher paying, or better performing. With the resulting compensation data in hand, the compensation committee – under the guidance of the CEO, human resources, and the consultant – sets the company's "competitive position" of the pay opportunity at the 50th percentile (the median) or the 75th percentile. Because no company wants its constituents to think that it hires executives with below-average skills and talent, which is the implication of a pay philosophy that sets pay opportunity below the 50th percentile, most companies adopt a philosophy of targeting pay opportunity above the median, and all companies end up chasing an ever-rising median to remain "competitive." This is referred to as the ratchet effect.

Even participants acknowledge that the percentile process is flawed. But compensation committees are desperate for objective information to help them set CEO pay. Committees have legitimate concerns about demotivating their CEO. They want their CEO focused on the success of the company, not on whether he or she is competitively paid.

Peer group selection and chasing a rising median are legitimate concerns with no obvious solutions. But any managerial influence is simply a normal part of the "bid-ask" negotiation process in any complex market for nonfungible goods, such as executive labor, and only one of the many forces that affect the board's decisions about executive pay levels.

The SEC in effect requires companies to use peer group data, disclosed in the proxy statement, for making benchmark comparisons of executive pay. Most companies discuss the peer group and their competitive position in their proxy, and many express pride about the effectiveness of their process and the care that went into setting pay. It is unfortunate that they sometimes are criticized for this. Companies that do not discuss their position relative to a peer group most likely pay well below a median and do not want to advertise that to their employees or the competition. Perfect competitive analysis, using perfect peer group data, size adjusted, would reveal that 50 percent of companies pay below the median and 50 percent pay above it.

Other Factors in Setting Pay

Under the business judgment rule, the law protects board members in making highly discretionary decisions with no clear answer a priori as long as they are highly deliberative, consult experts, explore alternatives, and use appropriate data. Although peer group data are essentially the only source of information, boards also consider other factors:

- The company's performance in the most recent year, in the last three and five years, and during the CEO's entire tenure
- The CEO's performance relative to his or her goals for the year. Some companies use a company-wide formula, with or without a discretionary factor; others simply rely on the judgment of the compensation committee or the full board. Some companies allow the CEO to receive a higher bonus as a percentage of target than the overall average for all employees. We think that future best practice will be

to have the CEO paid a bonus funded at the company average, irrespective of his or her individual performance.

- The strategic repositioning of the company, which may entail acquisitions, divestitures, new product lines, outsourcing, or financial engineering
- The likelihood of the CEO's possible voluntary departure
- CEO job tenure
- The costs, in hard dollars and business disruption, and difficulty of replacing the CEO
- The CEO's current stock ownership
- The CEO's compensation history
- The amount of the CEO's vested and unvested stock option profit and other stock, such as restricted stock
- The company's pay-for-performance culture

Many of these factors push compensation up. Talented CEOs at high-performing companies will historically have received high and increasing pay because they generate high returns and, despite what critics say, because economic theory indicates that it requires ever-increasing amounts of compensation to motivate the most talented and well-paid CEOs.

Underperforming companies, especially those with new CEOs, also must offer above-median pay opportunities to attract and motivate the CEO to undertake a turnaround. This may explain the loss of the historical statistical relationship between stock option grant sizes and subsequent TRS.

The media and investors are understandably critical when an underperforming company's CEO receives a big pay increase to turn the company around. In today's environment, boards are terminating these CEOs with greater frequency, as reflected in the declining tenures of CEOs in the last 10 years. But there are legitimate cases where a compensation committee may conclude that the company is better off with the current CEO.

The risk and cost of losing executive talent – in the form of disrupted strategy, hostile takeovers, loss of revenue, and other substantial costs – is clear to compensation committees, which have continued to provide high and rising executive pay despite outbursts of public disapproval, negative media attention, and personal attacks on board members. Some dramatic examples are Hewlett Packard, Boeing, 3M, and NCR. The net result is an upward bias in pay levels, tipping the scale toward retention and overpayment rather than underpayment and turnover.

This is where, for better or worse, the business judgment rule comes into play. The rule protects board members from being second-guessed in lawsuits filed after outcomes are known or more perfect information is revealed. Basically, the courts, particularly those in Delaware, where many U.S. corporations are incorporated, provide wide latitude and protections to directors to run their complex companies. However, some recent court cases and legal settlements have heightened the personal legal liability of directors with respect to their decisions.

Fixed Shares versus Constant-Dollar Techniques

The other aspect of how much to pay the CEO is whether there truly is a ratchet effect that drives pay ever upward. Three other related phenomena explain this effect or put it into perspective: (1) the distinction between pay opportunity and actual or realizable pay; (2) the technique of granting stock options using a fixed number of shares annually, irrespective of stock price; and (3) the dramatic downward slide in CEO and other executive pay trends in 2001–2003.

Compensation committees must constantly balance two goals: retaining and motivating an effective executive team and maintaining the cost structure of the company. Executive pay is only a small part of the total cost, but it can set the pattern for other major costs. But these committees also understand the huge difference between pay opportunity and pay received. The peer group and ratchet effect phenomena refer to pay opportunity. How much compensation the executive actually receives will depend heavily, and in some cases completely, on financial and stock market performance in the postgrant years.

The fixed-number technique, in concert with a rising and volatile stock market, is the key factor behind rising CEO pay opportunity. Many companies, especially in the technology sector, set the size of stock option grants by granting a fixed number of stock options annually, for a number of years, irrespective of the stock price. No precise data are available, but we estimate that historically more than 50 percent of companies have used this method.

For example, a CEO receives a grant of 1 million stock options in 2004 at an exercise price of $20 (the stock price on the date of award) for a total Black–Scholes (an economic model that places a present value in dollars on a stock option) value (at $10 per option) of $10 million. In 2005, the CEO receives the same 1 million stock options, but the stock price has risen to $60, with a Black–Scholes value of $30 per option and a total value of $30 million – an increase of 200 percent over the previous year. Market survey data for 2005 would have shown the $30 million.

Any company that used the survey data, including this company, would show a significant increase in the median or average values of the stock options granted. A company that was attempting to match its own compensation to the median in dollar value would experience an ever-rising median. The companies that did not use the fixed-number approach instead used a constant-dollar approach derived from surveys and other sources and also evaluated their target values annually or biennially. It is these companies that chased the ever-rising median, although the dollar value of stock options fluctuated with the stock market. Obviously, to the extent that a majority or even a significant plurality of companies use the fixed-number approach, the median will rise in proportion to the number of companies using it and to the increase in the stock prices of these companies.

Compensation committees stayed with a fixed number of shares for two simple reasons: (1) It was a relatively easy approach from an analytical and communications perspective, and (2) any reduction in the number of stock options granted because of the stock price rise would have been seen as a pay cut. In the example above, where the stock price went from $20 to $60, the number of stock options needed to sustain the original $10 million of value granted would have been 333,000, a reduction of two-thirds.

This is exactly the dilemma that a constant-dollar company faced. The company either raised pay (an economic cost) to keep its executives competitive with the marketplace and sustain motivation or kept pay and costs constant and demoralized the executives. Most compensation committees that faced this problem kept the number of stock options constant or mitigated the decrease mildly, which created a rising median. Although reducing the number of stock options after a stock price increase is not truly a pay cut, most executives would view it as such. They are particularly irritated because it seems their pay was cut after their stock price rose.

The fixed-number approach depends on the current stock price for the change in economic value. The stock market correction of 2001–2003 provided a laboratory test of the ratchet effect – of whether total stock option values could go down as well as up. If managerial power were driving these decisions, companies would have switched to a constant-dollar approach in the declining market, locking in the larger dollar value and higher number of options granted. That is, they would have increased the number of stock options granted to sustain the dollar value delivered for that particular year. This did not happen.

From 2000 to early 2003, the total value of stock option grants to CEOs fell steeply. Realistically, the ratchet effect has caused reductions in pay only a few times in the last 20 years. These declines were associated with recessions, stock market declines, or both. Conversely, the dramatic increase in stock prices in the last 20 years and the concomitant increases in U.S. wealth by trillions of dollars explain the upward bias. The data confirm that the ratchet effect works both up and down and belies the myth that executive pay only rises.

As we are now in a world of expensing stock options, most companies use the constant-dollar approach. As the stock price rises, the number of stock options will decline to preserve the original budgeted accounting cost.

Conflicts of Interest

The criticism that human resources staff provide upwardly biased, or at least self-serving, data to the CEO and the compensation committee came dramatically to light with the role of human resources in the Richard Grasso scandal at the New York Stock Exchange, where a senior HR officer acknowledged wrongdoing and returned a bonus.

Human resources employees are often put in the unfair position of recommending pay for their boss or their boss's boss. This conflict of interest is similar to but less dramatic than the one faced by audit and finance staff. The latter's dilemma has been resolved by giving it a reporting relationship independent of the audit committee of the board. Given that human resources matters have historically lacked the legal imperative of financial matters, the solution is unclear.

Critics claim that compensation consultants also are caught in a conflict of interest. But potential conflicts exist for virtually all professional advisers to major corporations: lawyers, strategy consultants, technology consultants, accountants, auditors, commercial bankers, insurance brokers, and investment bankers. All of these professionals, including compensation consultants, have standards and codes of conduct. Only a tiny proportion of these professionals succumb to these conflicts in an unprofessional or, even more rarely, illegal manner.

Some critics argue that it is better to retain independent compensation consultants from small firms. These boutiques may be in a better position to perform work solely for the compensation committee, but many of them also do other work for management, again raising the conflict-of-interest issue. And because the fees from any one client may represent a large percentage of a small firm's revenue, there is the same theoretical potential loss of independence. Finally, large firms, with their multiple relationships with the client, probably have a deeper understanding of the client's culture and strategy. The key factor in selecting a consultant should be whether it will provide objective, fact-based advice.

Most companies have concluded that a compensation consultant is necessary in the current corporate environment. These consultants bring expertise in both selecting the peer group and performing an analysis that is fraught with difficult issues, such as how to handle new-hire stock grants or special grants. And they often have access to proprietary data sources and a broad knowledge of accounting, tax issues, securities laws, ERISA (Employee Retirement Income Security Act) issues, investor relations, and other factors related to executive compensation.

Some companies use two consultants – one for the board and another for management. Others allow their CEO to hire an outside lawyer, typically paid for by the company, to represent him or her. Some use a large consulting firm but request that the consultants seek approval from the committee for all other work. In another major improvement, compensation consultants are now typically hired by the compensation committee rather than by management. These various solutions suggest that most companies think the conflict-of-interest issues are manageable.

Conclusion

In some ways, the perception that managerial power is overused has increased the pressure that executives, board members, HR staffs, and compensation consultants feel when discussing the most effective methods for tying pay to performance and ensuring the success of the company. But it has also contributed to discussions about corporate governance and raised the level of dialogue in boardrooms.

When the argument is blown into mythological proportions, however, it skews thinking about corporate behavior and leads to fundamental misunderstandings about executives, their pay levels, and their role in building successful corporations and a flourishing economy. Consequently, it leads many to reject a pay model that works well and is crucial to economic growth at both the corporate and the national levels. We need to address excesses in executive pay without abandoning the core model.

The flexible U.S. corporate governance model will continue to evolve and address any challenges to balance executive and shareholder interests as it continues to maximize shareholder value.

3 External Pressures: The New Context for Executive Compensation

Everybody should have an interest in controlling this explosion in executive pay. The wealth of America has been built through the returns of our public corporations, and if those returns are being redirected to company managements, then the people who get the short end of the stick are the people who hope to retire someday.

Frederick E. Rowe, Jr., chairman, Texas Pension Review Board

I feel nothing but contempt. They pay themselves like rock stars.

Don Hodges, president, Hodges Fund

Since the advent of the modern corporation, executive pay has been vilified by the media, targeted for reform by activists, and regulated by the government. For the most part, the free market forces that gave rise to and underpin the successful pay-for-performance model have enabled executive pay to withstand the onslaught. However, never before have companies witnessed such an intense confluence of events and a convergence of external forces seeking to reshape the design, delivery, and disclosure of executive compensation.

In a world in which executive pay will be scrutinized, regulated, and revealed in an unprecedented fashion, understanding the external pressures that are creating this new context is a precursor to effectively designing executive pay programs.

Characteristics of External Forces

Two characteristics mark these external pressures. First, their intensity rises and falls in a pattern that follows the broad outlines of the business cycle and cyclical movements in the stock market. Historically, during times of relative economic prosperity and rising stock prices, high levels of executive compensation received little attention. But in periods of economic uncertainty, recession, or poor stock market performance, media criticisms of executive compensation proliferate, shareholder activists decry "corporate greed run amok," and regulators and Congress create new controls and limits on executive pay. This historical tendency, however, has changed in recent years, with the pressures on executive pay continuing unabated despite an improved economy and stock market from 2004 through 2006.

The second characteristic of the external pressures is that they generate both intended and unintended changes in executive pay practices, corporate governance, and business performance. These changes commonly carry positive and negative implications for the companies that are affected and, ultimately, for shareholders, employees, and the broader economy. As we will show, all too often in the history of executive compensation, the unintended consequences of reform efforts frequently undercut their original purpose.

The United States has a rich history of executive pay scrutiny and reform efforts. During the Gilded Age of the late 19th century, Mark Twain ridiculed John D. Rockefeller, Andrew Carnegie, and other corporate "robber barons" who grew rich through corrupt means. Criticisms of executive pay continued through the early part of the 20th century. In the early 1920s, the *New York Times* and the *Wall Street Journal* ran a series of articles that revealed the large salaries paid to railroad executives. The first known shareholder lawsuit over executive pay occurred in 1933 against American Tobacco for its $1.3 million payment to its president, George Washington Hill. In *Rogers v. Hill*, the U.S. Supreme Court established that executive pay at public companies is subject to judicial review.[1]

Criticism of high pay was not limited to corporate executives but extended to professional entertainers and athletes. In 1930, after holding out for more money, Babe Ruth signed a contract for $80,000, which was $5,000 more than President Hoover's salary. When challenged by a reporter about whether he deserved to make more than the president, Ruth responded, "I had a better year than he did."[2] Clearly, he understood the relationship between pay and performance.

During the Great Depression, in response to public concern about executive bonuses and stipends, government agencies gathered information on executive pay levels. Efforts to force executive pay disclosure crystallized with the establishment of the SEC in 1934. Since that time, the agency has provided information about executive compensation to the public.[3] When the commission released enhanced executive pay disclosure requirements in early 2006, SEC Chairman Christopher Cox remarked that "disclosure of material information has been one of the priorities of the SEC for 70 years."[4]

Cyclical Reforms and Unintended Consequences

The cyclical nature of scrutiny and reform efforts highlights their reactive nature and may partly explain the substantial number of unintended consequences that arise from these efforts. More often than not, government intervention in and constraints on the operation of free economic and labor markets has hurt performance and led to unexpected results. At the same time, it often creates positive residual change that helps shape executive pay in a constructive manner.

For example, the high marginal tax rates in the 1950s and 1960s gave rise to vehicles not subject to onerous taxation. The 1950 Revenue Act created the restricted-stock option, which allowed for capital gains tax treatment – a rate of 25 percent – on stock options. The rise in the use of stock options in the 1950s and 1960s enabled corporations to retain their top talent in a tax-effective manner while providing appropriate incentives to enhance shareholder value.

A second example can be found in the 1990–1991 recession. This downturn inspired pay critic Graef Crystal's 1991 book *In Search of Excess: The Overcompensation of Executives*, in which he criticized a number of leading executives, including Steven J. Ross, then CEO of Time Warner, whom he dubbed the "prince of pay." He also criticized then-CEOs Robert Goizueta of Coca-Cola and Lee Iacocca of Chrysler. Crystal introduced the idea of comparing executive pay levels in the United States with those in other countries, where companies supposedly were performing better.

A year later, *Time* magazine published "Executive Pay: The Shareholders Strike Back."[5] The article quoted Robert Monks of Institutional Shareholder Services: "Pay masks a much bigger problem. The real problem is the lack of accountability. CEOs are today's absolute monarchs and their Boards are the House of Lords, and they feel they can thumb their noses at us shareholders without fear of being held accountable. But I guarantee you, the days of corporate royalty are over." The article noted that ITT's CEO, Rand Araskog, who was criticized in Crystal's book for the $7 million pay package he received in 1990, had agreed to replace his outright stock grants with stock options.

Concerns about excessive executive pay during the 1990–1991 recession also touched off new disclosure efforts. In 1992, the SEC issued rules that required companies to include nonbinding shareholder proposals about pay in company proxy statements. The SEC rules also resulted in enhanced disclosure of CEO pay in relation to performance and stock option values. As with most reform efforts, this, too, had an unintended consequence. With enhanced disclosure, executive pay levels were transparent to all, thereby benefiting apparently underpaid executives.

In the constant search for equilibrium, the pendulum swings too far to one side and tries to right itself. The forces that attempted to correct the "excessive" compensation of the late 1980s led to the meteoric rise of executive compensation in the 1990s. During the Clinton administration, the Tax Act of 1994, which generated IRC Section 162(m), led to a dramatic proliferation of stock options. Media and shareholder scrutiny of pay without performance resulted in a dramatic increase in performance-based pay, which was aided by the SEC's new proxy disclosure rules.

The Genesis of the Current Environment

Criticisms of executive pay and efforts to reform it diminished in the mid- to late 1990s as the economy flourished and shareholders reaped huge returns. Internet companies led a dramatic increase in the use of stock options at all levels in the organization. With stock options spreading rewards to large numbers of employees and institutional shareholders profiting from the boom, CEOs were once again admired as business leaders, and their pay packages were rarely disputed. Dilution was not an issue because, on a net basis, the returns to shareholders were enormous.

The stock market continued its climb virtually unabated, but strong concerns eventually emerged over the high valuations of many companies, especially those in the technology sector. Early in 2000, technology sectors began to experience declining sales and signs of overcapacity. Soon company revenue growth and profitability targets came into question. Equity markets responded sharply. By the end of 2000, the S&P 500 had declined by 10.1 percent for the year and 13.6 percent from the market peak in March.

As investors grew cautious of the disconnect between company valuations and their underlying economics, the downturn broadened to other sectors and the resulting recession further exacerbated stock market volatility, already at historically high levels.

It was clear that executive compensation played a role in the decline in performance at some companies. The excessive use of options by some companies had led to a short-term focus and, at a few companies, illegal behavior. Chief executive officers who had been lauded only a few years earlier were suddenly denounced. Even celebrity corporate leaders such as General Electric's Jack Welch came under attack for their high earnings and extensive, poorly disclosed perks.

When the Enron scandal broke in fall 2001, the government was forced to take action; too many employees had been hurt, and the nation was in an uproar. Reportedly, Enron employees were holding onto locked-up shares in retirement plans while executives cashed out their stock options. A rush of external pressures pushed open the door for radical changes in the laws and regulations related to executive pay, most notably the Sarbanes-Oxley Act.

The Enron scandal also marked the beginning of a series of shareholder and government agency lawsuits, all aimed at what many argued were excessive payments made to executives. The complexity of these lawsuits is best expressed in the series of suits and countersuits that unfolded after Richard Grasso, former chairman of the New York Stock Exchange (NYSE), received a 2003 compensation agreement worth $188 million. When disclosure and payment issues emerged, Grasso resigned.

In 2004, New York state attorney general Eliot Spitzer filed suit against Grasso and the chairman of the NYSE's compensation committee. The suit was supported by a report written by former prosecutor Daniel K. Webb, which was commissioned by interim NYSE chairman John Reed. It charged that directors overpaid Grasso based on "incomplete, inaccurate and misleading information and that Grasso influenced his awards."[6] The report is a scathing indictment of Grasso and poor corporate governance at the NYSE.

However, additional documents were revealed to the public in 2005, despite Spitzer's efforts to block their release. These documents, which describe lengthy interviews with various board members, reveal that, contrary to Spitzer's claims, many directors knew exactly what was being provided to Grasso and believed his performance and criticality to the continued success of the NYSE warranted the level of pay he was given. According to board member and former Merrill Lynch chairman David Komansky, "We knew what we were doing when we paid him. We did it purposefully, and we believe it was the right compensation."[7] Other board interviews reveal that peer group selection, criticized in the Webb report, actually reflected "a great deal of thought and work."[8]

Of course, there are valid concerns about what took place at the NYSE, but not to the extent portrayed by Spitzer and the media. A press hungry for salacious details of a fallen CEO built up a story that may have been overstated.[9] It remains to be seen what the legal outcome will be.

The Regulators

The cyclical nature of media criticisms of executive pay also appears in the pattern of regulation efforts by the various federal agencies, which accelerates during periods of economic and stock market decline and abates with recovery. In the process, the reforms and new regulations that proliferate often have unintended consequences.

SECURITIES AND EXCHANGE COMMISSION

The SEC did little in the 10 years after crafting its proxy disclosure requirements in 1992 to require improved executive compensation disclosure. But after the events at Enron, WorldCom, and several other troubled companies, its position changed, first through actions against specific companies, then through public pronouncements, and eventually through the release of new disclosure requirements in early 2006.

In a series of lawsuits and pronouncements in 2004, the SEC tried to enforce disclosure requirements that were already on the books. Most notably, it took action against General Electric for failing to fully and adequately describe the "terms and conditions" of its retirement agreement with its former CEO Jack Welch.

In its settlement with General Electric, the SEC stated that simply disclosing that Welch was to receive "facilities and services comparable to those provided to him prior to his retirement" was not sufficient because such disclosure did not inform investors that these benefits included the personal use of chauffeured limousines and of GE-owned aircraft and home security systems worth more than $1 million annually.[10]

On December 15, 2004, Tyson Foods disclosed that it had settled an SEC complaint that the company and its former chairman, Don Tyson, did not adequately disclose the perks Tyson was receiving while chairman. The perks were valued at $1.7 million.[11] Five days later, the SEC announced enforcement proceedings against The Walt Disney Company. Disney was charged with failing to disclose that the company employed three children of its directors and provided office space, secretarial services, a leased car, and a driver to a director, which were valued at more than $200,000 annually.[12]

As often happens, the market reacted more quickly than the regulatory bodies. In 2004–2005, the majority of the compensation committees we worked with – and, we suspect, many others – were already reviewing such disclosures as executive compensation "tally sheets," which provide a detailed ledger of total pay and show potential payouts under various termination scenarios.

Nevertheless, with the announcement in early 2006 of the SEC's enhanced disclosure rules, many companies must now revamp their pay disclosure processes. The new rules require the following:

- A new Compensation Discussion and Analysis section replaces the Board Compensation Committee report. This new report to shareholders must be written in "plain English." It should describe, in detail, the goals and objectives of the executive compensation program, the performance the program is designed to reward, and the process for determining compensation.
- Covered executives now must include the CFO in addition to the CEO and the next three most highly compensated executives based on total compensation. Compensation may also need to be disclosed for up to three additional policymaking executives if they are paid more than any named executive officer.
- A revamped Summary Compensation Table must show a total compensation figure along with the elements that compose it, including cash, the annual accounting accrual value of equity compensation, and all other compensation, which consists of the actuarial value of the increase in pension plan benefits, above-market earnings on deferred compensation, and all perquisites having a value greater than $10,000.
- Supplemental tables must provide additional details about equity awards, outstanding equity awards at fiscal year-end, option exercises and stock vested, and retirement and deferred compensation balances and earnings.
- Additionally, a narrative must be provided that describes and quantifies severance and change-in-control payments that would be due executives.

It remains to be seen what effects the rules will have. In certain cases, companies did not fully disclose compensation delivery, particularly with respect to deferred compensation and benefits and perquisites. The new rules will reduce the number of outliers and may reduce the use of non–performance-based pay. Enhanced disclosure helps create a healthy and efficient labor market. But for the vast majority of companies and their shareholders, the rules will simply improve what is already a successful executive compensation system.

FINANCIAL ACCOUNTING STANDARDS BOARD

Confronted with intense pressure from lobbyists and receiving little external support, in 1993 the Financial Accounting Standards Board backed off of its drive for the mandatory expensing of stock options and allowed voluntary adoption of FAS 123. But in the post-Enron era of greater scrutiny and with public support from influential people such as former Federal Reserve Board chairman Alan Greenspan and Berkshire Hathaway CEO Warren Buffett, FASB put in place mandatory stock option expensing under FAS 123(R), effective for fiscal years beginning after June 15, 2005.

FAS 123(R) requires the expensing of all stock-settled awards, including stock options, stock-settled stock appreciation rights, restricted stock, performance shares, and performance-contingent restricted stock. The expense must be measured on the basis of the fair value of the awards at the time of grant based on an estimate of the number of awards likely to vest.

The expensing rule has leveled the playing field for long-term incentive vehicles. No longer will companies automatically default to stock options. It is likely that this reform, like others, will produce a series of unintended effects. One of those effects we are currently seeing is the move by many companies to limit participation by no longer awarding stock options below the executive ranks. A second effect is the move to time-vested restricted stock, which lacks the performance orientation found in stock options.

INTERNAL REVENUE SERVICE

Past efforts by the IRS to address executive compensation "abuses" have met with resistance, with the courts generally interpreting IRS rules on deferred compensation provisions that are generally favored by executives. However, in a 2003 pilot program, the agency reviewed 24 companies' deferred compensation practices and found that executives were not following rules on the taxation of corporate fringe benefits and that some executives were not reporting income properly or even filing returns.[13]

Consequently, the IRS expanded its review to cover stock options and stock incentives, with particular attention to the timing of deductions, IRC Section 83(b) elections, and matching gains and deductions on stock option exercises. The agency also indicated that it would investigate the deferral of option gains to family partnerships. In fact, in early 2005, the IRS put in place a settlement offer for companies involved in these "schemes."

The IRS also scrutinized nonqualified deferred compensation plans, which led to legislation in the form of IRC Section 409A. This rule made it more difficult to defer current income and subsequently receive that deferred income. We suspect that the prevalence of deferred compensation has markedly declined as a result of Section 409A and the relatively low tax rates under the George W. Bush administration. That is unfortunate because deferred compensation denominated in company stock is an effective way to promote long-term shareholder alignment and share ownership.

NYSE AND NASDAQ

After the Enron debacle, both exchanges, first the NYSE and then the NASDAQ, revisited their listing requirements. The NYSE standards committee determined that "now, in the aftermath of the 'meltdown' of significant companies due to failures of diligence, ethics and controls, the NYSE has the opportunity – and the responsibility – once again to raise corporate governance and disclosure standards."[14] The NASDAQ instituted new requirements that largely paralleled the NYSE requirements. The SEC approved amendments to both the NYSE and the NASDAQ listing standards on November 4, 2003.

The NYSE listing requirements relevant to executive and stock-based compensation include the following:[15]

- **Director independence.** *Requirement*: Independent directors must constitute a majority of the board. Independence requires no "material relationship with the listed company," which is determined based on a broad consideration "of all the facts and circumstances." *Implications*: This requirement has contributed to the demand-and-supply imbalance in the market for director talent. Demand has increased because of the independence requirements and the need for audit or compensation expertise, while supply is constrained because serving as a director now requires considerable time and carries greater risk and exposure. Moreover, active CEOs are discouraged from serving on the boards of other companies because of concerns about the time commitment and the possibility of interlocking relationships. Basic microeconomics indicates that this imbalance has led to significant increases in director compensation.

- **Executive sessions.** *Requirement*: Nonmanagement directors are required to meet at regularly scheduled sessions without management present "to foster better communication among non-management directors." *Implications*: This rule has increased the prevalence of having a lead, or presiding, director who chairs these sessions. It also empowers the board and committees to consider, with their own independent advisers, various compensation-related proposals put forth by management. We have been involved in hundreds of these sessions. They ensure a deliberate and uninfluenced evaluation of executive pay program design and delivery.

- **Compensation committee.** *Requirement*: The committee must be composed entirely of independent directors. It must have a written charter, which should provide, among other things, that the committee has "the sole authority to retain and terminate" a compensation consultant as well as approve the firm's fees and other retention terms. The committee must review and approve corporate goals relevant to CEO compensation. The standards also stipulate that the committee must determine and approve the CEO's compensation based on an evaluation of the CEO's performance. The committee must also make recommendations to the board with respect to non-CEO compensation as well as incentive and stock-based compensation. In determining long-term incentive compensation for the CEO, the committee should consider the company's performance and relative shareholder return. *Implications*: Assessing relationships between pay and performance becomes of paramount importance. Also, the standards alter the relationship with the compensation consultant.

- **Shareholder approval of equity plans.** *Requirement*: Shareholders must have the opportunity to vote on all equity compensation plans as well as any material revisions to any equity plans, including an increase in the number of shares or eligible participants, an expansion of the types of awards, an increase in the number of eligible participants, an extension in the term, a change in the method for determining the strike price for options, and the deletion or limitation of any provision prohibiting repricing of options. Limited exceptions include employment inducement awards and certain other types of qualified plans. *Implications*: This new standard gives shareholders greater control over dilution from stock-based plans. It limits management's and the board's ability to make plan changes without going back to shareholders. With many companies now having to ask for shareholder approval for more shares, it is more difficult to get approval for plan changes.

CONGRESS

In the wake of the corporate scandals, U.S. senators and representatives generated a large amount of legislation to show voters that they were addressing the issues. Although many of these attempts did not go very far, two major pieces of legislation were enacted.

- **Sarbanes-Oxley Act**. This far-reaching legislation was signed into law by President George W. Bush on July 30, 2002, "to protect investors by improving the accuracy and reliability of corporate disclosures."[16] According to U.S. Chamber of Commerce president and CEO Thomas J. Donohue, "the pendulum has swung too far."[17]

One company, Monarch Casinos, described its experience complying with the act in the *Wall Street Journal*:

> We are in the process of our compliance efforts mandated by Section 404 of the Sarbanes-Oxley Act of 2002. As we have done our due diligence in trying to understand the requirements and corresponding work necessary to successfully document our system of internal controls to the standards and satisfaction of third parties, we have encountered egregious estimates of time, dollars, outside consultant fees, and volumes of paperwork. As our implementation has progressed, we have yet to realize any control, operations or governance improvements or benefits. Additionally, and most importantly, the estimated potential cost to our shareholders in relation to the benefits, or even potential benefits, is unconscionable.[18]

The often-denounced Sarbanes-Oxley Act contains many far-reaching requirements, but our focus relates to the implications for executive compensation. The act prohibits executive loans and imposes executive trading restrictions during blackout periods. Because of the loan prohibition, companies must be more creative in how they induce executives to join their companies, often leading to more costly alternatives such as restricted-stock awards, up-front signing bonuses, and enhanced severance – all of which are now being criticized as pay for nonperformance or pay for failure. But because of the trading restrictions, many companies have established executive trading plans under SEC Rule 10b5–1, which we view as a positive development. A 10b5–1 plan is a set of written instructions to a broker that specifies the amount, price, and date of future trades. The 10b5–1 plan must be entered into at a time when the executive is not aware of any material nonpublic information.

- **American Jobs Creation Act of 2004**. Signed into law by President George W. Bush on October 22, 2004, this act created IRC Section 409A, which provides that all amounts deferred under a nonqualified deferred compensation plan are taxable unless certain requirements are met. The initial election to defer must be made in the calendar year prior to the year in which the compensation is earned unless the compensation is performance-based, in which case it must be made up to six months before the end of the performance period. Distributions may occur only upon separation of service (with a six-month delay for top executives), death or disability, a specified time or schedule, or in the event of an emergency.

The act also eliminates the ability to get at deferred amounts early and limits flexibility for further deferrals. As it relates to equity compensation, the act does not extend to market-priced options and stock appreciation rights settled in stock but does cover restricted stock units. The act applies to amounts deferred after December 31, 2004. The new requirements make deferred compensation programs less attractive, but the economic advantages of pretax deferrals and tax-deferred capital accumulation will remain.

The Reformers

Institutional shareholders and their advisers control or influence hundreds of billions of dollars of shareholder wealth. Will they use that influence to help shape the pay-for-performance model in a way that benefits their own wealth, as many private equity firms have done? Or will they undermine their own well-being by attempting to reform executive pay through controls that are unrelated to market forces?

Many of the recent regulatory efforts were advanced or supported by institutional investors, who are one of the most powerful external forces involved in reshaping executive compensation. The most common types of institutional investors are mutual fund companies, such as Fidelity and Vanguard; retirement programs, including private company pension funds and 401(k) plans; public sector employee retirement programs and multiemployer plans; insurance companies; banks; and universities and foundations. In addition to institutional investors, large investors include venture capital and private equity firms, wealthy individuals, and family trusts.

As the ownership share of institutional investors grew dramatically in the 1990s, their power over boards and executives also increased. In addition, when the SEC changed the proxy rules governing shareholder communications in 1992 and essentially reduced the costs of coordinated shareholder actions, it further empowered shareholder groups to take an activist role and challenge boards and executives on management issues, including executive compensation.

Ironically, institutional investors were at least partially responsible for the dramatic increase in executive pay in the 1990s, but they are now its greatest critics. An article by Jay Matthews in the March 24, 1996, *Washington Post* titled "Their Riches Were Your Command" had as its subhead "Demands that executive pay be tied to performance are what led to downsizers' bonuses; pension funds add to pressure on companies to reform."

It is difficult to overestimate the power of U.S. institutional investors. The latest data show that they controlled $24.1 trillion in assets in 2005, up 39 percent since 2002, at which point they controlled $17.3 trillion in assets, according to The Conference Board.[19]

One of the more visible signs of the increased activism of institutional shareholders has been the dramatic increase in executive-pay-related shareholder resolutions on corporate proxy ballots. According to Institutional Shareholder Services (ISS) and the Investor Responsibility Research Center, there were 276 compensation-related proposals in 2005, up from 182 in 2004, 163 in 2003, and 25 in 2002. The increase, in part, reflects the large number of proposals for targeted companies to expense stock options. With the advent of required stock option expensing in 2006, the pace of shareholder resolutions has dropped off.

Moreover, activist shareholders, particularly building trades' pension funds, have become more targeted in their approach, limiting pay for nonperformance. For example, Amalgamated Bank and the International Brotherhood of Electrical Workers have submitted proposals at a number of prominent companies calling for a limit to golden parachute payments upon a change in control. The United Brotherhood of Carpenters and Joiners of America has submitted proposals at a number of companies that restrict equity awards to when companies outperform peers. This reflects a change in strategy; in the past, the Carpenters called for

FIGURE 3.1
Institutional Investors See Problems with the U.S. Executive Pay Model and Disclosure

Overall, the U.S. executive pay model at most companies . . .	AGREE	NEUTRAL	DISAGREE
Has hurt corporate America's image	85%	10%	6%
Has dramatically overpaid executives	90%	8%	2%
Is too heavily influenced by management	87%	8%	6%
Is an example of poor U.S. corporate governance	63%	15%	21%
Is properly disclosed	25%	11%	64%

Source: Watson Wyatt.

limitations on executive pay, which appeared to garner little support from other shareholders. However, some studies indicate that these proposals, even if rejected, have a chilling effect on compensation decisions, with lower executive pay awarded at companies that experience a shareholder proposal on executive compensation.[20]

INSTITUTIONAL INVESTOR PERSPECTIVES
In 2005, Watson Wyatt surveyed 55 institutional investors that manage more than $800 billion in assets.[21] We found that although U.S. equity markets have generally performed well in the last 25 years, there is a consensus among institutional investors that a good part of that performance was caused by major factors beyond the control or influence of management. Moreover, they believe that management, especially executives, captured a disproportionately large part of the stock market gains in the form of stock options and other pay elements.

Institutional investors think that more change is needed in the way U.S. executive pay is determined. Although some institutional investors are neutral, 63 percent say that executive pay is an example of poor U.S. corporate governance (see Figure 3.1). In addition, fully 85 percent think that the U.S. executive pay model has hurt corporate America's image, and 90 percent think it has created dramatically overpaid executives. For the most part, institutional investors blame this on management, who too heavily influence compensation levels, according to 87 percent of institutional investors.

Concerns with Lack of Pay-for-Performance

Overall, institutional investors believe executive pay is too high and are concerned over a lack of pay-for-performance, particularly at average- or poor-performing companies. But institutional investors also see some

FIGURE 3.2
Significant Share Ownership by Executives

Overall, the U.S. executive pay model at most companies ...	AGREE	NEUTRAL	DISAGREE
Has yielded high levels of executive share ownership	52%	31%	17%

In your opinion, how shareholder-friendly are ...	SHAREHOLDER-FRIENDLY	NEUTRAL	SHAREHOLDER-UNFRIENDLY
Stock ownership guidelines for executives	44%	12%	44%
Stock ownership guidelines for directors	46%	25%	29%
Requirements for holding shares following exercise or vesting of restricted shares	61%	18%	22%

Source: Watson Wyatt.

positive trends, including rising levels of executive stock ownership, larger amounts of performance vesting, and the increasing prevalence of the "right" financial performance metrics.

Most institutional investors think the current pay system has promoted significant share ownership by executives (see Figure 3.2). This is important because high share ownership results in a total executive pay package that is highly sensitive to the company's stock price performance, which encourages alignment between management and shareholder interests.

STOCK INCENTIVES

Institutional investors generally consider stock option and full-value share programs that have performance vesting much more attractive than programs with time-based vesting. About one in three institutional investors find time-vested stock options attractive. That number nearly doubles to 65 percent if the vesting is performance-based (see Figure 3.3).

FIGURE 3.3
Support for Performance-Contingent LTI Vehicles

LTI VEHICLE	PERCENTAGE FAVORABLE
Stock Options	
Time-vested stock options	35%
Performance-vested stock options	65%
Full-Value Shares	
Time-vested restricted stock	29%
Performance-vested stock	70%

Source: Watson Wyatt.

FIGURE 3.4
Pay-for-Performance Metrics of Importance to Institutional Investors

PERFORMANCE METRIC	SINGLE MOST IMPORTANT	TOP THREE MOST IMPORTANT
Return on equity (ROE)	12%	38%
Return on invested capital (ROIC)	6%	30%
Return on assets (ROA)	4%	26%
Cash flow return on investment (CFROI)	8%	26%
Earnings per share (EPS)	6%	32%
Sales growth	4%	8%
Total returns to shareholders (TRS)	38%	62%
Earnings (EBIT or EBITDA)	2%	16%
Operating cash flow	6%	18%
Economic value added	4%	24%
Others	10%	12%

Source: Watson Wyatt.

For full-value shares, the numbers are even more dramatic. Only 29 percent of respondents think that time-vested restricted stock – often derided by critics as "pay for pulse" – is attractive from the shareholder's perspective. That number increases to 70 percent if the vesting is contingent on meeting performance targets. Although performance vesting for stock options remains quite rare, there is a major move under way toward performance vesting on full-value shares, typically being granted in lieu of some stock options.

PERFORMANCE METRICS
Implementing performance requirements will, of course, depend on the trade-offs between shareholders and management. We asked institutional investors to identify the most important pay-for-performance metrics (see Figure 3.4). As expected, total return to shareholders was cited most often; 38 percent ranked it number one, and 62 percent listed it among the top three metrics. Twenty-two percent of the responses cited return metrics such as return on equity (ROE), return on invested capital (ROIC), and return on assets (ROA) as the most important metric.

SEVERANCE AND CHANGE-IN-CONTROL AGREEMENTS
An often-overlooked aspect of pay for performance is downside risk. From media accounts and institutional investor documents, it appears

FIGURE 3.5

Institutional Investors' Views on Pay-for-Failure and Change-in-Control

In your opinion, how shareholder-friendly are ...	SHAREHOLDER-FRIENDLY	NEUTRAL	SHAREHOLDER-UNFRIENDLY
Change-in-control agreements for top executives	17%	19%	64%
Automatic vesting for long-term incentives upon a change in control	6%	10%	84%
Executive severance plans for involuntary termination	6%	19%	75%

Source: Watson Wyatt.

that much of the anger in the marketplace about executive compensation is the perception that executives, and CEOs in particular, receive substantial compensation regardless of their performance. Extraordinary pay that can be justified by extraordinary performance is one issue (even if there is some sentiment that the pay ought not to be so high). But anything that smacks of pay for failure or pay for a transaction beyond the executive's control is another matter. Indeed, in March 2006, four union pension funds filed a lawsuit charging that Hewlett Packard's directors provided ousted CEO Carly Fiorina with a severance package that "greatly exceeded the maximum allowed under a board policy adopted in 2003."[22]

In this vein, it is not surprising that the data in Figure 3.5 show that institutional investors are strongly opposed to change-in-control agreements, automatic vesting, and severance plans for involuntary termination, all of which are regarded by institutional shareholders as shareholder-unfriendly.

It is extremely difficult to recruit a top executive into an organization without offering severance or change-in-control protection. These recruiting packages set the market and drive incumbent pay packages as well. Change-in-control payments to executives, while very large in the last 10 to 15 years, have helped feed the coincident – but not coincidental – takeover booms. Executives no longer resist deals and, in fact, seek them out, thereby creating higher returns for their shareholders. Change-in-control agreements allow the top executives to "sell" their "stake" in the company.

In mid-2006, a Watson Wyatt report called "Balance Under Pressure – Board of Directors' Views on Executive Compensation" found that nonemployee directors agreed that the U.S. executive pay model has hurt corporate America's image (79 percent of corporate directors compared with 85 percent of institutional investors), but there was significant disagreement between directors and institutional investors as to whether the U.S. pay model has improved corporate performance. Nearly two-thirds (65 percent) of the surveyed corporate directors felt that the executive pay model has improved corporate performance as compared with only 22 percent of institutional investors. Based on this finding, it is fair to assume that directors by and large believe that the negative perception of executive pay is unfair as it relates to the vast majority of U.S. companies.

The Financial Activists

The economic history of executive compensation in the 1970s and 1980s laid the foundation for what has happened since the 1990s. Basically, the underperformance of the U.S. economy in the 1970s, led by the underperformance of the corporate sector, yielded two sources of upward pressure on executive pay levels.

The first source was the number of leveraged buyouts. These created alternatives for executives, either as employees of LBO or management buyout (MBO) firms or as executives at public companies that responded to the rising demand for superior performance by improving their executive rewards with large grants of stock options. The net result was high levels of pay at the public companies, presumably linked to higher levels of performance, to keep executives from moving to these alternative employers.

The second source was the use and size of change-in-control severance agreements in the late 1980s. These agreements were necessary to reduce – or effectively eliminate – resistance to value-enhancing hostile takeovers. The plans did just that, but they also caused pay packages to rise. Compensation increased to motivate management to run companies effectively and to neutralize the large economic advantage gained from selling the company to obtain the change-in-control payments.

LBO Impact

The migration of top corporate talent to investment and venture capital firms has occurred for decades. These firms can be an attractive option for executives in the latter stages of their careers or for those wishing to avoid the constant publicity and risk that comes with being an executive in a public company. If there is further downward pressure on executive compensation, or more stigma and embarrassment associated with being an executive, the trickle of executives going into private investment firms could become a flood.

Randall S. Thomas, professor of business and law at Vanderbilt University, refers to this as the "opportunity cost theory."[23] One of the theory's components is that U.S. executives have many lucrative employment alternatives created by the financial revolution in the United States. These alternatives – venture capital, private equity, MBOs, and other entities outside the corporate sector – have logically, according to the laws of supply and demand, raised the executive's cost to their current employer.

Coming into the 1980s, there were trillions of dollars of underperforming assets managed by the private sector equivalent of civil servants. This low-hanging fruit was ready for picking by firms willing to try a new economic model, the LBO, which boosted returns to shareholders but also increased executive compensation at private and public companies. Leveraged buyouts involved using debt to purchase underperforming companies from the public shareholders or the parent company and creating strict internal operating expense discipline. And LBOs frequently used the same executives who had been underperforming and loaded them up with stock options and shares that were often purchased, usually on favorable terms. And what happened? In many cases, those new leveraged, private companies dramatically outperformed their public company history and their peers and created enormous wealth for the LBO firms and their executives.[24]

These executives were granted large amounts of stock options, which motivated them to improve strategy, sell or close underperforming assets, and make better acquisitions. Specifically, the executives were encouraged to reduce costs, especially through layoffs. While this created distress at the individual employee and family levels, fortunately the U.S. economy began to boom after 1983, and the labor market was able to absorb most of the newly unemployed.

The cyclical migration of talent could happen again. If criticism and overregulation of executive pay continue to increase, another migration of talented executives could occur. Numerous executives have left the corporate world to enter buyout or venture capital firms. These include executives with experience in investment banking, health care, the automotive industry, property and casualty insurance, asset management, hospitality, reinsurance, and many other industries. Opportunities – and the opportunity costs – force current corporate employers to raise executive pay levels. Fortunately, there is still a sufficient margin remaining for excellent returns to shareholders.

Thomas argues that in the U.S. economy power has shifted to highly skilled labor, including top executives. In conjunction with easy financing from the capital markets, skilled executives can easily start their own firms. "The implications of this shift in power for executive compensation are obvious: established firms will need to offer their most skilled employees, the ones that have the most alternative options for employment, a larger piece of the firm's surplus in order to retain them."[25]

IMPACT OF CHANGE-IN-CONTROL PROTECTION

A related phenomenon was the rise of hostile takeovers by LBO firms and other financial or strategic buyers, which also generated upward pressure on executive pay. These takeovers were hostile because the directors of the target, and especially its management, argued that the target company could create more value for shareholders by being independent. This has dramatically been proved false. The real reason for the resistance was that management did not want to lose their lucrative jobs.[26]

Eventually, most companies instituted change-in-control protection to make their executives relatively indifferent to keeping their jobs or being bought out. Although these agreements essentially eliminated hostile takeovers, they dramatically increased total takeover activity. But the pendulum may have swung too far, as some consider the $100 million change-in-control payments to some executives excessive. Some critics argue that CEOs are selling their companies cheap (at low premiums) to get their change-in-control packages. In fact, target shareholders have achieved excellent returns from those takeovers. Even Warren Buffett, who is largely critical of executive pay, noted that the nine-figure platinum parachute received by Gillette CEO James Kilts as a result of its takeover by Procter & Gamble was high pay for high performance. Buffett commented in his company's 2006 report to shareholders that "for his accomplishments, Jim was paid very well – but earned every penny."

Institutional investors may argue that U.S. CEOs are simply receiving extraordinary payments for making a decision they should make in the interests of the company. Executives need change-in-control payments – a "bribe" – to sell their company, and then they need a "bribe" not to sell. Nevertheless, these events create enormous value for target shareholders.

Target company shareholders gain when their company is acquired, but returns have historically been more uncertain for buyers. Sara B. Moeller, Frederik P. Schlingemann, and Rene M. Stulz added other dimensions to the discussion in a 2005 study.[27] First, the study found that more than half of the buying companies create value through the acquisitions. Second, with the growth of options as a form of managerial compensation in the 1990s, managerial wealth is more closely tied to stock prices, presumably making management more conscious of the impact of acquisitions on the stock price and less likely to make acquisitions that decrease shareholder wealth.

For the acquiring company, the CEO is – or so his or her boards believe – essential to approving, negotiating, integrating, and running the new company postacquisition.

HEDGE FUNDS

Hedge funds could well be the LBO agent of the early 21st century. They typically end up as short-term shareholders but exert tremendous influence on the companies in which they take large positions. Especially in the retail and banking sectors, hedge funds are demanding a larger role in managing the companies they invest in and determining executive pay levels.[28] The rising power, control, and influence of hedge funds may do more to shape executive compensation than any other external force during this period.

"A number of hedge funds have become the corporate activists of this generation," says Alan Jones, managing director and head of global corporate finance at Morgan Stanley.[29] Hedge funds have become increasingly aggressive in taking board seats and demanding executive compensation reform. They often insist that the company take actions to boost the stock price, including hiring outside strategists and forcing the CEO to give up certain compensation and retirement benefits.

Legendary investor Carl Icahn did just that at Blockbuster. With the support of hedge funds, Icahn and two other dissident candidates won seats on Blockbuster's board in May 2005 after long-standing disagreements with its CEO over the company's direction. With 8.6 percent of Blockbuster's overall voting shares, Icahn is the largest shareholder and is now in a position to wield power in the boardroom, with the blessing of large hedge funds that also hold significant amounts of stock. Icahn immediately made it clear that he would use his seat on the board to cut spending and increase dividends to shareholders. He also indicated that he would attempt to take control of the board in 2006 elections if the company continued down what he considers the wrong path.[30]

More recently, in early 2006, investor Kirk Kerkorian, who at the time owned nearly 10 percent of General Motors, called for significant pay cuts for top executives and directors at the company. Jerome York, one of Kerkorian's top lieutenants, told the *Wall Street Journal* that although cutting executive pay would not save "huge dollars, it would be a very important indication that we are all in this together."[31] As a result, GM executives agreed to a pay cut, with the CEO cutting his salary by 50 percent and top executives reducing theirs by 20 percent to 30 percent.

Media Critics and Public Figures

Scrutiny of executive compensation has always been with us, but the coverage took on a more caustic tone after the Enron scandal. In a June 25, 2001, article, "The Great CEO Pay Heist," *Fortune* referred to executive compensation as "highway robbery" and criticized "America's out-of-control CEO pay machine." The article cited Steve Jobs's large pay package at Apple, while acknowledging that "he deserves to be rewarded – handsomely – for bringing Apple back from the dead." The article also cited large stock option grants for Oracle's Larry Ellison and Dell's Michael Dell.

A May 6, 2002, *BusinessWeek* article quoted J. Richard Finlay, chairman of the Center for Corporate & Public Governance, as saying, "Excessive CEO pay is the mad cow disease of American boardrooms." The influential *Financial Times* ran a story on July 2, 2003, titled "CEO: (n) Greedy Liar with Personality Disorder," which stated that six senior U.S. professors thought that "a fair number of CEOs are sociopaths" because they were not concerned about their seemingly excessive pay packages.

Media scrutiny serves an important purpose. Although the media systematically draw negative attention to instances of nonperformance for pay – which are isolated, not systemic – in doing so they may help ensure that companies with appropriate executive compensation practices work harder to maintain them. But the media also distort the picture of executive compensation that is presented to the public and policymakers.

In addition to critics in the media, some public figures routinely denounce executive pay practices. Warren Buffett, for example, in his 2004 annual report to Berkshire Hathaway's shareholders, wrote: "In judging whether Corporate America is serious about reforming itself, CEO pay remains the acid test. To date, results aren't encouraging." He goes on to lambaste "consultants and human relations departments, which had no trouble perceiving who buttered their bread." He also faults directors, noting that "in recent years compensation committees too often have been tail-wagging puppy dogs meekly following recommendations by consultants." His statement on James Kilts notwithstanding, Buffett stepped up his vitriol in Berkshire's 2005 shareholders report, decrying that "too often, executive compensation in the U.S. is ridiculously out of line with performance. The upshot is that a mediocre-or-worse CEO – aided by his handpicked VP of human relations and a consultant from the ever-accommodating firm of Ratchet, Ratchet and Bingo – all too often receives gobs of money from an ill-designed compensation arrangement."

While he himself takes little in the form of compensation, Buffett sits on the boards of several companies that provide large executive pay packages. Buffett was on the board at Coca-Cola when it awarded CEO Roberto Goizueta an $8 million consulting contract and immediately vested 2 million shares of restricted stock when he left the company. He also sat on the board when it awarded a million shares of restricted stock in 2001, worth about $60 million, to CEO Douglas Daft and then lowered his performance targets when it became apparent that the company would not meet them. And he was on the board of Gillette when it fired CEO Michael Hawley but gave him $8.7 million in termination fees and increased his lifelong pension benefits.

Graef Crystal provided a reference point for criticisms of executive pay in *In Search of Excess*. But Crystal seems to accept the idea that real negotiations take place between boards and CEOs. He told The Conference Board in 2002 that, "[I]f the board is doing its job, it should be trying to get the CEO to work for a dollar a year. If the CEO is doing his job, he's going to try to get a pay package that's one dollar a year less than the revenues of the company. And after a lot of screaming and yelling and storming out of rooms, they're going to come to a deal."[32]

What We Can Learn

We have been taught from the early 1990s pay reform efforts that certain macroeconomic and sociopolitical events upset the equilibrium of executive compensation and cause the pendulum to swing to one side. In this case, the result was an onslaught of external pressures and change agents seeking to reform executive compensation.

But reform efforts often led to unintended consequences. The Omnibus Budget and Reconciliation Act gave birth to IRC Section 162(m). The net effect of Section 162(m) was a proliferation of stock options. The net effect of the 1992 proxy statement disclosure enhancements was an increased focus on pay and performance relationships but also an increase in the use of "stealth" compensation. These forces, however, ultimately led to the proliferation of options that helped drive and support the stock market boom of the mid- to late 1990s.

We see parallels in the early part of this decade, when corporate scandals and the stock market decline focused the spotlight on the inexcusable practices of the few and drew attention to the less than optimal practices of others. However, the intense scrutiny and regulatory zeal may create more problems than they solve.

The issues may have been best described in a January 21, 2006, editorial in the *Wall Street Journal*:

> Who knows what is "exorbitant" pay anyway? The modern CEO position requires a variety of skills and experience that aren't easily found. Especially in a Sarbanes-Oxley world, CEOs face more scrutiny and have shorter tenures. It's also notable that many of today's most informed and sophisticated investors are only too happy to pay handsomely, perhaps even exorbitantly, for the right CEO candidate. Private equity firms in particular have persisted in giving out large pay packages to the top managers they hire to turn companies around. And because they are paying with their own money, they have a big stake in getting it right.[33]

Ultimately, the market should be the final arbiter of the CEO pay debate. To the extent that the external forces limit or prevent the market from operating efficiently, current and potential talent may look for opportunities elsewhere. And if that happens, all stakeholders – shareholders, employees, and the economy in general – will suffer.

4 End of an Era: The Decline of the Stock Option

When you win [with options], you win the lottery . . . the variation is huge; much greater than employees have an appetite for . . . so what we do now is give shares, not options.

Bill Gates, Microsoft Corporation

On the eve of the 21st century, the buzzword in executive compensation was "airplane wealth": making enough money to buy an airplane. Top executives were leaving old-economy corporations in droves and joining upstart Internet companies with the idea of boosting their earnings to the level of "airplane wealth." Executives who stayed with their companies structured spin-offs and tracking stocks and joint ventures to try to capitalize on the value ascribed to their own quick-start, Internet-based ventures.

Stock options, the coin of the realm, were the preferred method of payment for top executives, employees, and anyone else connected with the company. Headhunters, law firms, and even compensation consulting firms were more than willing to take 10 cents on the dollar to have their fees delivered in the form of stock options.

And why not? At its peak, the NASDAQ composite stock index hit 5,048.62 on March 10, 2000, double its value from the previous summer. Stock options had no enemies. Shareholders and investors with bulging portfolios cared little that their own returns were being eroded by 4 percent or more per year when they were earning 40 percent a year. For the companies, options minimized their cash outlays and improved cash flow because they benefited from the cash inflow of proceeds from payment of exercise price and tax deductions when employees exercised their options. The tax benefits of option exercises at Cisco Systems added approximately $2.5 billion to the company's cash flow for the fiscal year ending in July 2000.[1]

But a little more than a month after its peak, the NASDAQ lost one-third of its value; in the next two-and-a-half years, it shed 80 percent. Aggressive bookkeeping at a number of companies – and criminal activity at a few – left executives with substantial wealth and employees with little or nothing. The heavy reliance on stock options was partly to blame, as it promoted a short-term perspective that was reinforced by analysts focused on quarterly earnings reports.

And finally, after years of pressing for stock option expensing, the Financial Accounting Standards Board saw its opening and installed an expensing requirement in the middle of 2005. Stock option expensing, coupled with increased shareholder activism concerning dilution, accelerated the reversal of the earlier trend and became the primary factor driving the decline in stock option use. The number of options awarded to CEOs at the nation's largest companies dropped by 7 percent in 2004 and 16 percent in 2005, according to an analysis by Watson Wyatt.

After this tumultuous rise and fall, it is now possible to reevaluate stock options as part of compensation. In the new world, stock options must be expensed. Their perceived value – and how they measure up in a cost–benefit analysis – are key considerations.

The 1990s: The Decade of the Stock Option

Stock options dominated the compensation landscape of the 1990s. At the zenith in 2000, annual awards of employee stock options at non-technology companies represented 2.9 percent of shares outstanding, a 44 percent increase from 1994. At new-economy companies, annual option grants rose from 4.2 percent to 7.4 percent of shares outstanding, a 75 percent increase in the same period.[2]

Watson Wyatt research shows that in 1990, the average stock option overhang for a firm in the S&P 1500 was 5.4 percent. By 2000, it was 14.6 percent, representing an 11 percent annual increase. During the same decade, the S&P 500 rose by 15 percent a year[3] (see Figures 4.1 and 4.2).

Much has been written about the reasons for the dramatic rise in the use of stock options during the 1990s. Academic studies posit two different theories.

Lucien Bebchuk and Jesse Fried represent the first view, arguing that CEOs and senior executives used their influence to make the design of option plans more favorable to them. Bebchuk and Fried say, "Managers

FIGURE 4.1
Stock Option Overhang and Stock Market Performance in the 1990s

	DOW JONES INDUSTRIAL AVERAGE	OVERHANG
1990	2,634	5.4%
1995	5,117	9.2%
1997	7,908	11.9%
1999	11,497	13.0%
2000	10,787	14.6%
Ten-year annualized growth rate	**15.1%**	**10.5%**

Source: Watson Wyatt.

have been able to use their influence to grab the reins of the options bandwagon and steer it in a direction that serves their interests."[4]

Bebchuk and Fried also claim that managers "prefer compensation practices that obscure the total amount of compensation, that appear to be more performance-based than they really are, and that package pay in ways that make it easier to justify and defend."[5] They contend that market-priced stock options are not performance-based because they are not indexed against a peer group or broader market.

However, their argument does not hold up. First, although senior executives certainly benefited from the increasing use of options, much of that increase reflected a growing practice of pushing stock option participation down into the organization. Second, option use is not camouflaged but is fully disclosed in public documents. Third, CEOs do not direct the use of conventional, nonindexed options because it is more advantageous; they do so in part simply because accounting was better before the new rules went into effect in 2006.

The opposing view put forth by Kevin J. Murphy, Brian J. Hall, and Michael C. Jensen states that Bebchuk and Fried's theory does not explain why options became so prevalent as a compensation tool for employees below the top executives.[6] As they note, in 2002, more than 90 percent of the stock options went to employees below the top five.

Murphy, Hall, and Jensen posit an alternative view. They argue that option decisions are made on the basis of their "perceived cost," which does not reflect their actual cost. They suggest that decisions on option awards are made with the consideration of the dilutive impact of options on fully diluted earnings per share but not on the basis of the economic

FIGURE 4.2
2000 Overhang Levels by Industry

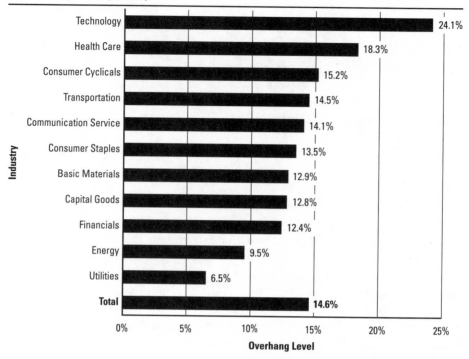

Source: Watson Wyatt.

cost of the options. Because of this, directors were more willing to grant options in substantial quantities to large numbers of workers.

Murphy, Hall, and Jensen have identified some key dynamics in the selection of long-term incentive vehicles. The primary consideration is the relationship between cost and perceived value. In practice, companies and their boards strive to deliver the highest perceived value for a given level of expense, and from a perceived value standpoint, options were unequaled in the mid- to late 1990s.

Led by the technology companies, corporations pushed stock options down through the organization to employees who were willing to take lower cash compensation in exchange for the upside leverage of options. And for many employees, it paid off in a big way. As the stock market climbed and stories of millionaire secretaries became public, the clamor for stock options grew. Old-economy companies had to follow suit, first to retain employees who might leave for start-ups and second because they sought to capture the valuation ascribed to Internet firms by creating their own Internet-oriented businesses.

The external and regulatory environments also stoked the options fire. Academics argued that options should be used more aggressively to avoid paying executives like bureaucrats. Congress pushed legislation that promoted option use at lower levels in organizations. And IRC Section 162(m) encouraged performance-based pay, which led to the proliferation of options as well.

Ultimately, however, their proliferation reflected a correcting mechanism in the market. Before the late 1990s, stock-based vehicles were underused. When the right factors were in place, companies used them more aggressively. As shown in Figure 4.1, in the early 1990s, companies were not fully tapping into the incentive power of stock options.

As stock option use accelerated, so, too, did stock market growth. But, at a certain point, too many options were awarded and the resulting rise in dilution dampened stock prices. The overuse of options in the late 1990s in part led to the burst of the stock market bubble in 2000.

2000–2002: A Turning Point

When the bubble burst, "irrational exuberance" (as Alan Greenspan put it) and sentiments about stock options were quickly tempered. In an up market, the leveraged effects of stock options work wonders, but in a down market, the opposite occurs. Executives and broader employee groups watched their options slip underwater. Employees who exercised incentive stock options and held shares to get favorable tax treatment, only to see their value plummet, were hit hard. Although they had to pay taxes on the exercised value under the alternative minimum tax, they then did not have the value in their held shares to cover the taxes.

Enron, the poster child of everything wrong with stock options, became the catalyst for the antioption movement. It appeared as though Enron executives cashed out millions of dollars of option gains while employees were inadvertently subjected to lock-up provisions on shares held in the company's retirement programs. The excessive use of stock options at Enron, Global Crossing, and other companies may have encouraged the use of tactics that boosted the stock price in the short term, regardless of the long-term consequences. For some companies, it all came down to meeting analyst expectations for earnings; if you could meet or beat the street, the stock would rise.

FIGURE 4.3
Run Rates, 2001–2004

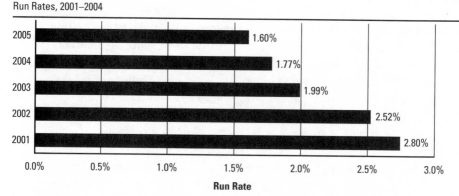

Source: Watson Wyatt.

What ultimately led to the reduction in the use of stock options was the effort by the Financial Accounting Standards Board to require stock option expensing. At the same time, President George W. Bush's tax policy drove down tax rates on corporate dividends. This development also supported a move away from stock options, which do not provide dividends, and a move to restricted stock plans, which do.

The Decline of the Stock Option

Watson Wyatt research reveals an across-the-board reduction in the number of stock option grants beginning in 2002. Many companies that had previously spread stock options across the organization either limited participation or eliminated options altogether. Even at the highest levels in the organization, stock option awards fell dramatically, although this reduction was offset by a move to restricted stock and long-term performance plans.[7]

This reduced use of stock options was reflected in declining annual share run rates (stock options granted in a particular year divided by common shares outstanding). As shown in Figure 4.3, annual share run rates dropped from 2.80 percent in 2001 to 1.60 percent in 2005 – a decline of more than 40 percent.

At the typical company, the reported fair value of the options granted in 2005 fell by 33 percent from 2004 and more than 70 percent from 2001 (see Figure 4.4). This decline crossed all industries and continued a trend that has emerged as organizations react to changes in the accounting

FIGURE 4.4
Fair Value of Stock Option Grants

	FAIR VALUE OF STOCK OPTION GRANTS	VALUE PER SHARE OF COMMON STOCK
Percentage change 2001–2005	−71%	−42%
Percentage change 2004–2005	−33%	−15%

Source: Watson Wyatt.

expense for stock options and increasing shareholder concerns about dilution and cost control. As a result, the expense per share at the typical organization has fallen sharply. In 2001, the fair value of options granted represented about 19 cents per share outstanding at the typical firm. By 2005, this number had fallen to 11 cents, despite the fact that earnings and share prices increased during the same period.

Between 2001 and 2005, the stock price at the typical firm in the S&P 1500 rose 41 percent (see Figure 4.5) − 12 percent in 2005 alone. If companies had simply continued to issue the same number of stock options, under the same terms, with no significant changes in their FAS 123(R) assumptions, then grant values could have increased dramatically. The fact that they fell can be attributed to two factors: Companies have dramatically reduced the number of stock options they are granting, and they have altered their FAS 123(R) assumptions to reduce the fair value of those grants expressed as a percentage of the security price. The two most important determinants of fair value, other than share price, are expected life and expected volatility. As shown in Figure 4.5, both determinants have declined from 2001 to 2005.

The Realities of Expensing

Under FAS 123(R), stock options result in an expense equal to the number of options awarded multiplied by their fair value on the date of grant.

FIGURE 4.5
Share Prices and FAS 123(R) Assumptions for S&P 1500 Firms

	2001	2004	2005	2001–2005	2004–2005
Share Price	$22.73	$28.69	$32.01	41%	12%
Fair Value/Share Price	43%	36%	35%	−18%	−4%
Expected Life	5.6 years	5.3 years	5.2 years	−6%	−1%
Expected Volatility	47%	43%	38%	−20%	−11%

Source: Watson Wyatt.

FIGURE 4.6
Performance Outcomes of Stock Option Award

STOCK PRICE PERFORMANCE SCENARIO	P&L EXPENSE	VALUE DELIVERY
Scenario A: Stock price remains at $24; no appreciation	$8M	$0
Scenario B: Stock price increases to $32, a 33% return over three years	$8M	$8M
Scenario C: Stock price increases to $40, a 67% return over three years	$8M	$16M

Source: Watson Wyatt.

This expense is amortized ratably over the service or vesting period. An initial reduction in the number of options is allowed for potential forfeitures and is subsequently adjusted based on actual forfeitures that occur during the service period.

This is the only adjustment allowed. There is no reversal of any accrued expense, even if the stock price declines and the options go underwater. Consequently, companies face a fixed cost that ultimately may or may not reflect the value that is being delivered to employees.

The following example illustrates this difficulty. Assume that a company awards 1 million stock options at a strike price of $24, the stock price on the date of award. Assume the Black–Scholes value of an option awarded at $24 is $8, or 33 percent of the grant value of the option. Thus, the total fair value or expense of the award, with no adjustments for forfeitures, is $8 million.

Figure 4.6 shows the different performance outcomes and a comparison of expenses incurred and value delivered over an assumed three-year vesting period. The key consideration in the use of options going forward concerns share price performance. The cost–benefit neutrality is attained only to the extent the share price increases by 33 percent over three years, or at a compounded annual growth rate of more than 10 percent. And this is share price performance only, not total returns to shareholders. Option recipients do not receive the benefit of any dividends paid on the stock.

Also, this example is based on a 33 percent Black–Scholes value, which is not the reality for many companies, particularly those that do not pay dividends and have volatile stock prices. For those companies, Black–Scholes factors of 50 percent or higher are not uncommon, although with FAS 123(R) now in effect, companies have become more

FIGURE 4.7
Annual Rates of Return Required to Achieve Cost–Benefit Neutrality

BS % OF FACE VALUE	TIME HORIZON IN YEARS					
	2	3	4	5	6	7
35%	17.1%	11.4%	8.7%	7.0%	6.0%	5.2%
40%	19.3%	12.8%	9.7%	7.9%	6.7%	5.9%
45%	21.5%	14.3%	10.8%	8.8%	7.4%	6.5%
50%	23.7%	15.6%	11.8%	9.6%	8.1%	7.1%
55%	25.8%	17.0%	12.8%	10.4%	8.8%	7.7%
60%	27.9%	18.3%	13.8%	11.1%	9.4%	8.2%
65%	30.0%	19.6%	14.7%	11.9%	10.0%	8.8%
70%	32.0%	20.8%	15.6%	12.6%	10.7%	9.3%
75%	34.0%	22.1%	16.5%	13.3%	11.2%	9.8%

Source: Watson Wyatt.

aggressive in managing their option valuation assumptions downward. Figure 4.7 shows the required compounded annual rates of return to achieve cost–benefit neutrality under different fair-value assumptions.

Perceived Value

In addition to the potential cost–benefit inefficiency, companies are pressured to reduce their use of stock options because employees undervalue them.[8] This is true for newly granted at-the-money options and underwater options. Practitioners, consultants, and researchers have known for some time that employees' perceived value of options is disproportionate to their cost to the company largely because employees are risk-averse and less than fully diversified.

On the rare occasions when companies sell stock options to their employees, they must discount the options by 50 percent to 75 percent of their Black–Scholes value to induce the employees to buy them. We have asked executives at dozens of companies whether they would pay the Black–Scholes value for an at-the-money stock option on their employer's stock. Like employees, they, too, would insist on a discount of at least 50 percent.

Even knowing – or at least suspecting – that employees undervalue stock options, employers increased their use of them in the 1990s, partly because they thought that stock options provided incentives for employees to behave in the interests of shareholders. Given the rise in stock prices, this worked in many instances. But for stock options to be cost-effective on a long-term basis, their incentive benefit must outweigh the gap between their cost to the employer and their perceived value to employees. For many companies, it is hard to justify offering a benefit that costs $1 when employees value it at only 50 cents.

Employees are not optimally diversified. With a disproportionate weight of company-related wealth in their portfolios – stock-based incentives, the value of their own human capital, and any other deferred or long-term benefits they expect to receive – they are exposed to significant firm-specific risk. But the market-based valuation models generally assume that equity holders can diversify their portfolios and are therefore compensated only for the systemic risk.

Moreover, employees with stock options may not easily hedge their options, whereas the Black–Scholes option-pricing model assumes that the option holders can perfectly hedge their options. Because people tend to be risk-averse, they place a higher value on a certain payoff – usually specified as a fixed cash amount to be paid under all possible outcomes, such as a salary increase – than they place on a risky payoff with the same expected value.

In a paper published in 2002, Hall and Murphy used an "expected utility" approach to estimate the certainty (cash) equivalent values for stock options to employees. In this model, employees who are more risk-averse and less diversified place a large discount on their options relative to the market value (cost).[9] For an executive with some risk aversion and 50 percent of his wealth already in company stock, a 10-year option granted at the money is worth only 63.5 percent of its Black–Scholes value.

Lisa K. Meulbroek, a professor at Claremont McKenna College, evaluated the reward-to-risk ratio of a stock option versus other vehicles.[10] She estimated that a manager of a typical NYSE-listed company values stock options at an average of 70 percent of their cost to the company.

Watson Wyatt surveyed 1,000 high-income employees (earning more than $50,000 per year) in a broad cross section of firms. Our study revealed that, on average, employees place a discount, or "haircut," as high as 49 percent on a grant of 500 stock options when compared with an estimate of the options' Black–Scholes cost to the company. For a grant of 100 options, the estimated average haircut is as much as 40 percent.[11]

These numbers indicate that employees discount the value of option grants substantially below their fair market value, that this haircut grows as the grants become larger, and that stock options cost the company

FIGURE 4.8
Estimated Average Discounts for 500 Options

		DISCOUNT ESTIMATES
All firms		49%
Large firms		46%
Small firms		58%
Positive three-year TRS		43%
Negative three-year TRS		51%
Conservative investors		53%
Aggressive investors		41%
Never exercised option before		51%
Exercised option before		46%
		DISCOUNT ESTIMATES
Do you know your company's stock price within $2?	Yes No	51% 36%
Accurate on TRS?	Yes No	52% 48%
What is your current annual salary?	$50,000–$74,999 $75,000 or greater	52% 49%
Is the current stock price higher than the average exercise price?	Yes No	50% 45%
What percentage of your shares are in-the-money?	75% or more Less than 75%	41% 54%

Note: Some totals do not equal 100% due to rounding.
Source: Watson Wyatt.

a great deal more than the employees value them (Figure 4.8). Finally, stock options are not the most effective vehicle for promoting share ownership. Most employees exercise options as soon as they vest, and the vast majority simply cash them in and do not hold onto any shares. Because share ownership drives superior company performance, encouraging stock ownership should be a key objective of every compensation strategy.

The Case for Stock Options

Although the prevalence of stock options has declined, we do not expect them to disappear from the compensation landscape. Concerns over dilution and cost–benefit efficiency have made stock options less desirable, but for certain companies and in certain situations, which we will outline, they remain a viable long-term incentive vehicle.

GROWTH COMPANIES

For options to deliver value equal to or above their cost, the company's stock price must appreciate above certain levels. Growth-oriented companies that expect significant stock price growth could be well served by using stock options. Stock options are arguably the most shareholder-aligned vehicle in that option holders, like shareholders, benefit only to the extent the stock price increases. There is also substantial risk: If the stock price falls below the exercise price, the option recipient can be left with a worthless benefit.

Some growth companies have remained steadfast supporters of stock options. John Chambers, chairman and chief executive of Cisco Systems, has stated that "broad-based employee stock options plans . . . foster the culture of ownership and associated behavior in which innovation and risk-taking . . . thrive; . . . it is key to the innovation and competitiveness on which our country's economy is built." IBM put in place a premium-priced stock option plan that awarded options with an exercise price set at 10 percent above the market price of the stock on the date of award. According to its CEO, Sam Palmisano, "These programs are unprecedented . . . [ensuring] that investors first receive meaningful returns . . . before IBM's top 300 executives can realize a penny of profit from their stock options."[12]

Indeed, for some companies, a decision to move away from stock options could be interpreted as a sign that the company has reservations about its future stock price performance. Although companies whose stock price has greatly appreciated tend to feel confident about their future stock price performance (and the perceived value of options by employees may be at its highest point), ironically that could be the wrong time to grant options because future stock price appreciation could be hard to come by. On the flip side, companies that have had recent poor stock price performance might be thinking of moving away from options, but it could be the right time to grant them.

SITUATIONAL CASES

New Hires and Promotions. Even if a company moves away from stock options, they remain appropriate in certain situations. For new hires who have yet to provide service to the company, options can be an effective

FIGURE 4.9
Stock Option Expenses Over Time (median)

	1999	2000	2001
Option expense	$7.5M	$9.7M	$11.8M
Option expense per employee	$763	$881	$1,032

Source: Watson Wyatt; based on data provided as part of S&P's Core Earnings calculations for S&P's Compustat database.

tool for providing incentive opportunity that is aligned with future service.

Top Five Executives. Options still represent a pay-for-performance vehicle. Companies that have moved to restricted stock have lost some of that performance alignment. They have also lost the tax deduction under IRC Section 162(m) for the top five officers. Restricted stock that vests based on time and not performance does not qualify as performance-based pay under Section 162(m), while options do qualify. Accordingly, options can ensure the maximum tax deductibility of compensation paid to the top five executives.

International Employees. In some countries, stock options are the most efficient vehicle for employees from a tax perspective. For example, in Canada, only 50 percent of stock option gains are subject to taxation. In many countries, restricted stock is taxed on the date of award, basically making its use unworkable. In those countries, companies will often use restricted stock units as a way around that, but some companies do not have shareholder approval of restricted stock units.

Costs and Stock Prices

Although the expense associated with stock options has caused companies to move away from them, studies have shown that the market has already fully reflected that expense in stock prices. The efficient market hypothesis argues that all publicly available information about a company – whether obtained from the income statement or the footnotes – is incorporated into the day's stock price.

Watson Wyatt conducted a historical analysis to explore this further. We went back in time and collected data on stock option expenses from the footnotes of 800 companies from the S&P 1500. Figure 4.9 shows the median size of this expense at both absolute and per-employee levels.

FIGURE 4.10
2001 Stock Option Expense and TRS (all figures are medians)

2001 OPTION EXPENSE	2001 OPTION EXPENSE/EE	TOTAL EXPENSE	2001 TRS	2002 TRS
Low	$282	$5.0M	14.9%	−4.0%
Medium	$828	$14.8M	1.4%	−10.4%
High	$5,127	$25.7M	−1.9%	−17.9%

Source: Watson Wyatt; based on data provided as part of S&P's Core Earnings calculations for S&P's Compustat database.

Our research found that in 2001–2002, the stock market had already factored the disclosed costs of historical stock options into the then-current value (see Figure 4.10). These findings are significant, both statistically and economically, and suggest the stock market's likely reaction to required expensing in 2006.

Back in 2004, an increase in stock option expense was associated with lower total returns to shareholders as investors became concerned that the cumulative dilution from stock options could overwhelm their motivational effect on employee behavior.

The market has been highly sensitive to changes in stock option expense (see Figure 4.11). Companies that have increased their stock option expenses have subsequently seen markedly lower shareholder returns. In fact, for the typical company, an increase in option expense is associated with more than a dollar-for-dollar reduction in market value. We expect this relationship to hold true in 2006 and beyond.

While companies have been penalized for increasing their stock option expense above competitive levels, we have also found that the stock market rewards companies that spread options around. One of the questions that the expensing issue raises is whether companies will reduce the eligibility for grants to reduce the total accounting expense. For example, some companies may sustain their grant levels for top

FIGURE 4.11
Change in Stock Option Expense and TRS (1999–2001)

CHANGE IN OPTION EXPENSE	% CHANGE	2002 TRS
High	227%	−15.1%
Medium	69%	−9.1%
Low	−16%	−6.7%

Source: Watson Wyatt.

executives while reducing the number of stock options for the employee population.

Our research, detailed here, and consulting experience have consistently shown that broader stock plan participation is correlated with superior financial performance. Our stock option expense analysis shows that companies with high levels of participation in stock option plans create greater shareholder value than companies with low participation. Balancing overall expense with broad eligibility appears to be a worthwhile effort.

During a three-year period for which we have collected data, an increase of one percentage point in the percentage of options allocated to broad employee groups (e.g., from 78 percent of the options to 79 percent) was associated with a nearly one percent increase in the firm's market value, or almost $15 million in market capitalization for the median firm in our sample.

Reducing the Expense

The two biggest assumptions that drive option expense are the expected life of the option and stock price volatility. Before the move to option expensing, many companies used the full term (typically 10 years) as the basis for expected life. For the vast majority of companies, of course, employees exercise stock options sooner than 10 years from issue and often as soon as they are vested, typically in three to five years. Companies can look at past exercise behavior to determine typical practice and lower the expected stock option life accordingly. More robust analysis using a lattice-based model can further lower the expense by using event-based analysis. For example, if recent history shows that a higher percentage of employees exercised options when the stock price rose 10 percent, this consideration can be built in.

For many companies, particularly in the high-tech industries, high volatility drives high expense. Again, there are ways to reduce assumed volatility. One way is to look at implied volatility as reflected in volatilities in publicly traded stock options. The net effect of managing assumptions and lowering stock option fair value expense is that options become more efficient from a cost–benefit standpoint.

Another strategy, used by just a few companies, is to cap the value of stock options. Schlumberger and Tech Data Corp. have both taken this step. In this approach, the company limits the upside of stock option gains; for example, it may grant options at a $20 exercise price and cap gains at a $40 stock price. This can substantially reduce stock option expense, but it also diminishes the value of options, which are designed to be a leveraged vehicle, by removing that upside.

Another approach is to put performance conditions on stock options. This lowers the expense because the probability of not attaining the performance goal reduces the fair value of the award. Additionally, this avoids the fixed-expense aspect of options; if the goals are not attained, the expense can be reversed (if vesting/earning of the award is not based on market conditions). But companies may need to grant more performance-based options to offset the risk associated with that vehicle.

We urge all companies to revisit their stock-based incentives with the goal of managing total expense, developing alternative programs with higher motivational value to employees, and developing programs that are more shareholder-friendly. Alternatives to stock options include restricted stock, performance shares (shares granted contingently based upon future performance hurdles), and management stock purchase plans.

Stock options will likely never again have the prominence they had in the 1990s. Nevertheless, companies should still consider them when evaluating long-term incentive vehicles.

5 The Future of Long-Term Incentives

You can't reward value added unless you can measure it. Since you get what you reward, and reward what you measure, you get what you measure. Make sure you're measuring the right thing.

Richard A. Brealey and Stewart C. Myers,
Principles of Corporate Finance

In this new era of stock option expensing, companies are moving to a portfolio of long-term incentive vehicles. Now that companies must expense options like every other form of compensation, the goal is to maximize value delivery, both real and perceived, for a given level of expense. This changed paradigm can be seen in Figure 5.1. The transformation to a portfolio approach is well under way. From 2002 to 2004, among approximately 1,000 companies, the Black–Scholes value of stock option awards for CEOs fell by 24 percent (see Figure 5.2). While this is a big decline even in a flat stock market, the fact that the share price for the vast majority of these companies shot up during the same period makes it even more meaningful. Some of the decline in value simply reflects a more aggressive management of Black–Scholes assumptions to reduce expense, but most of it reflects the dramatic drop – 30 percent – in the number of options awarded to these CEOs. In the same period, CEOs' restricted stock and long-term performance plan values increased by 46 percent and 51 percent, respectively – a major realignment of the delivery of long-term incentive values. The net effect of this realignment was that the total LTI values for CEOs increased by about 5 percent, once again demonstrating that executive pay is sensitive to company performance.

FIGURE 5.1
The Portfolio Approach

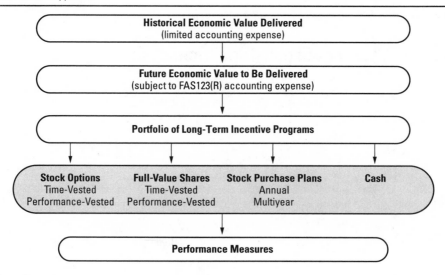

Source: Watson Wyatt.

A portfolio approach provides the balance that allows companies to accomplish multiple objectives. Restricted stock can promote retention in a cost- and share-efficient manner, and stock options can ensure shareholder alignment and leveraged incentive opportunities for exceptional stock price performance, while a long-term performance plan can focus attention and rewards on key underlying drivers of shareholder value. And unlike time-vested stock options, the expense associated with a long-term performance plan can be reversed if performance goals are not met.[1]

FIGURE 5.2
Decline in Stock Option Awards

	THREE-YEAR LTI CHANGE (2002–2004)			
MEDIAN	RESTRICTED STOCK AWARDS	LTIP TARGET	STOCK OPTIONS (B-S VALUE)	TOTAL LTI
FY02–03 Change	23.5%	24.7%	–30.0%	–9.9%
FY03–04 Change	18.3%	21.5%	9.1%	16.8%
FY02–04 Change	46.1%	51.4%	–23.6%	5.3%

Note: Sample size = 1,047.

Source: Watson Wyatt.

FIGURE 5.3
Internal and External Factors in Evaluating LTI Alternatives

Source: Watson Wyatt.

Factors Influencing LTI Design

Many factors, internal and external, shape the design and delivery of long-term incentives (see Figure 5.3). A move to restricted stock, for example, can open the company up to criticism that it is paying without performance. And while a company may want to be at the leading edge (like Microsoft in its early move to restricted stock), it should know what its peers are doing.

Internally, moving to an unfamiliar vehicle such as restricted stock units may involve a major effort to communicate the change to ensure the highest perceived value among employees. Such a move, if implemented on a global basis, can dramatically increase administration requirements.

Designing an LTI Program

The first step in designing a long-term incentive plan is to assemble a cross-functional team – human resources, finance, tax, legal, and communications – as well as outside compensation consulting support. We also recommend creating a steering committee of senior executives that represent major business areas and support functions.

FIGURE 5.4
Example of Prioritized LTI Objectives

OBJECTIVE	PRIORITY
1. Maintain shareholder alignment	High
2. Minimize shareholder dilution	High
3. Maximize perceived value of award	High
4. Motivate the attainment of key internal objectives	High
5. Maximize company cash flow	Medium
6. Foster long-term retention	Medium
7. Minimize plan design complexity	Medium
8. Reward for outperforming peers	Low
9. Encourage employee "skin-in-the-game"	Low

Source: Watson Wyatt.

After receiving steering committee input, the team should seek input from the CEO and the compensation committee. While the CEO and the committee provide approval at the end of the process, their input is vital along the way.

- Understanding key objectives

The purpose of the interviews is to understand the perspectives of various stakeholders on the following issues:

- Desired relationship between risk and reward
- Use of cash rather than equity
- Key drivers of long-term value creation
- Retention concerns
- Value delivery expectations
- Appropriate competitive frame of reference
- Views on complexity

It is essential to know the priority that outside directors and senior management assign to each of these items. For example, is the goal to minimize plan complexity or to focus attention on internal performance goals? Because each LTI vehicle varies in its ability to deliver on specific objectives, selecting one over another will inevitably involve trade-offs.

Figure 5.4 shows a simple approach to ranking key objectives and constraints that can be customized to the organization and its makeup. It may be appropriate, for instance, to have separate objectives for top management and the broader employee population because their priorities may vary significantly.

- Understanding the competitive perspective

Peer and broader market practices and trends can provide a point of reference. Comparing and contrasting with other companies – of similar and different growth and maturity profiles and industry dynamics – that have moved or not moved in a particular LTI direction can also provide a valuable reference point.

- Conducting internal analyses

In considering plan objectives, it is important to understand the company's internal situation. Key analyses include determining the retention value of current outstanding awards, assessing executives' current share ownership position, looking at past long-term incentive cost–benefit relationships, and understanding and quantifying executives' perceived value of various LTI vehicles.

- Identifying viable alternatives

Aside from stock options and their variations (time-vested, performance-contingent, performance-accelerated, premium, indexed), other LTI vehicles can accomplish specific objectives and operate independently or in conjunction with each other. The new accounting rules for stock-based compensation not only level the playing field but also provide a better field position for share-based plans that measure performance using metrics that are not based on share price. Figure 5.5 shows various long-term incentive vehicles and summarizes their advantages and disadvantages. (See Appendix A for the tax and accounting treatment for each vehicle.)

- Evaluating restricted stock and restricted stock units

Figure 5.6 compares restricted stock and restricted stock units and outlines their advantages and disadvantages to the employer and the employee. Generally, restricted stock units offer more tax flexibility. The executive can defer receipt of the shares to a future date when he or she may be in a lower tax bracket.

The first problem with a time-vested restricted stock plan is that it does not comply with IRC Section 162(m). For the top five executive officers, the value of shares may not be tax-deductible to the company when they vest. (When restricted stock vests, it also is a taxable event for the executive.) If vesting occurs during a blackout period, the executive is

FIGURE 5.5

Advantages and Disadvantages of LTI Vehicles

VEHICLE	ADVANTAGES	DISADVANTAGES
Stock Options Option, but not requirement, to purchase shares at stated price (strike or exercise price) over a given period of time (life).	• Well understood • Shareholder alignment • Leverage • Cash flow positive	• High dilution • Inefficient cost–benefit • Lacks retention value in down/flat market
Stock Appreciation Rights Rights to receive a payment (in the form of cash or stock) equal to the intrinsic value on the date of exercise.	• Shareholder alignment • Leverage • Requires fewer shares	• Inefficient cost–benefit • Lacks retention value in down/flat market • ISS may value them as full-value shares
Time-Vested Restricted Stock Actual award of shares of common stock that carry restrictions that lapse over a period of time (vesting period). Eligible for dividends.	• High retention value • Promotes share ownership • Positive cost–benefit • Fixed expense	• Not performance-based (not 162(m) qualified) • Negatively perceived by shareholders
Restricted Stock Units Similar to restricted stock but represents a promise to pay shares in the future rather than an up-front delivery. Can structure with dividend equivalents.	• Same as restricted stock • Additional benefit of tax flexibility	• Same as restricted stock • Delayed tax deduction for company • Deferral elections subject to 409A deferred-compensation rules
Performance Shares An opportunity to earn shares of common stock contingent on the attainment of preestablished performance goals. Performance period is typically three years with overlapping performance cycles. Ultimate value of award is contingent on stock price performance and the number of shares earned at the end of the performance period.	• Performance-based • 162(m) qualified • Flexibility to use a variety of performance measures • Fixed fair value expense • Reversible expense	• Can be difficult to set long-term performance goals
Performance-Lapse Restricted Stock Similar to restricted stock (can also be structured as units), with the primary difference being that, in addition to time, restrictions only lapse upon the attainment of preestablished performance goals. Unlike performance shares, there is no upside opportunity.	• Performance-based • 162(m) qualified • Flexibility to use a variety of performance measures • Fixed fair value expense • Reversible expense	• Can be difficult to set long-term performance goals
Performance Cash/Units Analogous to an annual cash incentive plan but based on the attainment of multiyear (typically three years) performance goals. With units, can be structured so that the unit value varies based on one performance goal, with the actual number of units earned varying based on a different performance goal.	• Minimizes dilution • Performance-based • 162(m) qualified • Flexibility to use a variety of performance measures • Reversible expense	• Can be difficult to set long-term performance goals • Lacks shareholder alignment • Full value of award delivered must be expensed
Management Stock Purchase Plan (MSPP) A tax-effective way for companies to allow executives to increase their level of management ownership of company stock. Using a nonqualified deferred compensation plan provides highly compensated employees with the opportunity to defer bonus (and sometimes salary) into company stock. A match is typically provided, yielding a discount to the purchase price.	• Promotes share ownership • Promotes retention through vesting on match • Allows for "skin-in-the-game" through the deferral of earned bonus	• Similar to double jeopardy in that if the bonus plan does not pay out, there is no opportunity to defer and get a match

Source: Watson Wyatt.

FIGURE 5.6
Overview of Restricted Stock and Restricted Stock Units

	RESTRICTED STOCK	RESTRICTED STOCK UNITS
Description	Award of actual full-value shares that carry restrictions that lapse over time	Promise to pay shares at some point in the future (either the vesting date or at a later date selected by the recipient)
Shareholder	Yes	No
Beneficial Ownership	Included	Not included (can footnote)
Voting Rights	Yes	No
Dividend Rights	Yes	No (can pay dividend equivalents)
Accounting	Market value on date of grant; amortized over the vesting period	
Tax	Ordinary income upon lapse of restrictions	Ordinary income upon receipt (date of vest or later if deferred)
162(m)	Not qualified unless performance-based	Can avoid 162(m) impact if deferred until termination of employment
Proxy Disclosure	FAS 123(R) fair value on date of grant shown in Summary Compensation table. Number of shares (or units) awarded shown in Grants of Plan-Based Awards table. Aggregate number of shares (units) outstanding and value shown in Outstanding Equity Awards at Fiscal Year-End table. Number of shares (units) vested and value realized shown in Options Exercised and Stock Vested table.	

Source: Watson Wyatt.

prohibited from selling shares to meet the tax obligation and must come up with the cash to pay the taxes owed. One solution is to use share units so that vesting may occur during a blackout period, but executives can defer receipt and thus taxation.

The use of restricted stock also is often not feasible on an international basis, so most multinational companies use share units instead. Many countries – including Canada, France, Germany, Sweden, and Switzerland – tax restricted stock on the date of grant instead of when it vests. In these cases, the executive must pay taxes on the shares before he or she has received any value from them. The solution, again, is to use restricted stock units, which are taxed only when they vest and the individual takes receipt. The tax flexibility of restricted stock unit plans also applies to performance shares and performance-lapse restricted stock, which can also be denominated in units.

- Evaluating alternatives

In determining the most appropriate long-term incentive vehicle, companies should evaluate the ability of each potential vehicle to meet the company's high-priority objectives identified in Figure 5.4. For example, stock options are more effective than restricted stock in providing leveraged incentive opportunities and generating cash flow from the proceeds made by payment of the exercise price. However, stock options are potentially more dilutive than restricted stock and may not be as cost-efficient unless there is significant stock price appreciation. A company may rate the alignment of incentives with internal financial goals as a high-priority objective. In that case, time-vested options and restricted stock do not fare as well as stock- or cash-based performance plans.

For many companies, the diversity of high-priority objectives supports a portfolio approach to long-term incentives. A balanced portfolio could be comprised of stock options and restricted stock to accomplish shareholder alignment, retention, and cost–benefit efficiency, or a portfolio could be comprised of a combination of time- and performance-vested restricted stock to achieve a balance between retention and linkage to internal financial goals. Beyond vehicle combinations are vehicle variations, as shown in the following two examples.

Example 1: "Home Run" Plan. This consists of a base-level award of time-vested restricted stock (a "single") with an opportunity to earn multiples of that award ("double," "triple," or "home run") based on attainment of preestablished performance goals measured over a multiyear period. For example:

Award Level	Shares	Conditions on Vesting
Base-level ("single")	10,000	Continued employment
2 × ("double")	20,000	6% annual EPS growth
3 × ("triple")	30,000	10% annual EPS growth
4 × ("home run")	40,000	15% annual EPS growth

This approach, while not suitable for every situation, accomplishes multiple objectives:

- Retention (through the base-level share award)
- Performance alignment (through the opportunity to earn additional shares based on EPS growth)
- Shareholder alignment (the underlying vehicle is stock)
- Cost efficiency (any accrued expense for the performance-based feature is reversible if the performance goals are not met)
- Share efficiency (the use of full-value shares requires fewer shares than with options, and to the extent the goals are not attained, the shares go back into the plan)

Example 2: Performance-Contingent Restricted Stock. Selecting metrics and setting goals are two of the most difficult aspects of moving to long-term performance vehicles. One solution is to make restricted-stock awards contingent on annual performance. This is the reverse of the program in which vesting is contingent on long-term performance. For example, a company can set an annual earnings per share (EPS) goal and, based on the degree of attainment, a number of restricted shares will be awarded subject to a vesting requirement, typically one or two additional years following the performance period. With an annual performance period, however, this approach in some respects is a duplicate of the short-term incentive plan. It does not create the desired dynamic tension between short-term and long-term incentives that is a key objective in developing long-term measures. This is somewhat mitigated by placing subsequent vesting requirements on the actual shares awarded.

SETTING PERFORMANCE GOALS AND METRICS

Companies' strategic business planning often lacks the support of a long-term performance plan to reinforce its goals and reward their attainment. When companies look at what drives long-term value, they often reassess short-term drivers and can end up redesigning their annual incentive plan and establishing line-of-sight performance goals for employees.

- Performance metrics

Performance metrics signal the company's strategic imperatives to executives and shareholders. The appropriate metrics and goals are to:

- Align executives with shareholders
- Focus executives on increasing market value
- Provide a consistent framework for rewarding behavior

At Watson Wyatt, we follow a three-step process to help our clients select performance metrics and set goals:

Step 1: Understand Performance Framework

Activity	Review existing business strategy
Activity	Understand value drivers in strategic plan
Activity	Examine market expectations
Outcome	*Baseline performance summary*

Step 2: Review Potential Metrics

Activity	Review the relationship between various metrics and historical shareholder returns
Activity	Review value driver impact on shareholder value
Activity	Consider industry convention

Outcome	*List of appropriate metrics*

Step 3: Set Appropriate Performance Goals

Activity	Establish historical peer group performance norms
Activity	Review analyst expectations
Activity	Understand stock price implied expectations

Outcome	*Reasonable performance goals*

Figures 5.7, 5.8, and 5.9 show the prevalence of various metrics used by large-cap companies for performance share and cash plans and the number of measures and performance cycles typically used. The most common approach is to use two measures and a three-year performance cycle, with a maximum payout of 150 percent.

FIGURE 5.7
Prevalence of Metrics Used, General Industry
(large-cap companies that recently adopted LTI plans)

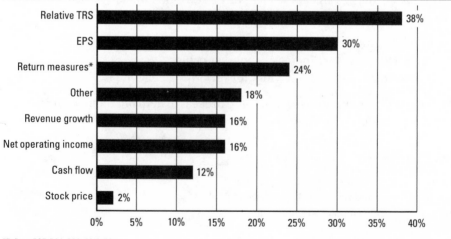

*Reflects ROE, ROA, ROC, ROIC, ROI.
Source: Watson Wyatt.

FIGURE 5.8
Number of Measures Used

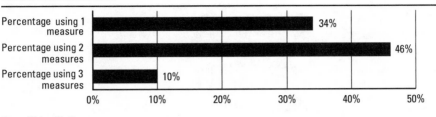

Source: Watson Wyatt.

The choice of performance metrics reflects the tension between companies and analysts, who generally rely on financial metrics based on GAAP (generally accepted accounting principles) accounting, and institutional shareholders, who often distrust these measures. The marketplace in general uses typical financial metrics, such as earnings per share and price/earnings multiples, to evaluate corporate performance. But institutional investors think these metrics can be easily influenced and manipulated. For example, companies may include or exclude certain factors, such as "nonrecurring" or "extraordinary" items.

However, we expect that financial metrics such as EPS will remain prevalent because they are important measures of a company's profitability and are a primary benchmark used by analysts in valuing companies. And under the new accounting rules, the main alternative – total return to shareholders – has substantial drawbacks. With share-price–based metrics, such as TRS or share price performance, the company must use a fixed accounting expense that is not reversible if the company does not meet the performance goal. With EPS and other metrics that are not based

FIGURE 5.9
Performance Cycles (median performance cycle (years): 3.0)

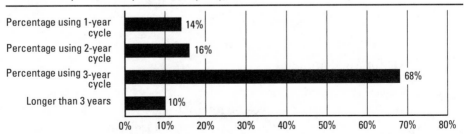

Note: Median maximum payout = 150% of target incentive opportunity.

Source: Watson Wyatt.

FIGURE 5.10
Best Correlations with Ten-Year TRS

ECONOMIC SECTOR	GROWTH	RETURNS
Overall	Sales	ROIC, ROE, ROA
Consumer discretionary	Sales, EPS	ROIC
Consumer staples	EPS	ROIC, ROA
Energy	Sales	ROA
Financials	EPS	ROE
Health care	Sales	ROA
Industrials	EPS	ROE, ROA
Information technology	Sales	ROIC
Materials	EPS	ROE
Telecommunications	EPS	ROA
Utilities	EPS	ROE

Source: Watson Wyatt.

on share price, the company can reverse the expense if it does not meet the goal.

We also expect that more companies will use capital-based metrics, such as return on invested capital, which are more attractive to institutional investors. These measures reflect the cost of the capital the company uses to generate profits and helps executives focus on generating returns in excess of that cost. The question arises, however, of how much control executives have over capital allocation. The challenge here is to balance complexity with the desire for line-of-sight metrics.

Watson Wyatt analyzed the correlation of various financial metrics with TRS. Because a key criterion in selecting metrics is their ability to drive shareholder value, a high correlation is desirable. Figure 5.10 shows which metrics are highly correlated with shareholder returns in various industries.

Basis for Measurement

Every metric has advantages and disadvantages. Total return to shareholders provides a good check on internal goals and represents ultimate value delivery to shareholders, but the expense is not reversible and many influences on share price are beyond the control of management. Earnings per share is viewed negatively by institutions, and it may not

FIGURE 5.11
Alternative Approaches to Performance Measurement

APPROACH	DESCRIPTION	PROS/CONS
Internal goals	Company performance measured against long-term threshold, target, and maximum performance goals	• Enables linkage of LTI to long-term business planning • Difficult to set long-term measures
Peer/index comparison	Company performance measured against peer performance or performance of an index	• Avoids difficulty of establishing long-term goals • Difficult to communicate performance during cycle
Internal/external hybrid	Combination of above two approaches; independent or matrix measurement	• Provides check and balance to goal setting • More complex and cumbersome

Source: Watson Wyatt.

be highly correlated with shareholder value, but it is the common metric used in performance plans and by analysts.

Revenue growth is highly correlated with shareholder returns for some industries, but it may encourage companies to achieve growth at the expense of profitability. A cash flow metric allows companies to measure both balance sheet performance and income statement performance, but it adds complexity. In addition, only certain employees can affect balance sheet items.

Some companies use two metrics: a financial measure, such as EPS or free cash flow, and a TRS metric indexed against a peer group. The financial metric helps the company focus on internal goals and performance, which are not subject to the vagaries of the stock market. At the same time, comparing TRS with a peer group provides a balance against the internal metric; it will, for instance, show whether the company's financial metric is too easily met. The internal, external, and hybrid approaches to performance measurement are outlined in Figure 5.11.

INTERNAL GOALS

Internal goals measure company performance against a target or long-term threshold. For example, in a performance share plan with a contingent award of 750 shares and TRS and EPS goals, the configuration might fall along the lines shown in Figure 5.12.

EXTERNAL GOALS/INDEXING

A purely external approach – in which the ultimate payout of a plan depends on how the company performs compared with its peers or an

FIGURE 5.12

Internal Goals in a Performance Share Plan

	THREE-YEAR COMPOUND EPS GROWTH		
THREE-YEAR TRS	**MINIMUM 8%**	**TARGET 9%**	**STRETCH 10%**
Minimum 15%	500 Shares	600 Shares	750 Shares
Target 20%	600 Shares	750 Shares	900 Shares
Stretch 25%	750 Shares	900 Shares	1,000 Shares

Source: Watson Wyatt.

index – is one way to deal with the difficulty of setting longer-term internal goals. For example, assume 1,000 contingent shares awarded and three-year compounded annual growth in EPS as the performance measure. The number of shares awarded for each level of performance relative to peer companies is shown in Figure 5.13. The obvious downside is that the plan could end up paying out for poor performance on an absolute basis but good performance on a relative basis. For example, the company's TRS over three years may be minus 10 percent, but because that is the peer group median, a payout is triggered.

HYBRID GOALS

A hybrid approach combines metrics based on internal goals and an external peer group. Although the approach is complex and often

FIGURE 5.13

External Goals Based on Peer/Index Comparison for Performance Share Plan

PEER COMPANY	COMPOUND EPS GROWTH	PERCENTILE RANK	SHARE AWARD
Company 1	20.00%	100th	2000
Company 2	19.45%	95th	2000
Company 3	17.33%	90th	1750
Company 4	14.24%	85th	1750
Company 5	13.22%	80th	1250
Company 6	12.19%	75th	1250
Company 7	11.01%	70th	1000
COMPANY	**10.45%**	**65th**	**1000**
Company 8	10.39%	60th	750
Company 9	10.22%	55th	750
Company 10	9.89%	50th	500
Company 11	9.22%	45th	0
Company 12	8.31%	40th	0

Source: Watson Wyatt.

FIGURE 5.14
Hybrid Approach for Performance Unit Plan

INTERNAL COMPOUND EPS GROWTH RATES	EXTERNAL COMPOUND EPS GROWTH VS. PEERS (PERCENTILE)		
	50TH	65TH	75TH
9.89% EPS growth	$50	$75	$100
10.45% EPS growth	$75	$100	$200
12.19% EPS growth	$100	$200	$400

Source: Watson Wyatt.

cumbersome, it avoids the shortcomings of a purely internal or external approach. For example, assume that a plan is based on performance
units with 1,000 units awarded having a target value of $100. The com-
pany uses two goals for performance measurements: EPS compared with
internal goals and EPS compared with peers. In the plan shown in Figure
5.14, the actual performance is at the 75th percentile of the peer group,
and the resulting unit value of $200 generates a total award of $200,000.

Goal Setting

Many companies have trouble setting goals for an annual plan, so a three-
year time frame may seem particularly daunting. Some companies try to
avoid the problem by simply adopting indexing, but this has obvious
drawbacks.

Companies that want to establish internal goals can follow some
broad rules (see Figure 5.15). The threshold commonly represents a
70 percent to 80 percent probability of a payout. The company pays 50
percent of the target incentive opportunity at that level. The slope of the
line shows that the steeper the slope, the more difficult it is to achieve that
level of performance. With a steep slope and only a 10 percent chance
that the company will hit that level of performance, the payout will be
commensurately higher than it would be for a flatter slope and a 30 percent chance of achieving the goal.

The goals and probabilities should reflect the company's long-term
business plan, its past performance, the peer group's performance,
industry-specific factors (such as product demand and supply issues),
analyst expectations, and macroeconomic factors (such as the growth
rate for the national economy). For our client companies, we often determine the probability of various outcomes based on the performance of
a peer sample. By looking at the distribution of previous outcomes, we
can evaluate the degree of difficulty of performance goals. To illustrate,

FIGURE 5.15
Setting Goals and Payouts

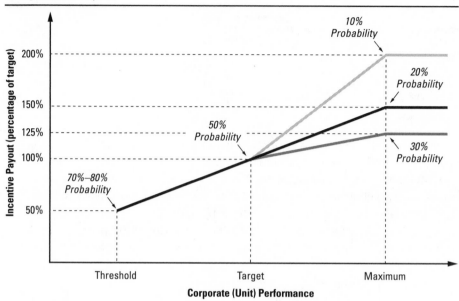

Source: Watson Wyatt.

in Figure 5.16, a sample analysis of year-to-year revenue growth goals shows that 10 percent to 15 percent compounded annual revenue growth has a roughly 50 percent probability of attainment.

Another solution to the problem of setting long-term goals is to set annual goals within a long-term cycle. Companies operating in industries where the dynamics change quickly, such as biotechnology or life sciences, may find it particularly difficult to set long-range goals because new developments can force them to change direction quickly. For example, a company with a three-year performance cycle can set a goal for every year, measure performance at the end of every year, and then either fix the award as of that date and defer payment until the end of the three-year period or take the award earned and carry it into the next year, where it is placed at risk and subject to performance goals for that year. This approach allows these companies to operate in a long-term framework and sustain performance over time.

Companies should set long-term goals whenever possible. The process forces them to push past their short-term thinking. Setting long-term goals can also generate dynamic tension with short-term goals such as boosting earnings or making specific investments. The best way to

FIGURE 5.16

Three-Year Revenue Growth Goals

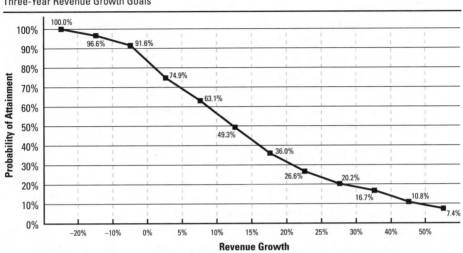

Source: Watson Wyatt.

measure the success of these short-term objectives is to look at long-term results for return on capital employed and other long-term goals for generating value.

Determining Share Award Sizes

In the 1990s, companies determined competitive awards by pulling survey data for long-term incentive values. The process was relatively simple and based purely on competitive value. The vast majority of the awards were in the form of stock options, for which there was no direct income statement expense. And, back then, dilution was not the concern that it eventually became.

After the stock market bubble burst in 2000, conditions changed. Survey data, which by their nature are dated, were based on LTI values that were considerably higher before the market dropped. When companies subsequently used those data to develop competitive grant levels, it was a recipe for disaster. These companies, which also suffered from the stock market decline, were now trying to deliver competitive value that was too high using their own low share price. As a result, it took significantly more shares to deliver competitive value, and share burn rates and dilution escalated.

In addition, establishing competitive share award levels can be counterintuitive. As a company's share price increases, it takes fewer shares to deliver competitive value, so the company must reduce the number of shares awarded to remain competitive. Employees will question why they are receiving fewer shares even though the company is performing well. In contrast, as a company's share price declines, it takes more shares to deliver competitive value. Shareholders, investors, and directors will question why the company is awarding more shares when performance is down.

Because of this inconsistency – and as a result of the market downturn and the resulting pressure from shareholders and shareholder advisory firms to restrain share dilution – companies began to focus on dilution rather than value in setting long-term incentive awards. A dilution-based approach would start with establishing a competitive share pool by looking at peer group share run (burn) rate statistics. For example, if the median share run rate among peer companies was 3 percent of common shares outstanding, the company would start with a share pool of 3 percent of its common shares outstanding. The allocation of that pool would then reflect various factors, including the percentage of common shares outstanding awarded to the CEO and other named executive officers, competitive values, and internal equity.

The approach worked fairly well in the early 2000s. Stock options were still the predominant vehicle, so using share run rate as a competitive benchmark allowed "apples to apples" comparisons. But this changed with the advent of stock option expensing in mid-2005, and two key considerations have come into play. First, with many companies transitioning to full-value shares, the definition of what constitutes a share for dilution purposes is in flux. Clearly, one option does not equal one restricted share, which does not equal one performance share. Second, because options are now being expensed, expense has become a relevant benchmark. While not on par from a dilution standpoint, $1 of option expense does equal $1 in restricted stock expense, which does equal $1 in performance share expense. In the current environment, program expense has become a key driver of LTI award levels and design.

Accordingly, in determining share award levels, we recommend that companies consider four factors equally: expense, competitive value, dilution, and internal equity and pay philosophy. As to the last factor, companies and their compensation committees should develop award levels that take into consideration how egalitarian the desired approach is, but within a reasonably competitive range of expense, dilution, and value. If the company is in an industry that does not push equity far down into the organization, yet the company wishes to allow broader participation, it may be appropriate to have the aggregate program expense and dilution above market and/or the value delivered below market.

A Look to the Future

So much has changed in executive compensation and long-term incentives in such a short time that it is difficult to envision additional major changes in the next three to five years. In that light, here are our near-term predictions for long-term incentive design and delivery:

- **Stock options will remain a core incentive for senior executives**. While overall stock option use will continue to decline as companies stop extending grants to broad employee groups, we expect the decline at the senior ranks to level off. First, over the long term and from the perspective of senior management, stock options are efficient from a cost–benefit perspective. (A company with a 40 percent Black–Scholes value requires 12 percent compounded annual share price growth to break even over a three-year period, but that declines to 7 percent over a five-year period – and most options have terms longer than five years.) Second, stock option fair values (as a percentage of grant values) have been declining as companies employ more robust valuation methodologies such as lattice models, which have effectively reduced reported expenses through assumption management. The use of lattice-based valuation models to derive expected life and the use of implied rather than historical volatility has reduced expenses for many companies. As a result, the required rate of return to break even continues to decline. And, finally, stock options remain a source of shareholder alignment, because the executive benefits only to the extent that the shareholders benefit.
- **Performance shares and vehicles that promote share ownership will proliferate**. In all their variations – for example, performance contingent, performance lapse – performance shares are fast becoming the stock options of the new era. By providing the flexibility of allowing a variety of company financial metrics while retaining the shareholder alignment through the use of a share-based vehicle, performance shares will continue to gain in prevalence. In connection with these plans, we also expect that the prevalence of net share holding requirements will continue to increase. Under these guidelines,

executives must hold a certain portion of earned shares net of payment of any taxes (a) for a specific time, (b) until an ownership level is attained, or (c) until they retire.

- **Cash-based long-term incentives will increase in prevalence.** The increasingly aggressive actions taken by institutional investors and their advisers are making it more difficult for companies to get share plans approved by shareholders. As a result, we expect – and are already seeing – an increase in the prevalence of cash-based long-term incentive plans. The downside for shareholders is that these plans are not directly aligned with long-term shareholder value creation. The downward trend in dilution will have a negative impact on the incentive effect that stock-based awards have on increasing the stock price.
- **The prevalence of long-term incentive plans for nonmanagement employees will continue to decline.** The unfortunate and unintended outcome of stock option expensing is that efforts to curtail dilution and reduce expense will affect broad-based employee groups more than top executives. We encourage companies to maintain broad-based eligibility and, if expense is a constraint, limit participation to top performers.

6 Executive Stock Ownership: The Solution to the Executive Compensation Crisis

> These results illustrate that when managers with below-equilibrium equity ownership are required to increase their ownership levels, there are improvements in firm performance.[1]
>
> John E. Core, professor of accounting, Wharton School, University of Pennsylvania, and David F. Larcker, professor of accounting, Graduate School of Business, Stanford University

A basic assumption of executive compensation – that more stock ownership is better than less – is as solid as the theory that supports it. The theory is that companies flourish if their executives act like owners rather than hired hands. If the executives own only a small amount of stock in the company, their self-interest may be paramount and not completely aligned with the interests of the shareholders. However, we also need to factor in the desire of executives to have a balanced personal portfolio.

Companies use a number of techniques, such as stock options and cash incentives, to push executives to "act" like owners. However, companies can make them actual owners through stock ownership. But does executive ownership really work? And how does a company get its executives to take on the added risk of owning high levels of stock in the company?

Agency Theory and Costs

In 1932,[2] Adolph Berle and Gardiner Means articulated for the first time "agency theory" and its implication for corporate America. This theory describes the conflicts of interest or gaps that naturally occur between economic principals (typically, owners and shareholders) and their agents who run the organizations (typically, employees or executives). Agency theory, frequently described as the "separation of ownership and control," remains relevant today.

Agency costs are huge but difficult to quantify. However, the differences in total returns to shareholders among companies in a given industry can provide an estimate. While many factors may explain those differences, agency costs are clearly one of them. For example, consider a company with a $2 billion market capitalization in a given industry. A high-performing, "low agency cost" company has a 15 percent TRS. A "high agency cost" company has a 10 percent TRS. This difference of 5 percentage points in annual return could yield as much as $100 million of higher market value annually.

In the early history of corporate America, agency costs were less of an issue because the major firms, such as U.S. Steel and Ford, were owned and operated by the same people, often the founders and their families. But today's corporations are owned by tens of millions of dispersed and diversified shareholders and operate in a litigious environment, with risk-averse investors looking for safe places to invest literally trillions of dollars.

These conflicting issues are larger than Berle and Means could have imagined. But the short answer to the problem of separation of ownership and control has already been found: using aggressive amounts of stock incentives and encouraging or requiring large amounts of executive (and, indeed, employee) stock ownership. Ownership by executives keeps them focused on increasing the stock price through improved operational performance and not on increasing their own power.

While the ownership/control gap can be vast, principals and agents easily agree on the survival of the firm. If the company goes bankrupt, the principals suffer a capital loss. But the agents – the executives – suffer damage to their reputations and finances as well. Even so, conflicts of interest remain, creating costs that must be mitigated to maximize long-term shareholder value.

The classic examples are executives who want to make the most amount of money for the least amount of work, and to accumulate power and prestige, usually by increasing the size and prominence of their company. To the extent that the company succeeds and has a high and rising stock price, everyone's interests are aligned. But to the extent that size and prominence can be achieved without true underlying profitability and true shareholder value creation – as opposed to temporary spikes in the stock price – the executives' interests are served and the shareholders' are not.

We have seen examples of this at the industry level, in the automotive and airline transportation sectors, in recent decades. At the company level, examples include Tyco and WorldCom, during their acquisition binges of the 1990s, as well as the Enron and Adelphia disasters. Remembering how successful these latter companies seemed in their heyday, it becomes clear that it is difficult to recognize these agency costs in real time. In addition to huge stock option grants, the management teams at some of these companies had very large stock holdings. Boards must not abdicate their monitoring and oversight roles simply because they have created strong incentives.

Nevertheless, the primary solution to this agency problem and its associated costs is to create high and rising amounts of executive stock ownership, ideally with some of it purchased by the executives. When companies require stock ownership, the agents become principals, thereby partially closing the gap.

Some people worry about pushing too much stock into the hands of executives, as executives worry about becoming narrowly diversified. This problem can be managed, however. Executives should receive some of their stock free and be given highly leveraged incentive plans, including stock options, to achieve a balance that solves the agency problem without creating too much risk.

Stock ownership is not a panacea; it is part of an architecture and process for boards to use to manage publicly traded corporations. Nevertheless, our research, as demonstrated in Figure 6.1, shows that high levels of executive stock ownership both predict and drive high levels of financial and stock market performance. A company with high CEO stock ownership is also more likely to have high stock ownership among those who report directly to the CEO as well as the employee population as a whole.

Moral Hazard

Another economic concept – moral hazard – is also helpful in analyzing the importance of executive stock ownership. Moral hazard is typically created after an owner insures an item and then becomes less diligent about taking care of it. The classic example is found in fire insurance on a business. Without the insurance, business owners are extremely careful

FIGURE 6.1

Executive Stock Ownership and Company Performance in 2004

	2004 CEO STOCK OWNERSHIP (MM$)*	2004 STOCK OWNERSHIP NEXT 4 (MM$)	THREE-YEAR ANNUALIZED TRS*	FIVE-YEAR ANNUALIZED TRS*	ROE*	ROA*	ONE-YEAR EPS GROWTH*	TOBIN'S Q**
High	$24.6	$3.4	13.1%	12.3%	13.7%	4.9%	23.0%	1.32
Low	$1.9	$0.6	8.3%	6.9%	9.2%	3.4%	21.0%	1.22
All	$7.4	$1.4	10.7%	9.8%	11.6%	4.1%	22.1%	1.28

  * *Significant at .05 level.* EPS: Earnings Per Share = Net Profit/ Average Shares Outstanding.
** *Significant at .1 level.* Tobin's Q = [stock market valuation + long-term debt]/replacement cost of assets].
Note: CEO ownership (excluding stock options) and financial information as of December 31, 2004.
Sample size = 1,414.

Source: Watson Wyatt .

with electrical appliances, kitchen equipment, and other possible fire hazards. After obtaining insurance, they may be more casual because they are now protected by a third party if the business is destroyed by fire.

Stock options create an analogous moral hazard. If the stock price rises, the executives share in the appreciation – and if it declines, they are protected; they have no loss and can keep their salaries, bonuses, and pensions. However, the shareholders suffer from the stock price decline. At some companies, the employees hold 15 percent or more of the upside in their company's stock price appreciation through stock options but none of the downside risk.

Encouraging or requiring executives to buy stock can address this moral hazard. The combination of stock options and stock ownership balances the upside and downside for executives and presumably creates advantages for both executives and shareholders. In essence, stock ownership can address the biggest challenge in executive pay today – ensuring that executives act in the best interests of the shareholders.

But the question remains: Can we prove that executive stock ownership drives superior returns to shareholders?

Driving Superior Returns

Watson Wyatt has been studying the impact of executive stock ownership on financial and stock market performance for more than 10 years, with an impressive and consistent finding: Companies where the CEO and all of the executives – and frequently the entire employee population – hold an above-average amount of stock, excluding stock options, significantly and persistently outperform companies where the CEO owns a relatively small amount of stock.

Watson Wyatt's fiscal year 2004 study collected data on the stock ownership and compensation levels of CEOs at 1,420 large public companies as reported in S&P's ExecuComp database. The companies, a subset of the S&P 1500, filed their annual proxy statements before June 2005. They had a median revenue of roughly $1.4 billion and a median market capitalization of $2.0 billion. The pay data in the study represent salaries and bonuses for 2004.

We measure CEO stock values in several ways: present values of new grant opportunities (namely, new stock option grants + restricted stock + long-term incentive plan [LTIP] target); realized values (actual exercised value of stock options + LTIP payout); and total value of in-the-money options (unrealized value). We focus here on findings that show the strong, positive relationship of CEO stock ownership to corporate performance.

- Companies with CEOs who own a significant amount of the company's stock perform better

Figure 6.1 shows the end of fiscal year 2004 stock ownership levels for the CEO and other named executives relative to various financial performance measures. To determine the relationship between executive stock ownership (excluding options) and company performance, we split companies into high and low CEO ownership based on stock owned at the end of 2004. The CEOs in the high-ownership group had a median stake of $25 million; the median holdings of CEOs in the low-ownership group were just $2 million. Our analyses for 2004 and for earlier years have consistently shown that companies with high executive stock ownership have stronger financial performance as measured by TRS, ROA, ROE, and earnings growth.

Our research also indicates that the median stock ownership of other named executives (the average ownership among the second through fifth most highly compensated executives) in companies with high CEO ownership was $3.4 million. This level of ownership is nearly six times as high as that of companies in the low-ownership group. Our results indicate that companies that have CEOs with high stock ownership extend the high-ownership levels below the top position.

Companies whose CEOs have high stock ownership were superior investments – a three-year annualized total return of 13.1 percent and a five-year annualized total return of 12.3 percent for their shareholders

FIGURE 6.2

Investors Pay a Premium for Companies with High CEO Stock Ownership

	CEO STOCK OWNERSHIP IN 2000 (MMS)*	CURRENT TOBIN'S Q*	FIVE-YEAR EPS GROWTH*
High	$33.3	1.33	58.9%
Low	$1.8	1.20	36.4%
All	$7.8	1.27	47.9%

* Significant at .05 level.

Note: CEO ownership (excluding stock options) as of January 1, 2000.
Sample size = 721.

Source: Watson Wyatt.

at the median – while companies with low CEO ownership saw a much lower return on their investment for the period ending December 2004.

• Investors pay more when senior management's and shareholders' interests are aligned

We used an economic concept called Tobin's Q to research the alignment of senior management and shareholder interests. Tobin's Q is calculated as [stock market valuation + long-term debt]/replacement cost of assets. A Tobin's Q of 1.0 indicates that a company is valued at the replacement cost of its assets. Values above 1.0 imply that the market sees the company as more valuable than the sum of its assets. The Tobin's Q of companies with high CEO ownership was 8 percent higher than that of companies led by CEOs with lower stock ownership.

To confirm this relationship and to test whether CEO stock ownership causes the superior financial performance, we also looked at CEO stock ownership in 2000 and compared it with the companies' current Tobin's Q and five-year annualized TRS from 2000 through 2004. This analysis similarly shows that companies with higher CEO stock ownership levels subsequently are more highly valued and have better performance (see Figure 6.2).

The current Tobin's Q of companies whose CEOs had high ownership in 2000 is almost 10 percent greater than that of companies led by lower-ownership CEOs – again indicating that investors are willing to pay more for companies that align the interests of executives and shareholders. We also interpret this to indicate that those high-ownership CEOs in 2000 developed and executed strategies superior to those of CEOs with

FIGURE 6.3
Stock Ownership and TRS, EPS Growth, and Tobin's Q

YEAR	CEO STOCK OWNERSHIP	THREE-YEAR TRS	CUMULATIVE THREE-YEAR EPS GROWTH	TOBIN'S Q
1994	High	12.2%	63.4%	1.60
	Low	6.6%	31.0%	1.08
1995	High	14.4%	60.2%	1.46
	Low	9.6%	30.0%	1.04
1996	High	19.1%	67.4%	1.54
	Low	9.2%	31.5%	1.08
1997	High	33.7%	64.5%	1.66
	Low	19.1%	30.9%	1.20
1998	High	26.2%	54.3%	1.62
	Low	10.2%	19.1%	1.08
1999	High	18.1%	56.9%	1.75
	Low	2.2%	20.1%	.97
2000	High	11.5%	50.2%	1.44
	Low	−1.1%	30.6%	.97
2001	High	7.6%	24.4%	1.33
	Low	4.5%	−5.9%	1.03
2002	High	3.8%	23.4%	1.09
	Low	−4.5%	−17.5%	.87
2003	High	9.0%	22.2%	1.26
	Low	6.3%	−3.2%	1.14
2004	High	13.1%	67.3%	1.32
	Low	8.3%	51.1%	1.22
2005	High	19.7%	16.4%*	1.28
	Low	17.0%	13.1%*	1.19

*One-year EPS growth.

Source: Watson Wyatt.

lower ownership. Our research, which is detailed here, also shows that higher-performing companies, as measured by the five-year annualized EPS, had CEOs with high ownership.

Figure 6.3 shows a 12-year history of the relationship between stock ownership and various financial metrics through 2005. It consolidates data from our studies of the approximately 1,000 largest U.S. corporations. In every year, high levels of CEO stock ownership are highly correlated with TRS, EPS growth, and Tobin's Q.

STOCK INCENTIVE LEVELS AND STRUCTURES ARE IN TRANSITION

It is important to look at the history of stock options as a context for creating stock ownership. Stock options have played a role in creating the high executive stock ownership described in this book and the concomitant superior performance. However, it appears to take time for this phenomenon to take effect. We compared the total new long-term incentive opportunities of CEOs from 2000 through 2004 with their company's five-year annualized TRS. Because the purpose of LTI is to motivate executives to focus on their firm's future performance, we expected it to correlate with the company's subsequent stock market performance. However, we did not find a relationship between LTI and five-year TRS. It seems to have lost its incentive effect around 2000, given the bear stock market. Further analysis showed that the size of the five-year LTI correlated with firm performance for previous years but that the correlation has progressively decreased over the years (see Figure 6.4). Watson Wyatt research for 2005 continues the trend of no statistical relationship between new LTI opportunity and recent financial performance. It appears that both high- and low-performing companies are using large new stock grants to motivate their employees. However, as shown in this book, there is a strong relationship between realized pay and performance.

We believe that stock incentive levels and structures are in transition, with no perfect solution yet discovered. However, our findings suggest that high levels of stock ownership are more consistently shareholder-friendly than high levels of stock options, which leads us to the conclusion that the design of stock incentives is more important than the amounts.

Stock Ownership Guidelines

In a 2002 study, John Core and David Larcker tested some of the basic assumptions about stock ownership and stock ownership guidelines.[3] They built a database of hundreds of companies over six or seven years in the late 1990s, when only about 10 percent of companies had ownership guidelines. Today, more than 50 percent of major companies report some type of guidelines, and many more have them but do not disclose them.

Because so few companies had ownership guidelines, Core and Larcker could examine whether there were economically and statistically important distinctions between the types of companies that did and those

FIGURE 6.4
Five-Year LTI Opportunities of CEOs and Company Performance

	2000–2004		1999–2003		1998–2002		1997–2001		1996–2000	
SAMPLE SIZE	732		710		550		426		373	
	FIVE-YEAR TOTAL CEO LTI (MM$)*	FIVE-YEAR ANNUAL-IZED TRS*	FIVE-YEAR TOTAL CEO LTI (MM$)*	FIVE-YEAR ANNUAL-IZED TRS*	FIVE-YEAR TOTAL CEO LTI (MM$)*	FIVE-YEAR ANNUAL-IZED TRS*	FIVE-YEAR TOTAL CEO LTI (MM$)*	FIVE-YEAR ANNUAL-IZED TRS*	FIVE-YEAR TOTAL CEO LTI (MM$)*	FIVE-YEAR ANNUAL-IZED TRS*
High	$18.0	10.0%	$19.7	8.1%	$18.5	4.5%	$18.6	15.1%	$14.4	18.5%
Low	$3.5	9.8%	$2.7	7.4%	$2.7	2.4%	$2.2	7.8%	$2.0	8.8%
All	$7.9	9.9%	$7.9	7.8%	$7.7	3.1%	$6.6	12.0%	$5.3	12.8%

* Significant at .05 level.
Note: Only includes companies that had the same CEO in the five-year period in study. Sample differs for each five-year period.

Source: Watson Wyatt.

that did not. They also examined whether implementing target owner-ship guidelines improved the companies' performance. They found that this was, indeed, the case.

Core and Larcker found that:

1. Companies whose top five executives had low levels of stock owner-ship were much more likely to implement stock ownership guidelines than companies with high ownership levels.
2. Underperforming companies implemented stock ownership guide-lines.
3. The target ownership plans increased executive stock ownership.
4. Once these higher-ownership companies had increased their stock ownership, they outperformed others.

The study has implications for almost all companies today. Even if an organization has relatively high ownership – with or without ownership guidelines – and relatively high performance, it makes sense in terms of both governance and shareholder alignment to encourage even more executive stock ownership.[4]

Stock Holding Requirements

According to Bruce Ellig, an expert on executive compensation, the first company to implement stock ownership guidelines was Warner Lambert in 1989.[5] Arguably, this began to level the playing field between executives and shareholders. Before then, executives were reluctant to own stock in their companies. Since then, hundreds if not thousands of companies have implemented stock ownership guidelines.

These guidelines are typically structured as

a multiple of base salary (by far the most common approach),

a multiple of total cash compensation (salary plus bonus),

a fixed dollar amount, or

a fixed number of shares.

Under guidelines that use a multiple of base salary, for example, stock ownership is easily determined:

CEO salary = $1 million

Ownership guideline multiple = 5 × salary

Value of shares to be owned = $5 million

Today's stock price = $20

Number of shares needed to meet guideline = 250,000

One issue that has arisen is the impact of stock price volatility. In our example, if the executive owns the 250,000 requisite shares and the stock price drops to $10, he or she will have to go into the market and buy $2.5 million worth of stock at a time when the stock price is declining. Companies are exploring alternative solutions to this problem, such as using an average stock price over a period of several months or a year.

Some companies fix the number of shares to be owned based on the current stock price and stay with that number for a period of time. Obviously, a large stock price increase would reduce the number of shares the executive needed to purchase.

This policy and all others must be periodically evaluated for fairness; a sound targeted stock ownership policy is attractive to the shareholders without being unduly unfair to the executives. As in all corporate policies, a fair amount of judgment goes into administering the program.

Net Share Retention Requirements

Many companies have also implemented a complementary executive stock ownership technique. This is a stock holding program in which the executive is expected to hold for a period of time – anywhere from one year to retirement – a proportion of the shares obtained after the vesting of restricted stock or the exercise of a stock option. But, in this case, the holding requirement could be in addition to the number of shares required under the ownership guidelines.

The thinking behind these requirements is twofold. First, because the executives receive large grants of stock incentives, primarily stock options, every year, their ownership should be expected to rise somewhat proportionately. Second, holding requirements discourage the premature exercise of stock options using cashless exercise, minimizing the value of 10-year stock options, and encourage the deferral of vested restricted stock or restricted stock units beyond the vesting date. Recent tax law changes may reduce the ability to defer the taxes on stock.

Holding requirements are generally denominated as a percentage of the net shares obtained by the executives, assuming sufficient sales of stock to pay the proceeds on stock options and the taxes on both stock options and restricted stock units. Typically, holding requirements range from 25 percent to 100 percent, with very few at the latter level, although Citigroup used that requirement for its top executives under CEO Sandy Weill.

The following case shows how holding requirements work. For example, assume the following conditions:

1 million stock options with a strike price of $20

Today's price = $50

Tax rate = 50 percent

Net holding requirement of 25 percent

If the executive exercises today and sells enough stock to pay exercise proceeds and taxes, the scenario might look like this:

The executive sells 400,000 shares for proceeds to pay the exercise price ($20 million).

The executive sells an additional 300,000 shares ($15 million) to pay taxes on a $30 million profit.

The executive is required to hold 75,000 ($3.75 million) of the remaining 300,000 net "profit" shares.

The final 225,000 profit shares can be held or sold at the executive's discretion, assuming no other ownership guidelines or other sales restrictions.

Other Mechanisms for Creating Ownership

Companies grant stock-based incentives, primarily stock options, to align the interests of executives and shareholders and (potentially and indirectly) to create executive stock ownership – or, in other words, to reduce agency costs and moral hazard.

Companies used to say that they granted these incentives specifically to create higher levels of executive stock ownership. But given the reality of the last 10 to 15 years, where many shares from stock options or restricted stock were sold after exercise or vesting, companies have stopped making that claim. Interestingly, despite the vast amount of stock sales by executives after vesting or exercise, their stock ownership has increased – another indication of the size of the grants made to these executives.

Direct stock ownership, especially if the executives purchase the stock, creates the best and clearest alignment with shareholders. Stock options have only upside and no direct downside; that lack of symmetry can encourage executives to undertake riskier strategies than the shareholders desire. (This is ironic because stock options were invented partially to overcome executives' natural risk aversion.)

Some commentators have argued that stock options have a downside in the form of a loss of economic upside opportunity. Say, for example, the stock options were granted in lieu of salary or a cash bonus, perquisites, or even a pension – which certainly occurs in some sectors, especially the technology sector. If this is the case, and the CEO of company A receives a large grant and does not increase his company's stock price, he gets paid less, in terms of actual realized pay, than the CEO of company B, who also received a large grant but increased his company's stock price. However, that forgone opportunity argument has lost much of its power in the last decade as the size of executive stock option grants has exploded. Stock options at most companies are not in lieu of other components of compensation but in addition to them. This arguably reflects the rising market value of executives.

Even restricted stock, which solves the "no downside loss" problem, does not balance the interests of the executive and the shareholders because the executive wins even if the stock price falls. Restricted stock is the economic equivalent of giving an executive $1 million in chips at a casino and telling him that, win or lose, he can keep the change. Obviously, a moral hazard is created as well; the executive behaves differently than if he were playing with his own money.

Our solution is a balanced portfolio of incentives and stock ownership programs in which executives are either required or allowed to purchase stock pretax, typically with a discount or a match. As mentioned earlier, executives desire a more balanced personal portfolio. By skipping over stock incentives and going directly to stock ownership with purchased shares, the management stock purchase plan (MSPP) described in this book solves the agency and moral hazard problems.

The challenge is getting the executives to buy the stock, or even to hold significant amounts of stock received as incentives and overcome their natural proclivity to sell immediately. The compensation committee must determine how to overcome the risk aversion that stems from a lack of diversification, given that so much of the executive's worth and human capital is tied up with the company.

The classic stock-based incentive portfolio contains stock options, time-based restricted stock, and performance shares, with the grant of shares being forfeited if the performance goal is not achieved. Numerous bells and whistles are associated with all of these; for example, premium strike prices, indexed strike prices, accelerated vesting, and combinations of performance and time vesting.

All of the programs should be linked to design features that mimic or create stock ownership; for example, longer vesting and holding requirements. In this context, two major points must be considered, one regarding cash long-term incentives rather than stock and the other the use of MSPPs.

Many companies use a cash-based multiyear long-term incentive plan (cash LTIP) to complement their stock incentive plans. Companies have used these plans for years with excellent success. This type of plan gives the executive some portfolio diversification – a fine goal – but diminishes the effectiveness of directly linking executive stock interests to shareholders' interests. To overcome that problem, many companies use a TRS measure inside the plan.

This, of course, does not solve the stock price risk problem. Other companies use internal or relative financial measures as the payout mechanism, a preferable solution. But it is better to denominate the grants in shares rather than in cash for two reasons. First, the share plans have more favorable accounting treatment under FAS 123(R). Second, and more important, companies should provide share-based incentive plans to their executives at every opportunity.

Management Stock Purchase Plans

An MSPP is one of the most cost- and tax-effective ways for a company to boost the level of stock ownership. Executives and managers purchase company restricted stock units (RSUs) on a pretax basis out of income they would otherwise receive as salary or bonus. Restricted stock units are notional accounts established for participants, who are credited with amounts equivalent to shares of company stock subject to designated restrictions. At the time of payout, participants receive a number of actual shares of company stock equal to the number of their RSUs.

The purchased RSUs are fully vested, but their delivery and taxation are delayed until they are delivered at a preestablished future date. Under IRC Section 409A, RSUs are considered nonqualified deferred compensation that must meet the deferral election and distribution form and timing rules. To help the executive balance the risk of forgoing current compensation to purchase RSUs, the company contributes a matching RSU, ranging from 25 percent to 100 percent for each purchased RSU, with a vesting schedule of two to five years, three years being the most common. During the restricted period, the stock cannot be sold, assigned, transferred, hypothecated, or pledged.

The company determines whether it will deliver shares underlying the RSUs when the matching RSUs vest or permit deferral of RSU delivery until a later date. In accordance with the new rules, if the program permits continued deferral, the executive should decide when the RSUs will be delivered at the same time he or she elects to purchase them. If the executive terminates before the matching RSUs vest, he or she receives a distribution of only the purchased RSUs.

TAX IMPLICATIONS

Management stock purchase plans carry tax advantages for both the participant and the company. When the participant's compensation is reduced mandatorily to buy shares, there is no need to meet the deferral-timing rules under Section 409A. The grant of the RSU is not currently taxable. When compensation is reduced voluntarily to buy shares, the rules of Section 409A must be met for a pretax purchase.

When the payout occurs, the participant will have ordinary income on the fair market value of the stock or the amount of cash he or she receives. There are no current tax consequences from dividend equivalent units (DEUs) credited to the RSUs until paid. Whether paid in additional RSUs or cash, these amounts are taxed as ordinary compensation income when distributed. The company is liable for tax withholding on MSPP distributions.

For the company, although there is a delay in the corporate tax deduction, the size of the deduction will increase with any stock price increase.

FAS 123(R)

Under FAS 123(R), MSPPs continue to have the same predictable and controllable accounting costs as they did under prior accounting rules. Purchased RSUs, which by design are fully vested on the purchase date, do not require any expense to be taken on the grant date. This is because the employee purchases the shares with cash compensation earned for services previously rendered and pays the then-current fair value, usually the quoted market price of the stock on the purchase date. An accounting expense is incurred for MSPP matching RSUs, as these are granted in consideration for services to be rendered by the employee over the "requisite service period," which is the vesting period. The compensation expense for the grant will ultimately yield a tax deduction for the company.

Management stock purchase plans provide a distinct advantage over option plans because of their retentive nature. Under FAS 123(R), both an MSPP and an option plan will cause the company to incur an expense, but an option program has a weaker retentive value unless the company stock price has greatly appreciated. In almost all cases, the MSPP will provide the executives with more real equity value than the option program. This is certainly true in the early years (before the options vest) and could be true even longer if the shares from the option exercise are sold at the time of exercise.

Companies find that using both stock options and an MSPP creates an ideal portfolio that emphasizes leverage, retentive value, and stock ownership through purchase opportunities. An MSPP also adds another equity-based component to the company's executive compensation portfolio and increases the portion of total direct compensation that is based on creating shareholder value. These plans help retain management by increasing the portion of compensation they leave on the table if employment is voluntarily terminated. They also provide incentives for voluntary savings among executives and managers.

Finding the Right Solutions

Executive pay may be in flux, but the paramount objective – aligning executive and shareholder interests – has not changed. Stock options and other incentives align interests and motivate executives, but they do not truly create executive stock ownership or serve as a substitute for stock ownership.

Companies can adopt various mechanisms to increase ownership: guidelines and holding plans, grants of stock options and restricted stock, and preferential MSPPs that allow the pretax purchase of stock with a significant match for holding the shares. Increasing executive stock ownership is a way to drive superior returns to shareholders.

7 Director Compensation in the New Environment

> The trade-offs of becoming a director of a corporation don't look nearly as attractive these days. The compensation hasn't gone up that much, the hours have gone up a lot and the liabilities have increased.
>
> John A. Thain, CEO, New York Stock Exchange[1]

Wanted: To serve on the board of directors of a Fortune 1000 company, an individual (current or former chief executive or financial officer most desirable) of high moral character and strength of convictions. Must have the ability to engage in constructive dialogue with the CEO and other senior management while maintaining strict independence. Must be willing to take on significant financial and reputational risks. Substantial time commitment. Annual pay: approximately $170,000, nonnegotiable.

For many years, serving as an outside director of a prominent company was a coveted role. A seat on the board of a Fortune 1000 company earned its holder the respect of peers and the opportunity to interact with other prominent people from other high-profile companies. While the pay was never comparable to what most directors made in their full-time jobs, it gave many retired executives a continued income stream and a valuable benefits package. Moreover, the time commitment and the work were not particularly strenuous, and there was little risk to reputation or finances. All of this changed in the early 2000s.

The Sarbanes-Oxley Act and stock exchange listing requirements have forced many companies to bring on new independent directors who have no interlocking relationships with the company and who must represent a majority of the board and constitute the compensation and audit committees. Expertise in various governance matters is at a premium, especially given the new requirement that one of the members of the audit committee be qualified as a financial expert.

But as demand for top director talent has been increasing, the pool of potential candidates has been shrinking. In 1997, CEOs in the S&P 500 sat on an average of two outside boards. In 2005, that number had fallen to less than one (0.9).[2] In addition to concerns about risks to finances and reputation, the increased time commitment is another factor driving this change. As a result of Sarbanes-Oxley, audit committees held an average of eight meetings in 2004, compared with five just two years earlier. And the average number of hours a director spent on board matters for a company increased from 13 hours a month in 2001 to 18 hours a month in 2004,[3] or 216 hours a year – more than five full-time workweeks.

Median total director pay among S&P 500 firms is $170,000,[4] according to Watson Wyatt data, and it has increased 10 percent to 15 percent a year in the last few years. When considered on an hourly basis, that $170,000 translates into $787 an hour – on its own, not a particularly bad deal. But compared with an hourly rate of $884 in 2001, director pay has declined, while the risk, workload, and complexity have risen.

Also, compare that hourly rate with the pay that board members routinely received as CEOs. The median total pay for a CEO of an S&P 500 company was $7.4 million in 2004. The CEO position is not an eight-hour-a-day job; assume that the CEO works 10 hours a day for 300 days a year. This translates into $2,467 an hour, more than triple the hourly director pay.

When Michael Capellas was the CEO at Compaq, he also served on the board of Dynegy. The board met four times a year, and Capellas would "read the material the night before," he told the *Wall Street Journal*. Today "you have to attend many more board meetings," and the reading material is "much more voluminous." Now, he serves on no other boards and has turned down dozens of offers.[5]

Because of the increased time commitment, more and more companies are either limiting the number of external directorships their CEO may take on or prohibiting it altogether. In 2004, 51 percent of companies limited the number of other boards on which their CEO could serve, up from 23 percent in 2001.[6] Another factor is retirement age. Nearly 70 percent of Fortune 1000 companies have a mandatory retirement age for directors, with an average age of 71. Because most board members are retired executives, age restrictions constrict supply.

Finally, concern about potential liability has reached new proportions. In the WorldCom and Enron settlements, directors had to pay a total of $33 million out of their own pockets to settle shareholder law-suits. And although Disney "won" its case in the shareholder lawsuit over Michael Ovitz's severance pay, the case nevertheless called into question directors' protection under the business judgment rule. As a result, com-pensation committees have become much more active and involved in scrutinizing the full spectrum of executive compensation and benefits.

The forces of increasing demand and contracting supply are pushing director compensation up. Although pay levels have increased, it is not yet clear whether the amount is sufficient to attract and retain the quality of directors needed to provide guidance and oversight in this new world of corporate governance. The most qualified directors may not want to be exposed to the risks – to finances or reputation.

The unintended outcome is that if less qualified directors take on the role, corporate governance could be damaged, and the advisory and monitoring roles that directors play could decline as well. Companies and their shareholders would suffer as a result. Beyond questions about the level of compensation, key questions remain about how to struc-ture and deliver this compensation so that directors can carry out their responsibilities: namely, "engage, monitor, and, when necessary replace company management."[7]

The Evolution of Director Compensation

Agency theory posits that the interests of management (the agents) and owners (the principals) are at odds because managers will generally act in their own self-interest, which can be at odds with maximizing value for shareholders.[8] One of the solutions to this principal/agent problem was to install a board of directors that would act as an intermediary between owners and management, thus monitoring management and taking action where appropriate to the benefit of the owners.

Before the rise of the modern corporation, companies were generally owned by a few large shareholders who could control the appointment of directors – also large shareholders – so the board was fully aligned with shareholder interests. But with the rise of the modern corporation, ownership became more diffuse and control of the corporation increas-ingly came under management, because the shareholder base lacked the collective ability to monitor management's actions. Of course, over time, other entities came into being that effectively monitored management performance, most notably the LBO associations of the late 1980s and hedge funds most recently.

The threat of a hostile takeover was an effective, market-based means for monitoring management performance and served as a form of discipline in evaluating company performance. Nevertheless, board members were increasingly hand-picked by management. These directors joined the company with little in the way of stock ownership and thus little in the way of shareholder alignment. But they provided a service and were, in exchange, compensated.

The compensation was typically cash, and the only extra benefit was that directors could often participate in the company's pension plan. One of the first companies to construct a more modern board approach was Texas Instruments (TI). In the 1960s and 1970s, TI put in place a board with two insiders (the CEO and the president) and 10 outsiders, most of whom were former TI executives, which is not common today. They worked between 35 and 65 days a year. In return, they were paid an "unheard of retainer of $35,000 plus fees for every meeting they attend[ed]."[9]

From the late 1980s through the mid-1990s, director compensation fundamentally changed. Although the level of direct compensation – a cash retainer and meeting fees – remained relatively stable, the pay package expanded to include perquisites and benefits normally reserved for the CEO. As depicted in a May 1995 *Fortune* article titled "The Cosseted Director," the pay package of the 1990s director was soon dominated by perks and cash, matching gifts, charitable contributions, life insurance, pensions, airplane use, and medical and dental coverage for life, but little use of stock.[10]

The outrage factor was in high gear. Beginning in the mid-1990s, partly in response to recommendations from the National Association of Corporate Directors (NACD), the vast majority of director pensions were frozen or eliminated and cashed out or converted into restricted stock. Today, the percentage of companies with pensions for directors is in the low single digits. To fill the vacuum, companies began to incorporate stock (largely in the form of stock options) into the director compensation package, paralleling the increased use of stock in the compensation of executives.

Move Away from Stock Options

After the scandals at Enron, WorldCom, and other companies – where, it was thought, option-dominated executive pay packages promoted a short-term perspective and directors were asleep at the switch and cozy with management – the attitude toward stock options began to change. If

FIGURE 7.1
Stock Option and Full-Value Shares

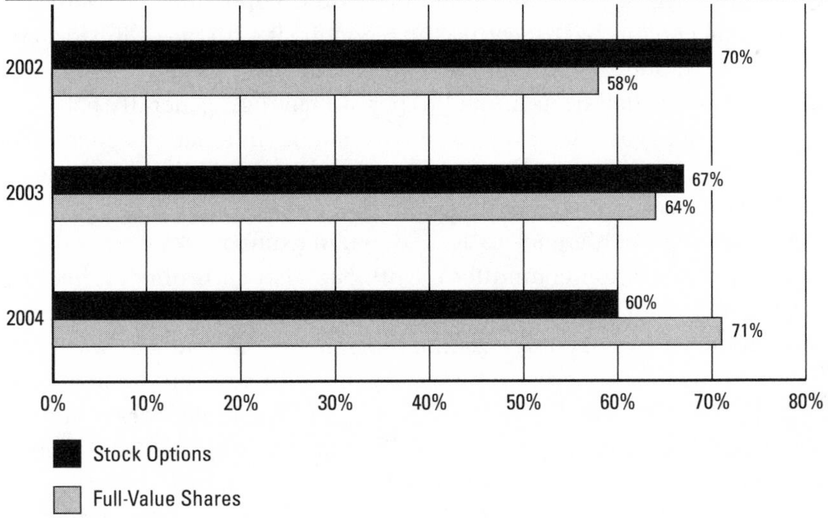

Stock Options

Full-Value Shares

Source: Watson Wyatt.

options were criticized as encouraging executives to engage in short-term actions at the expense of long-term value creation, then it was even less appropriate for directors to be receiving them. Because directors were supposed to be independent and have the proper checks and balances over executive actions and behaviors, they should have had a separately constructed pay package that aligned them with long-term shareholders.

The outcome was a noticeable shift in director compensation. Stock options were castigated as too aligned with executives and short-term interests and not effective in promoting long-term share ownership and alignment. According to Albert Dunlap, "It's the last dirty secret. You've got directors taking large sums of money but holding incredibly few shares in the company they're serving."[11] In a trend that accelerated in 2005 and 2006, more companies began to eliminate stock option awards and deliver the annual retainer in a mix of full-value shares or share units and cash.

Watson Wyatt's analysis of director compensation practices among S&P 500 companies shows that while the use of stock options declined from 70 percent of companies in 2002–2003 to 60 percent of companies in 2004–2005, the use of full-value shares or share units increased from 58 percent to 71 percent (See Figure 7.1).

Activity-Based Compensation

As the number of board meetings increased, companies struggled to define what constituted a meeting and reconcile it with the desire to compensate directors for the increased workload. Historically, interaction among directors had been limited to board meetings, generally between 4 and 12 each year. In the new environment, interactions increased significantly, particularly for the audit and compensation committees. For the audit committee, the impact of Sarbanes-Oxley led to more and longer meetings, conference calls, and e-mail exchanges.

The compensation committee's workload also multiplied, reflecting both the increased scrutiny of executive pay and the efforts of many companies to revamp their compensation programs as they moved away from stock options to alternative vehicles. Again, with so many interactions, defining a meeting was difficult. As a result, it is becoming more common, although still a minority practice, to eliminate meeting fees in exchange for enhanced retainers. One of the first companies to take this step was Intel in 2002. As it noted in its 2003 shareholder proxy statement:

> The Board's current view is that per-meeting fees are inappropriate, because attendance at all meetings is expected, and a substantial amount of the Board's work is done in Committee meetings and outside of formal meetings. On this basis, the Board decided to combine the former retainer and per-meeting fee amounts, and increase the retainer in recognition of the Board's increased workload and responsibilities in recent years. For similar reasons, the Board increased the additional fees payable to the Lead Independent Director and the chairs of the Board's committees.

In looking at the S&P 500, we found that the prevalence of meeting fees continued to decline slightly, from 72 percent of companies in 2003 to 68 percent in 2004. The use of committee chair and member retainers has increased, particularly for audit committee chairs and members (see Figure 7.2).

Compensating Committee Chairs and Members

Companies have adopted a variety of practices in awarding additional pay to committee chairs and members. A 2005 survey of the top 100 firms on the NYSE and the NASDAQ by Frederick W. Cook & Co. found that 27 percent of the largest NASDAQ companies pay members of the compensation and audit committees an additional retainer, with a median

FIGURE 7.2
Use of Retainer and Meeting Fees

Chair Retainer — 69%, 81%, 87%

Member Retainer — 16%, 22%, 28%

Member Meeting Fees — 70%, 72%, 68%

0% 10% 20% 30% 40% 50% 60% 70% 80% 90% 100%

■ 2002
▢ 2003
▨ 2004

Source: Watson Wyatt.

of $10,000; some 20 percent of top NYSE firms have a similar prac-
tice, with the median extra retainer $7,500 for compensation committee
members and $8,250 for audit committee members. In another 2005 sur-
vey, by Executive Compensation Resources, 28 percent of the companies
paid premiums for audit committee service, ranging from 25 percent to
200 percent above regular retainers.

The number of companies providing additional pay for committee
chairs increased significantly, especially at the NASDAQ companies,
according to the Cook study. Sixty-eight percent and 61 percent of the
100 largest NASDAQ firms provided additional audit and compensation
chair retainers, respectively, in 2005, up from 47 percent and 41 percent
in 2004. The percentage of large NYSE companies providing these extra
retainers also rose, from 84 percent for audit chairs and 79 percent for
compensation chairs in 2004 to 89 percent and 87 percent, respectively,
in 2005.

Dow Chemical's 2005 proxy statement provides an example of one
approach to committee chair and member compensation (see Figure 7.3).

FIGURE 7.3
Dow Chemical's Committee Compensation

Annual Retainer Fee	$60,000 annually
Meeting Retainer Fee	$40,000 annually
Audit Committee Chairmanship	$15,000 annually
All Other Committee Chairmanships	$8,000 annually
Audit Committee Membership	$12,000 annually
All Other Committee Memberships	$8,000 annually
Presiding Director Service	$20,000 annually

Source: Dow Chemical 2005 proxy statement.

In addition to the annual retainer and stock-based compensation, Duke Energy awards $7,500 to the chairs of the compensation, corporate governance, finance and risk management, and nuclear oversight committees, and $20,000 to the chair of the audit committee. During the 2005 fiscal year, each nonemployee director at Cisco Systems was paid a $75,000 regular annual retainer fee. The Cisco audit committee chair received an additional annual retainer of $25,000 and the compensation committee chair an additional $10,000. Each nonemployee member of each standing committee received an additional fee of $2,000 per meeting attended.

Another board role that has risen in prominence and compensation is that of lead director. Typically structured as a role between that of a nonexecutive chairman and a presiding director, a lead director presides over board executive sessions but also serves as an intermediary between the CEO and the board and is the leading spokesperson for the independent board members. Compensation for lead directors varies based on the degree of involvement but typically involves a premium annual retainer ranging from $20,000 to $60,000 but topping $100,000 at the largest companies or where the lead director has a more involved role.

General Electric as a Reference Point

In 2001, General Electric replaced its director pension program with deferred stock units for all directors hired in that year or beyond. The mix of director compensation in 2004 compared with 2002 can be viewed as a microcosm of changing pay practices.

FIGURE 7.4
Compensation Mix for GE Directors in 2002 and 2004

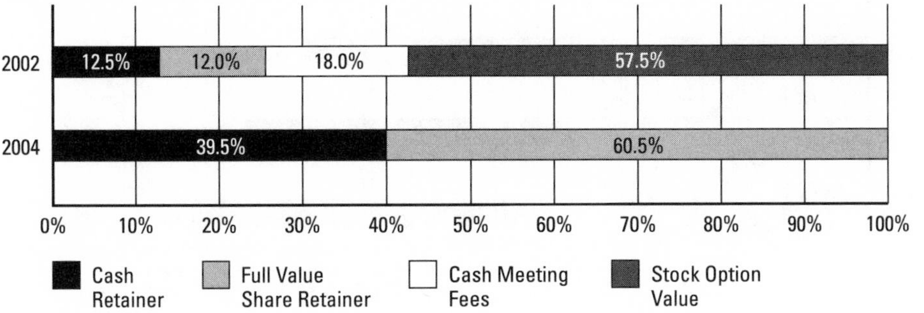

Source: General Electric 2003 and 2005 shareholder proxy statements.

As shown in Figure 7.4, in 2002, more than half of compensation value delivered to outside directors at GE was in the form of stock options, with full-value shares representing just over 10 percent, although directors had the opportunity to defer cash into stock units. During the next two years, GE, like many other companies, simplified its director compensation delivery, eliminating meeting fees and stock options and instituting an annual retainer reflecting a mix of cash (40 percent) and equity (60 percent).

Starting in 2003, GE began offering additional retainers for audit and compensation committee members equal to 10 percent of the total retainer, or $25,000 each, to reflect "the workload and broad-based responsibilities of these two committees." The company also modified its director charitable award program and eliminated life and accidental death insurance.

Director Compensation Levels and Mix

Reflecting supply and demand, director compensation has increased since the early part of this decade. As shown in Figure 7.5, median director pay among S&P 500 companies was $173,000 in 2004–2005, up 15 percent from the prior year and up 12 percent annually in the last two years. This outpaced the increase in CEO compensation, which rose by 6.7 percent in 2004 and just under 5 percent annually in 2002–2004.

These findings are consistent with the NACD 2005 director pay study, which showed a 2004–2005 median pay level for the top 200 companies

FIGURE 7.5
Median Director Pay at S&P 500 Companies, 2002–2004

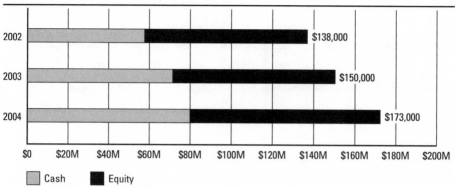

Cash   Equity

Source: Watson Wyatt.

of $177,000, up 14 percent from 2003–2004. Interestingly, the mix of cash and equity has remained relatively stable in the last few years, with 45 percent cash and 55 percent equity on average.

Director Share Ownership

Given the desire to align the interests of directors and shareholders, it would be expected that using stock to compensate directors would be standard practice. But a Korn/Ferry study of the Fortune 1000 shows that in 2004, 21 percent – more than one in five companies – did not use stock at all to compensate directors.

Watson Wyatt data show that among companies that compensate their directors with stock, options remain the most prevalent vehicle (46 percent of the companies), with restricted stock gaining ground and in place at 37 percent of the companies (see Figure 7.6). The Korn/Ferry study also reveals that 78 percent of directors surveyed among Fortune 1000 firms believe that the majority of director compensation should be in stock, up from 54 percent in 2003. Yet, as was shown for the S&P 500, the portion of compensation delivered in stock has remained relatively stable, at just above 50 percent of the total package, for the last several years.

A 2005 Executive Compensation Resources survey found that most companies in its sample have shifted to full-value stock grants, with only 19 percent of the companies still using stock options as part of

FIGURE 7.6
Stock Plans in Director Compensation

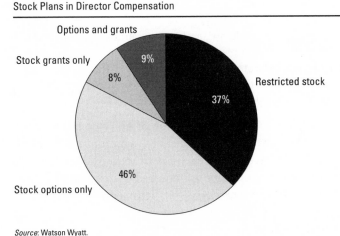

Source: Watson Wyatt.

their director compensation. Among the major corporations that shifted to restricted stock in 2004 were MCI, Microsoft, Exxon Mobil, Altria Group, and Goldman Sachs.

Stock Ownership Guidelines

With the move to stock-based compensation and the desire to promote long-term share ownership, it is becoming common practice to institute stock holding requirements. In 2004, 65 percent of the Fortune 1000 reported having stock ownership requirements for directors, up from 51 percent in 2002, according to a Korn/Ferry survey.[12]

A growing number of companies are requiring directors to own a minimum amount of company stock and in many cases to hold it until retirement. A 2005 Frederick W. Cook & Co. survey found that 67 percent of the NYSE companies and 26 percent of the NASDAQ firms require directors to maintain specific stock ownership levels and disclose either formal ownership guidelines or share retention schemes.[13]

Stock requirements generally come in two forms. The first, and more traditional, is the use of stock ownership guidelines. This is typically structured as a requirement that directors hold shares either equal to a percentage of their annual retainer (typically ranging from three times to five times the retainer) or, if a fluctuating stock price is a concern, equal to a certain number of shares. The following example is from 3M's 2005 proxy statement:

> The Board also approved stock ownership guidelines that provide that each director should attain over her or his three-year term an investment position in 3M's stock (including deferred stock) equal to two times the annual retainer [or $300,000]. All directors currently meet these stock ownership guidelines.

At eBay, directors are required to hold shares of eBay common stock with a value equal to three times the amount of the annual retainer and must achieve the guideline within three years of joining the board. At Aetna, each nonmanagement director is required to own, within five years of joining the board, shares or stock units with a dollar value equal to $400,000. As of February 25, 2005, all of Aetna's nonmanagement directors met these guidelines.

Although stock guidelines are well intended and are adhered to for the most part, difficulties arise with their enforceability and their meaningfulness. As the name implies, these are guidelines – not requirements – and typically the only punishment for not following them is that other directors are made aware that the individual has not met the guidelines. Guidelines also result in disparate treatment in that some directors already meet the guidelines when they are put in place, while other directors, particularly new ones, need time to meet the guidelines.

Net Share Holding Requirements

The alternative or complement to stock ownership guidelines is the use of net share holding requirements, whereby directors are required to hold all or a portion of the shares awarded for a period of time or until termination of board service. To the extent that the shares vest or options are exercised, the director is required to hold shares net of payment of taxes (in the case of restricted stock) or net of payment of the exercise price and taxes (in the case of options).

To promote greater ownership, companies are increasingly using restricted stock units. An example of share holding requirements and the use of RSUs is found in United Technologies' 2005 proxy statement:

> Under the Directors' Restricted Stock Unit Program, each nonemployee director receives on the date of election to the Board a one-time grant of restricted stock units valued at $100,000, based on the closing price of Common Stock on the date of grant. Dividend equivalents are

credited on the units. The units awarded vest ratably over five years, but may not be sold or otherwise transferred until the director retires or resigns from the Board.

U.S. Steel Corporation's 2005 director compensation package combined cash and stock-based compensation with holding requirements:

> Each director is required to defer at least 70 percent of his or her annual retainer fee as stock-based compensation until his or her departure from the Board. Directors are paid an annual retainer fee, a committee membership fee for each committee on which they serve, and a meeting fee for each Board and committee meeting they attend. In addition, if a director purchases common stock of the Corporation on the open market within 60 days after joining the Board, he or she is eligible for a matching grant from the Corporation of up to 1,000 book-entry shares payable in cash when he or she leaves the Board. The Corporation has no retirement program for directors.

Boeing's principles state that director compensation should be a mix of cash and equity-based compensation, with a significant portion of such compensation in the form of the company's stock or stock-equivalent units. Nonemployee directors receive a substantial portion of their compensation in deferred stock units, which must be held until retirement or other termination of board service.

Ownership Effectiveness

So, does director share ownership work? Research indicates that it does. In a 1999 study, two professors, Sanjai Bhagat and Charles M. Elson, and Dennis C. Carey, the vice chairman of Spencer Stuart, set out to test two hypotheses.[14] First, they asked whether companies where the directors hold more stock outperform companies where directors hold fewer shares; their rationale was that the greater the alignment of share holdings, the more the directors would monitor activity and hold executives accountable for performance. However, it could be argued that these directors had insider knowledge that performance was set to improve and simply acquired more shares to benefit from that improvement. Second, the authors hypothesized that the greater the share ownership, the more likely directors would be to take action against CEOs.

The study analyzed data from more than 1,700 companies. Bhagat, Elson, and Carey found a tight link between significant outside director stock ownership and effective monitoring and firm performance. They also found that the greater the value of directors' equity holdings, the more likely a disciplinary-type CEO turnover in a poorly performing company would occur. The authors conclude:

> The results were consistent with the initial hypothesis of a connection between substantial director share ownership and better monitoring. First, there was a significant correlation between the amount of stock owned by individual outside directors and firm performance (based on a variety of performance measures). Second, and more important for the analysis, the greater the dollar value of the individual outside director's equity holdings in the enterprise, the more likely a disciplinary-type CEO turnover in a poorly performing company would exist.[15]

With respect to director ownership and the resignation or removal of CEOs at poorly performing companies, Bhagat, Elson, and Carey conclude:

> A correlation between the dollar amount of a director's personal equity holdings and the likelihood of a disciplinary-type CEO succession in a poorly performing company is consistent with the hypothesis that the equity positions of the outside directors created the kind of heightened awareness among the board of the impact of an inadequate management team leading to its early termination.[16]

Finally, they state: "We believe board equity will create the kind of effective boards that the shareholding public expects and demands."[17]

Their findings are supported by other studies. An empirical study by Paula Silva in the October 2005 *Journal of Managerial Issues* assesses the relationship between directors' motivation and pay in evaluating CEO performance.[18] Silva found that the nature of the board members' decision making differs depending on the compensation structure; directors who receive stock as compensation use quantitative, verifiable criteria to a greater extent in measuring CEO performance. Directors with higher cash make greater use of qualitative measures in assessing CEO performance, and firm performance has a significant negative correlation with qualitative measures. "This suggests that equity ownership is necessary to align the board's interest with that of the shareholders," Silva concludes.

Another study, by professors Benjamin E. Hermalin and Michael S. Weisbach, found that increases in director ownership are correlated with increases in firm performance.[19] A study by Leslie Kren and Jeffrey L. Kerr, based on an analysis of 268 large corporations, found that boards with significant stock ownership are more likely to maintain a stronger link between CEO compensation and firm performance. This study also found that directors' contributions to corporate wealth are greater at higher levels of ownership.

Structuring the Optimal Director Compensation Package

As compensation consultants, we are often asked to assist with developing and recommending appropriate and competitive director pay packages. "Appropriate" and "competitive" are not necessarily synonymous. Interestingly – compared with CEO pay levels – director pay levels across the S&P 500 fall within a tight range. The spread between director pay at the 25th percentile of the S&P 500 and the 75th percentile is 100 percent ($122,000 and $250,000, respectively). In contrast, the spread for CEO pay is 200 percent ($4.3 million versus $13 million).

The more pronounced spread for CEO pay reflects the fact that the CEO plays a larger role in the company and has a more direct impact on its performance. Additionally, CEO pay is more sensitive to performance than director pay; companies that outperform the norm generally pay above market, whereas companies that underperform generally pay below market. Director compensation remains within a relatively tight range because the level is so heavily based on market practice.

Witness the audit committee chair premium retainer. With the exception of the lead director, the audit committee chair more than any other board member has taken on enormous responsibility and liability. Meetings are typically monthly and can last for hours. The preparation is intense and covers a lot of financial detail. Yet the premium for audit committee chairs has been essentially unchanged at a median $10,000 per year, compared with $8,000 for the compensation committee chair and $7,500 for the nominating and governance chairs among S&P 500 companies.

To attract and retain top director talent, director compensation will need to be adjusted to the economic realities of the marketplace. Accordingly, we recommend the following:

1. **Simplify the pay package**. The basic package should consist of an annual retainer, with a targeted mix of cash and stock. For example, a company might provide a $150,000 retainer, with 67 percent in stock and 33 percent in cash. Determining what constitutes a meeting has become difficult, so we recommend that companies consider

FIGURE 7.7
Disclosure of Director Compensation

DIRECTOR	CASH RETAINER	TOTAL MEETING FEES	EQUITY RETAINER	STOCK OPTION VALUE	TOTAL COMPENSATION
Joe Director	$50,000	$15,000	$50,000	$40,000	$155,000
Mary Director	$50,000	$25,000	$50,000	$40,000	$165,000

Source: Watson Wyatt.

eliminating per-meeting fees. However, because board members on certain committees spend more time on company matters than other directors, the additional activity and involvement should be recognized through higher pay. We recommend differentiated retainers. Thus, if the base-level retainer is $150,000, an audit committee member may instead receive $175,000, while the chair would receive $200,000. If the audit committee chair also serves as a member of the compensation committee, he or she might get an additional $15,000.

2. **Eliminate benefits and perquisites.** Eliminating benefits and perquisites can not only achieve greater separation between management and directors but can also result in improved company performance because the forgone benefits can be replaced with stock to promote shareholder alignment. A 2006 article in the *Journal of Pension Economics and Finance*[20] found that "there is a significant increase in the stock return performance of those firms terminating the pension plans for a quid-pro-quo increase in equity compensation."

3. **Improve director pay disclosure.** As required by the SEC, beginning in 2007, director compensation must exhibit improved disclosure. A straightforward summary of the compensation elements and the total pay delivered to each director is a transparent way to disclose director compensation (see Figure 7.7).

4. **Encourage directors to acquire shares.** If directors have their own skin in the game, they are more likely to actively monitor company performance and provide guidance. One way to encourage ownership is to structure the pay package as a mix of cash and full-value shares and to encourage directors to own additional stock by giving them the opportunity to defer the cash into stock units with a match. For example:

   a. $50,000 cash retainer, $50,000 full-value stock
   b. Stock price at $10
   c. Company provides for a 1:1 share match for every share purchased with the cash retainer

    d. Thus, if the director defers the entire $50,000 cash retainer into the stock, he or she receives 10,000 shares ($50,000 divided by $10 multiplied by 2). This is in addition to the 5,000 shares received through the $50,000 stock retainer

    e. If the company has a management stock purchase plan, the director plan provisions could match those of the executive plan

5. **Use full-value share units (or deferred stock awards) rather than stock options**. Before 2006, many companies used stock options for directors not only to promote shareholder alignment but to take advantage of the fact that options did not count as a direct expense on the income statement (under the rules, directors were treated on the same basis as employees). But with options now an expense, what is the most effective way to align directors with shareholders and create a dynamic tension with management? We recommend full-value shares. Stock options may focus attention on short-term stock price movements, but full-value shares foster a longer-term horizon.

6. **Implement stock ownership guidelines or net share holding requirements**. There is a positive relationship between board ownership and pay-for-performance linkages at the executive level. The best way to structure this ownership is a combination of stock ownership guidelines and net share holding requirements. For example, the board could institute a requirement that directors retain all shares (net of taxes) until a certain ownership level is attained – for example, three times the annual retainer. At that point, directors would be free to dispose of the shares as they saw fit.

The Future of Director Compensation

Reflecting simple supply and demand, the market for director talent will continue to be tight. We expect boards to have fewer members and directors to serve on fewer boards. And consistent with recent trends, the number and length of meetings will increase. As a result of all this, director pay will also increase. The move away from stock options to full-value shares/share units will accelerate, and we expect that the mix of director pay will strike a balance of roughly 40 percent cash and 60 percent stock.

    We also anticipate that while the prevalence of meeting fees will decline slightly, that trend will be moderated as companies try to reward directors for the increased activity of certain committees. Promoting director stock ownership will be at the forefront of program design, with ownership guidelines and net share holding requirements becoming more common.

In the end, despite the increased time commitment and risk, serving as a director will continue to be a desirable job. The enhancement of an individual's reputation in the business community and the opportunity to interact with peers and assist companies in important governance efforts will remain an attractive proposition. Director pay will evolve to ensure that top director talent will continue to carry out their duties in monitoring executive performance.

8 The Compensation Committee: Creating a Balance between Shareholders and Executives

> To attract a successful incumbent CEO from another company, you've got to give him a good incentive. You couldn't expect James McNerney to leave [the CEO position at] 3M if we weren't going to make him whole [as the new Boeing CEO].[1]
>
> John Biggs, director, Boeing, and former president, TIAA–CREF

Despite the efforts of compensation committee members to be scientific, there is tremendous variation in CEO pay. Much of this can be explained by differences in tenure, industry, and company size and performance. But substantial variation – up to 50 percent in some instances – is not explained by any conventional objective metrics. Cynics attribute this variation to cronyism or the randomness of executive pay. We attribute it to the highly subjective nature of CEO compensation and, in a shareholder-friendly sense, to the judgment, fine-tuning, care, and deliberation – for example, factoring in differences in business strategy and culture – that go into these pay decisions.

Other elements contribute to the difficulty of the task. Compensation committees historically have dealt piecemeal with management recommendations that came in – bonuses and salary increases in January, stock options in March, SERP enhancements in September – with no tally sheet that added it all up. Although pay-for-performance has clearly increased, the linkage could have been clearer. And finally, CEO contracts and severance plans (especially after a change of control, with the associated gross-up payments) were considered necessary merely for the company to be competitive. But the cost and consequences of those agreements were often not thought through.

Some of these problems are behind us; however, the pressures and liabilities that compensation committees face are greater than ever. Committee members worry about alienating or demotivating their CEO as much as they fear getting "no" vote recommendations from Institutional Shareholder Services or ending up in a *Wall Street Journal* headline. The gap in the perceived effectiveness of executive pay between investors and boards poses a huge challenge.

Legal Context

The legal context in which directors operate has changed in a way that may be better for shareholders but is certainly worse for directors. The difficulty of recruiting directors for the boards of major companies may only increase as the NYSE continues to impose new director-independence reporting requirements on companies.

In this new environment, committees must increase their own independence and the objectivity of their key advisers. They must put more emphasis on pay at risk and pay-for-performance. They must move away from plain-vanilla stock options and add performance hurdles to restricted stock awards. They must push for stock ownership and examine SERP costs and designs. Taking a holistic approach to pay, they must create tally sheets that add it all up and consider severance cost exposure at any given moment – both of which are now mandated by the SEC as required proxy disclosures. These are all positive outcomes. But pushing much further toward bureaucratic control over management will be bad for business and the economy.

The growing responsibilities placed on compensation committees and directors will make it more difficult to recruit top talent to these positions. The scandals at Enron, Disney, Tyco, the NYSE, and WorldCom speak to the accountability and liability issues that these committees now face. The Enron and WorldCom lawsuits required personal payments of millions of dollars by former directors.

In 2003, *In re The Walt Disney Co. Derivative Litigation* signaled potentially heightened fiduciary standards, greater scrutiny, and higher risks for compensation committee members.[2] The plaintiffs claimed that the directors had intentionally breached their fiduciary duty of due care in approving former CEO Michael Ovitz's employment agreement. When Ovitz was terminated, his contractual severance payments, including stock option profits, were well over $100 million.

The allegations stated that the compensation committee simply rubber-stamped an agreement and compensation package negotiated by Disney's CEO, Michael Eisner, with his close friend Ovitz. In ordering the original trial, the court stated: "Where a director consciously ignores his or her duties to the corporation, thereby causing economic injury to its shareholders, the director's actions are either 'not in good faith' or 'involve intentional misconduct.'"

Normally the business judgment rule would protect directors operating in good faith. But the claim in the *Disney* litigation was that the directors were so uninvolved that they should not be entitled to protection from personal liability. Because Delaware corporate law and similar state laws prohibit companies from indemnifying an officer or director unless he or she acted in good faith, a compensation committee member's failure to fulfill his or her fiduciary responsibilities to the company and its shareholders can result in personal, out-of-pocket liability. The fact that this case went to trial indicates a new world for directors.

While the Delaware Chancery Court eventually ruled that the board had acted in good faith with adequate information, the judge's ruling has several ramifications for compensation committees:

1. The business judgment rule remains intact. This is fortunate and essential for the continued success of the U.S. corporate model. Board members need to rely on management, outside experts, and their own judgment to maximize shareholder value.
2. There is now an even higher standard of behavior for management and boards than there was when Ovitz was hired in the mid-1990s. Certainly, by today's standards, the Disney board did not follow best governance practice. Today, more formal meetings and processes must be followed instead of the more casual one-on-one discussions that took place in 1995.
3. The severance plan was fair and justified. Ovitz had been making more than $20 million a year at his previous company, which he partially owned, and he had concerns about Eisner's willingness to share power with him in order to turn Disney around. Given his opportunity cost and this perceived – and, as it turned out, accurate – career risk, he negotiated protection for himself.

The lesson for today's compensation committee and institutional investors is that it is difficult, if not impossible, to recruit top talent without protecting them from the potential downside. Investors and directors may not like this, but it is the reality of the executive labor market. Recruiting senior human capital is the same as investing financial capital, with similar upside and downside potential.

A growing number of shareholders are placing initiatives on corporate ballots that deal with executive compensation. Although most of these proposals have been rejected, some studies indicate that lower executive pay is awarded at companies that experience this.[3]

Our biggest concern is that the combination of lawsuits and shareholder resolutions will have a chilling effect on entrepreneurialism in both the selection of candidates and the design of compensation programs to motivate them. If there are legal challenges to compensation committees' business judgment, committees will have to operate more conservatively either in process or in pay.

This could have a huge impact on the selection and performance of executives – and ultimately on the performance of the companies. Some experts predict that forthcoming legal cases, primarily in the Delaware Chancery Court, will place the business judgment rule under stricter standards than before.

Right from Wrong?

We predict that the courts will not move in this direction. But if they do, it could have negative consequences for shareholder value creation as committees recruit inferior candidates for both management and boards and create insufficient motivation for them. Some pundits, however, think that compensation committee members would develop much more shareholder-friendly programs and the governance process to develop those programs. But there is no consensus on what these designs and processes would look like. The following five subsections give some examples.

ARE STOCK OPTIONS PERFORMANCE-BASED?

Virtually all of the hundreds of compensation committee members that we meet with believe that stock options are an entirely performance-based compensation program. In a major change from their 1990s position, many institutional investors and pay critics do not share this view, harkening back to the rising-tide theory. Some investors in the last two to three years initially preferred time-vested restricted stock to stock options because far fewer shares are eventually issued under these plans.

For example, John Bogle, founder of the Vanguard mutual fund group and author of *The Battle for the Soul of Capitalism*, is an extreme critic of executive pay and what he calls "managerial capitalism," a concept similar to managerial power. In his book, he is very critical of stock options as too easy a manner for executives to get huge rewards for below-average performance: "These problems [with stock options] were well known, and simple solutions to the executive compensation morass were readily available. Restricted stock in which executives are awarded shares of the company and required to hold them to earn their rewards, were one obvious alternative."[4] Other critics think time-vested restricted stock is much too "executive friendly."

ARE PERFORMANCE SHARES THE PERFECT SOLUTION?
Although performance shares with challenging goals are shareholder-friendly, executives would be unhappy with them in many circumstances. And while the balance of power has shifted somewhat from executives to shareholders and boards in the last five years, executives will remain in the dominant position until the CEO labor market "corrects" – in other words, when most companies use performance vesting on their shares and the executives have no alternative employment opportunities that will provide them with something more "employee-friendly." There is some indication that this correction has started, but with 10,000 CEOs at publicly traded companies who must be tracked, it's too soon to draw conclusions.

SHOULD DIRECTORS BE REQUIRED TO OWN COMPANY STOCK?
Virtually all U.S. companies have decided that increasing director stock ownership is a priority. We have read critics who say that director stock ownership reduces director independence.

SHOULD PEER GROUPS BE USED TO SET EXECUTIVE PAY?
Some critics say that committees rely too heavily on peer groups to determine pay, thereby creating the upward ratchet effect on pay opportunity. However, directors fear that moving away from the data will require more subjectivity, creating even more legal exposure for them.

WHAT CONSTITUTES A GOOD BOARD MEMBER?
Another area lacking clarity is the issue of who is and who is not an excellent board member. James Kilts, the former CEO of Gillette, came under media criticism in 2005 for reaping a very large severance payment after he sold the company to Procter & Gamble. Interestingly, in February 2006, he was nominated to be on the board of Coca-Cola as an "excellent" board member. He was nominated by Warren Buffett, a major critic of

executive pay and stock options, who was resigning from the Coca Cola board.

With no standard, obvious answers to these questions, compensation committees must use a range of executive compensation strategies. We expect that these will be linked to each company's unique business needs, culture, and entrepreneurial philosophy. We also expect that these variations will have a positive impact on financial performance.

Some pundits applaud the predicted narrowing of the business judgment rule and see it as a potential major improvement in corporate governance and a major benefit for shareholders. We disagree on all counts. We predict that the courts will not move in this direction, as they think both that this area is working properly and that the results in terms of corporate performance and overall governance are both positive and effective. However, we also believe that if, in fact, the courts move to create a higher standard for the business judgment rule, this will not be beneficial for shareholders and may have actual negative consequences for corporate America and shareholder value creation. The major reason for these negative consequences would be the risk of recruiting inferior candidates for both management and boards and the insufficient motivation it would create for them.

Foundations for Best Practices

Despite all of this turmoil, the compensation committee's primary responsibility has not changed: to ensure management continuity through compensation and other human resource techniques, such as promotions and management development. That means ensuring the long-term survival and success of the company by attracting the best people and retaining and motivating them to maximize shareholder value.

It is possible that institutional shareholders could push companies so far that the resulting pay packages would be insufficient to attract top entrepreneurial talent away from strategy consulting firms, venture capitalists, hedge funds, LBO firms, investment banks, and law firms. Leaving the bureaucrats to run corporate America has occurred before, and it worked poorly. We can look at the 1970s to see the effect of lower executive quality and lower levels of motivation: poor corporate performance and, by the way, low pay by today's standards.

Clearly, executive compensation is in flux. But there are three key steps for establishing best practices in designing and implementing executive pay: creating excellence in corporate governance, setting the

CEO's pay as rigorously as possible, and building a pay-for-performance environment.

Creating Excellence in Corporate Governance

The most important issue the committee faces is creating a strong culture and process for managing executive and stock-based compensation. This sets the pattern for the rest of the board and the company, and it is the most visible process to shareholders. In the annual proxy disclosure, shareholders have a clear window into the committee's task: setting executive compensation. Many shareholders worry that if executive pay is too high relative to the company's performance, the whole pay decision process is bad – and that if this is the company's most disclosed process, there must be other hidden abuses of power, process, and governance that are even more detrimental to shareholders.

But if governance over executive pay is sound, if the company performs at high levels, if there is rigorous pay-for-performance, and if the executives buy and hold their stock, then the company may get the benefit of the doubt on other unseen aspects of corporate governance, including issues related to audit, board composition, takeover defenses, and management succession.

What does good governance look like for executive pay and stock-based incentives? First and foremost, executive pay must be commensurate with corporate performance. Second, the compensation committee must guard against the dilution of the shareholders' stock and equity as if the shares were their own. Third, the board and management should be significant shareholders.

To improve the governance of executive compensation, the committee should:

1. Conduct an annual study of the relationship between pay and performance, including the difficulty of attaining various financial goals.
2. Annually review a tally sheet of total executive pay (salary, bonus, long-term incentives, pensions, and perquisites). The new proxy rules will make the use of a tally sheet a virtual necessity.
3. Periodically review executive pension plans (provisions, annuity and lump-sum values) relative to the market.
4. Review severance plan cost scenarios – including voluntary, involuntary, and change-in-control costs – annually for the top five executives. This should include a "total walk-away value" that accounts for previously vested amounts.

5. Hire and manage a compensation consultant. Discourage executives from hiring their own experts; if they do, do not pay for it.

6. Develop a compensation philosophy and compare it with actual payments and plans. If the philosophy indicates that the company will have modest fixed costs, for example, do not sweeten the SERP.

7. Minimize perquisites, especially personal financial planning (which encourages stock sales).

8. Encourage members to ask the tough questions that critics might ask.

9. Hold an executive session every meeting without management present, and perhaps a second executive session without the consultant, to ensure complete candor.

10. Bring in other points of view – for example, from prior employers or other current board relationships – while factoring in the unique aspects of the company: its business strategy, people, and culture.

11. Ensure that the full board, minus management, reviews and approves the CEO pay package for good governance reasons but also so the CEO understands that the full board supports the decision.

12. Involve the board's lead director or chair in any critical executive pay and stock-based compensation issues.

13. Schedule a formal performance review of the CEO immediately after the board's approval with either the full committee or its chair and perhaps the board's lead director or chair in attendance.

14. Discourage the CEO from using the head of human resources or executive compensation to negotiate the pay package on his or her behalf and from doing his or her own competitive analysis. However, it can be helpful to get some indication from corporate staff about the CEO's expectations. (Some of the most successful CEO pay communications we have seen occurred when the committee had behind-the-scenes information. Obviously, there is a fine line between this type of information and actual negotiations that needs to be handled carefully.)

15. Encourage high levels of executive stock ownership through plan design, ownership guidelines, and holding requirements.

Institutional and Regulatory Governance Recommendations and Mandates

Compensation committees should be aware of the growing number of regulatory and shareholder recommendations and mandates related to executive compensation. The following list summarizes the best practices encouraged by shareholder activists, institutional shareholders, and regulatory authorities.

1. **Ensure compensation committee independence.** Directors serving on the committee must be independent in a legal and operational sense.
2. **Establish the committee's roles.** Construct a formal compensation philosophy and policy to ensure consistency with the company's strategic plan and shareholder considerations. The committee should:

   a. Conduct a performance appraisal of the CEO and other senior management at least annually.
   b. Determine and approve officer compensation levels, including salary, annual incentives, long-term incentives, benefits, and perquisites.
   c. Review and approve officer employment agreements, change-in-control agreements, performance targets and measures, aggregate incentive plan payments, equity pool use, merit budget funding, election of officers, succession plans, and director compensation arrangements.
   d. Ensure that all compensation and benefit plans are administered in accordance with current tax law, accounting principles, SEC requirements, company strategy, shareholder interests, and executive performance.
   e. Review and approve committee responsibilities and named executive officer (NEO) compensation for inclusion in the annual proxy report.
   f. Conduct an executive session at each meeting.
   g. Conduct a committee self-assessment annually.
   h. Report committee activities to the full board and advise it of necessary actions and exposure to public and shareholder criticism.
   i. Create and approve the meeting agenda and calendar for a full year.
   j. Communicate with shareholders on important compensation issues.

3. **Create a performance focus.** To ensure that executive pay is linked to corporate performance, the committee should:

   a. Ensure that a meaningful portion of total compensation is performance-based.
   b. Avoid executive pay increases during periods of negative TRS.
   c. Use annual and long-term variable compensation in a competitive and cost-effective manner.
   d. Reinforce strategic goals through performance-based pay.
   e. Consider alternatives to stock options, especially performance-based equity awards.

   f. Use stock ownership guidelines and share holding requirements to create a long-term focus.

4. **Administer executive compensation effectively**.

   a. Provide advance notice of executives' intent to directly or indirectly dispose of stock.
   b. Establish a practice of fixed-date stock option awards.
   c. Do not offer severance payments for termination for cause.
   d. Establish double-trigger change-in-control provisions (change in control and termination).
   e. Avoid "open-window" provisions that allow the executive to quit unilaterally for any reason for a given period (typically a month) a few months to a year after the deal closes.
   f. Seek shareholder approval for performance-based compensation to avoid tax-deduction limitations imposed by IRC Section 162(m).

5. **Engage independent consultants**. These consultants should report directly to the committee but work with management as necessary to perform certain analyses. This is discussed in more detail in the following section.

Consultant Independence

The compensation committee should also observe best practices in its relationship with consultants. In response to a number of corporate governance proposals, compensation consultants should clarify their relationships with their client boards and compensation committees.

The committee must have the authority to retain and terminate any consulting firm it uses to help evaluate director or senior executive compensation. Restrictions on providing other consulting services and related disclosures can help safeguard the consultant's independence. Boards and compensation committees can further ensure the consultant's objectivity and independence by following these protocols:

1. **Client definition**. The parties should agree that the compensation committee is the client but that cooperation and collaboration with management are necessary to ensure effectiveness. In short, the consultant will work with management but always on behalf of the committee.
2. **Consultant selection**. The committee should have the final say on which consultant to hire, but – in the interest of cooperation and

collaboration – with input from management on the strengths and weaknesses of various firms.

3. **Clear objectives**. The parties should agree on the objectives and scope of the consultant's work. This agreement may be reached through private interviews with the committee members and management, but joint agreement ultimately is necessary to make sure that the key points are on the table.

4. **Open access**. All parties should agree that the consultant will have ongoing access to the committee chair as well as the CEO and management to independently discuss all relevant matters.

5. **Human resources staff collaboration**. All parties should make it clear that the consultant will work closely with the company's human resources and compensation staff as required to obtain the necessary data, provide background on the program's history and operation, and clarify key issues.

6. **Information sharing**. All parties should agree on when and how the consultant will share findings, conclusions, and preliminary recommendations. Management should have an opportunity to review and comment on the advice and recommendations but not to override them or control which materials are sent to the committee.

7. **Presentations**. When formally presenting findings and recommendations to the committee, the consultant will be actively involved with management in a supporting role as required, and the committee is free to meet privately with the consultant at any time.

8. **Periodic assessment**. The committee – and, as appropriate, management – will regularly evaluate the consultant's effectiveness, with the consultant either informed of the findings or actively involved in soliciting feedback.

Setting the CEO's Pay as Rigorously as Possible

Setting the CEO's pay requires as much art and psychology as science. Although there is extensive literature about what motivates a CEO, from a desire for power to a need for affiliation, money plays a huge role.

We have seen dozens of situations where the committee came up with a bonus and stock grant only to worry about the CEO's reaction and further negotiate among themselves even before they had spoken with the CEO. The pay decision process for a CEO – unlike that for almost all other employees – is not one where the manager (the compensation committee) tells the employee about his or her raise and there are no further negotiations. In some cases, the CEO comes back with a counteroffer. This speaks to the unique nature of the position and its labor market.

The CEO pay package sets the tone for other executive compensation and should influence the pay packages for the broader employee population. It also signals to shareholders how the company is operated and governed. In fact, some institutional investors look at the CEO pay package and its evolution over time at the company and use that evaluation as one of the factors in determining which shareholder proposals to endorse and which to recommend voting against.

We explore an example of how one of our clients handled a CEO pay package in the following section.

Case Study of an Internal Promotion

The compensation committee must determine CEO pay in four situations: the annual review, a financial event (transaction), an outside hire, and an internal promotion.

The 15 percent to 20 percent of executives who change companies each year have a major impact in boosting pay for the additional executives at many other companies who either do not change jobs or are internally promoted. Obviously, most CEOs are aware of their pay opportunities because they can obtain nearly perfect information from their competitors' proxy statements. The compensation committee must factor these considerations into their pay decision for all CEOs. This is particularly important for a newly promoted CEO.

An internal promotion to CEO is the closest thing to a clean sheet of paper that the committee has in setting CEO pay. It is the occasion when the committee has the most equal footing with the employee and resembles the classic manager/subordinate relationship. The committee can deliver several messages, from a simple "congratulations," to "we want you to be highly motivated to drive financial and stock market performance," to realistic messages about what the CEO can expect in terms of pay for performance and fixed pay.

This is a unique opportunity for the committee, as the candidate is usually extremely eager to take the job after years of hard work and success. The internal labor market also has fewer advantages for the employee than for an externally recruited candidate. The internal promotion also provides fewer advantages than the circumstances surrounding the negotiations covering an existing, presumably successful, CEO regarding his or her annual increase in pay.

We recently encountered a situation that brought these issues to life. A $5 billion market capitalization technology company had been experiencing a flat stock price for several years. Although reasonably well positioned for growth and profitability, the company had not developed the right formula for executing its strategy and bringing it all together. The retiring CEO was extremely well paid in pension, salary, bonus, stock options, and restricted stock. But the flat stock price had yielded fairly limited exercises and profits.

The board unanimously chose the president as the CEO's successor. He was in his late 40s, had been with the company for most of his career, and had performed well by internal standards. Here are the facts about his pay relative to the market before his promotion:

Item	Salary	Bonus (% of salary)	LTI Value (% of salary)	Total Direct
Market	$900,000	100%	400%	$5.4 million
CEO candidate (pay in prior position)	$600,000	60%	150%	$1.86 million

The committee looked at the data and considered a number of other factors:

- An emphasis on incentives to motivate driving the stock price up (stock options for leverage and restricted stock for retention)
- An MSPP to drive stock ownership
- The relative youth of the CEO and, therefore, the lower value of his SERP to him
- The need to leave room for further increases

This is what the committee decided:

Salary	$800,000
Bonus	100%
LTI value	350%
Total direct compensation	$4,400,000

This amount significantly boosted his current pay package but still left room for increases. Based at least partially on these incentives and high levels of stock ownership, the stock price performance has tripled since his promotion.

Beyond attracting, retaining, and motivating the best talent, CEO compensation sends a signal to the outside world and sets the pattern for pay for those who report directly to the CEO and throughout the organization. This last issue is important in terms of fairness, equity, and morale; other employees want to see that the captain is on the same ship. The CEO's package also sets the cascading pattern for those who report directly to the CEO.

Academic studies and our own experience show that highly paid CEOs tend to have highly paid senior management teams, which can be a problem if the entire management team is overpaid. Low-paid CEOs have low-paid teams, which can be either a bargain for shareholders or a problem for recruitment, retention, and motivation. We always come back to this question: "How is the performance of the company relative to that high or low pay level?"

Some companies worry that the subordinates are underpaid if the top subordinate's pay is less than 50 percent of the CEO's. In fact, some executive pay critics have proposed capping CEO pay at a 50 percent premium to the second-highest-paid executive. This bears investigation, but a highly paid CEO and more modestly paid subordinates can be justified if the organizational structure (e.g., no chief operating officer or president), labor market, results, and turnover support it. There are clearly examples of this in the marketplace.

The more intractable problem occurs when the CEO is a founder or major shareholder and artificially keeps his or her pay low, thereby compressing the pay for senior subordinates. Again, this is a problem only if those subordinates are voluntarily leaving or if it is difficult to recruit senior executives.

Creating a Pay-for-Performance Environment

Creating and maintaining a pay-for-performance environment is complex but manageable:

1. **Minimize fixed compensation**. Limit salaries, pensions, and other forms of fixed compensation. Top executives are risk-averse and therefore want higher salaries. But too much fixed pay is expensive, sends the wrong signals to employees and shareholders, and might discourage an appropriate amount of risk. The expense of a high salary is compounded in two ways: It may raise the salaries for many other employees, and it is often used as the starting point for

determining pensions and annual and LTI opportunities in the form of multipliers. Unfortunately, CEOs frequently view a salary increase as part of their year-end report card and overemphasize its importance. This should be discouraged.

2. **Put half of pay at risk**. Make sure that at least 50 percent – a percentage based on our meetings with institutional investors – of total annual pay opportunity is at risk, which means that this portion could be zero at the end of the performance cycle. The following table categorizes various pay elements:

No Risk	Risky	Debatable
Salary	Annual incentives	Time-vested restricted stock
Pensions	Performance shares	
SERPs	Performance-granted restricted stock	
Perquisites	Stock options	

3. **Limit time vesting**. Minimize the amount of pure time vesting, primarily regarding restricted stock. A clear exception would be if the company had a one-year performance hurdle that needed to be achieved to earn the restricted stock, which would be subject to further time vesting. Although pure time vesting is not as easy to attain as some critics think – senior executives may lose their jobs and forfeit some or all of their pay – it should be minimized as part of a total portfolio. Reasons for using time vesting include special retention circumstances and replacing a SERP.

4. **Reduce perquisites**. Reduce or eliminate perks, especially financial planning services and personal use of company jets. While executives love these, they have no tax advantage and are a lightning rod for critics. The problem with company-paid financial planning is that these professionals advise their clients to diversify their assets away from their company's stock. This may be good financial advice, but it directly contradicts the shareholders' desire to increase executive stock ownership.

5. **Emphasize stock ownership**. Develop executive pay programs with a bias toward creating stock ownership. The company should have ownership guidelines for all senior officers and directors expressed as shares or a multiple of salary. It should also have a share retention policy whereby 25 percent to 50 percent of net shares are held until retirement or termination. Ideally, some of the shares should be

purchased by the executives – either on the open market or through special deferred plans. The committee should compare actual stock ownership with the guidelines annually and review sales and purchases quarterly.

6. **Select the right peer group**. The committee, with help from its consultant and management, should carefully choose the peer group for executive pay and performance comparison – typically 10 to 20 companies. Avoid companies that are clearly too large (more than 100 percent larger in revenue or market cap), too small, or that have uncharacteristically high or low or unusual compensation. Examine the recruiting and retention patterns for the company to determine the appropriate labor market. Review senior management recruiting and turnover patterns several times a year. Companies that are the largest in their industry or among the largest, or where there is no obvious peer group, should use companies of similar size in related industries. In such cases, the committee should place less emphasis on the peer group when setting pay.

7. **Adopt industry norms for severance payments**. Set severance payments at industry norms and not higher. While critics and institutional investors would like severance to be set very low, this appears to be impossible given the current state of the executive labor market, especially when recruiting from outside. In today's seller's market, executives have the upper hand in negotiations.

8. **Choose a fixed date of grant for stock incentives**. Recent SEC and accounting rules encourage the use of a fixed grant date for stock programs, especially stock options, preferably early in the fiscal year. This should minimize critics' claims that grants are deliberately made before good earnings reports or after bad news depresses the stock price.

9. **Align executive pay with broader compensation programs**. Executives are expected to earn more, but their compensation programs should be similar to employee programs in terms of risk. When companies do not align pay programs, employee morale – and the company's public image – can plummet. In a clear lack of alignment, executives have:

a. Perquisites
b. Higher salary increase budgets
c. Different financial metrics for incentives (especially if those incentives end up paying out higher than employee incentives)

   d. Time-vested restricted stock grants, while employees lower in the organization have stock options (so that when prices decline, the executives still have value but the other employees do not)

   e. High or increasing stock grants, while the value of the employee stock purchase plan is reduced or eliminated

10. **Create superior proxy disclosure practices**. The SEC is now requiring improved disclosure as of 2007. The disclosures will probably change the designs of some programs, but the transparency will likely be seen as shareholder-friendly. Many of the suggestions made in this chapter will become de rigueur in future proxy disclosures.

11. **Review performance metrics**. In conjunction with the full board and committees, the compensation committee should review at least annually the performance metrics in the incentive plans, especially executive plans, for several dimensions and linkages:

   a. The measures should be linked to the company's strategic success. In other words, if the managers and the company achieve or exceed the target levels of the given financial metrics, the company will be considered successful.

   b. Use the same or similar metrics for incentive plans and in public reports. For example, if return on invested capital is an incentive plan metric, report it as such in the annual report, even though it is not required under GAAP. Also minimize exceptions to the accounting treatment of the metrics illustration – for example, relating to divestitures. This allows the financial results for an incentive plan to match publicly reported financial metrics as closely as possible.

   c. Make sure that various constituencies, especially the executives themselves and the stock market, support the measures. However, some institutional investors' opinions may differ from conventional wisdom, particularly that of "sell-side" analysts. Use ROIC and cash flow metrics in addition to EPS.

   d. Use other measures besides the stock price and TRS. While the stock market is the ultimate arbiter of the value and execution of a business strategy for a public company, the board can signal its own views of how value is created by choosing the ideal and optimal strategic metrics.

   e. Evaluate the correlation of incentive plan metrics over the medium and long terms with the creation of shareholder value, especially TRS. Lower correlations over the short term (quarterly, one year) may be desirable (particularly in LTI vehicles) to encourage longer-term thinking by management and strategic longer-term investments.

f. Compare the company's performance with a benchmark group of competitors on a number of measures, including the incentive plan metrics, to determine how difficult or easy the goals have been to achieve. Link this historical analysis to pay levels to measure the relative success of pay-for-performance. This analysis can also help to identify strengths and weaknesses and determine the proper mix of metrics in the incentive plans.

g. Review whether to use all *absolute* metrics (e.g., EPS in dollars, ROE in percent, ROI in percent) or include more *relative* metrics (e.g., TRS percentile compared with a peer group, ROIC compared with peers). There are advantages and disadvantages with each type of metric.

12. **Disallow hedging**. Do not allow executives or directors to hedge their owned shares or stock options to protect themselves from a decline in the stock price. These hedges can take the form of short sales, pooled mutual funds, put options, or any economic equivalent. While these may not be illegal, they must be disclosed in SEC filings. And, more importantly, hedging is not within the spirit of stock ownership and the annual granting of large amounts of stock options and other stock incentives.

13. **Scrutinize change-of-control language**. Review and modify any change-of-control language in contracts, severance plans, and cash and stock incentive programs that is out of line with current corporate governance standards or may result in excessive payments (in absolute dollars or as a percentage of the deal). This review should include a cost estimate of the language before any transaction. The preferred percentage is usually 2 percent to 4 percent but varies based on company size. Institutional investors do not like single triggers or IRS Section 280G excise tax gross-ups because of their expense. However, it is competitive practice to provide the latter to top management. The number of participants can be kept to a minimum to satisfy shareholders, but there will be many disgruntled employees if they have to pay the 20 percent excise tax on "excessive" amounts.

Another area of concern is where the change-of-control trigger is inadvertently pulled at the buyer's company because of a technical issue, such as a percentage of the shares changing hands, the number of board members, or a required move by the CEO. These issues should be identified before the deal and negotiated out, or – in the worst case – eliminated after the deal is announced but before closing.

14. **Set the calendar well in advance**. Schedule meetings and agenda items for the full year before the start of the year so that members can keep track of all programs and payments throughout the year.

15. **Require preannounced plans to sell stock**. Require or encourage all officers and directors to use 10b5–1 trading plans to exercise stock options or sell the stock. These plans are considered an affirmative defense regarding insider trading, but they are not a safe harbor. In other words, they are good but imperfect vehicles for insider stock sales. Nevertheless, we think their use is an emerging best practice. These plans have many forms, some more or less advantageous to the executive and to the shareholders, but they all signal an intention to sell or, infrequently, to buy stock.

Rule 10b5–1 Plans – Preannounced Purchases or Sales of Stock

One of the great criticisms of executives and executive pay in the early 2000s was that executives sold their stock to preserve their wealth before bad earnings news or, in the worst cases, bankruptcy. Because the executives were presumed to have had inside information, this gave them a huge advantage – certainly immoral and possibly illegal – over other employees and outside shareholders.[5]

Executives incur high levels of risk when they hold large amounts of a single stock, including their own company's. But if they try to liquidate or diversify their holdings, they face various restrictions. Companies may restrict stock sales or limit their executives' ability to trade to open-window periods. These executive holdings may be difficult to liquidate because the stock price may become volatile if the executive makes a large trade in a designated open-window period. Executives also face tax implications and requirements for public reporting of their transactions.

A 10b5–1 plan provides for the sale or purchase of company stock in a systematic manner. The plan limits the executive's ability to influence the timing of purchases or sales and gives him or her an affirmative defense to any claims of insider trading. These plans commonly use a formula to determine the number of shares and prices of the transaction. They typically include selling dates that correspond to an executive's need for liquidity or diversification.

In order for the plan to provide an affirmative defense, it should be established when the executive is not aware of relevant, material, nonpublic information. The plan must specify the number of shares, price, and date for purchases and sales or provide a formula to determine these factors. Also, the plan cannot include an offsetting hedge position to protect the shares under the plan.

The executive can terminate the plan at any time, even if he or she is aware of material nonpublic information, but cannot modify it under those circumstances, for example, by changing the sale price. The executive can terminate the plan and immediately enter into a new one only if he or she is not aware of material nonpublic information.

Each executive may adopt a separate written plan prepared by his or her financial adviser. The company is not party to the plan, but general counsel or the corporate secretary should review it to ensure compliance with company policies. The executive must notify the company if the plan is terminated.

These plans allow executives to trade outside of the open-window periods (although there may be negative publicity if an executive sells stock automatically under a plan before some negative news during a blackout period. This should be weighed against the advantages). The plans may also be implemented before stock options vest, enabling a securities sale upon vesting and exercise.

In general, 10b5–1 plans trade executive flexibility in selling stock for a soothed market and an affirmative defense. The company can maintain a disciplined approach to trading with a reduced need for monitoring. The plans separate the executives' trading activities from the release of corporate earnings and encourage investors to view those trades as part of the executives' financial plan rather than a signal about corporate developments. They also allow the company to accommodate executives' financial and estate-planning needs without additional costs to the company. We estimate that executives at about 20 percent of major companies use these plans and the number is increasing.

Although there is no mandatory public disclosure for 10b5–1 plans, we recommend that companies announce any plans established by Section 16 officers. The press release should identify the executives and note that they are in full compliance with the company's stock ownership guidelines and will remain so for the duration of the plan.

Best Governance Practices in Designing Annual and Long-Term Incentives

Designing an executive pay program, especially an incentive plan, requires all of the considerations discussed earlier, but with some additional steps. Begin by interviewing top management, the full board, and employee focus groups as appropriate, generally using an outside consultant who reports to the compensation committee. The committee can then develop the strategy, philosophy, and goals of the program. The committee should conduct a competitive benchmark study, including pay levels and types of programs, as well as special features, vesting, and termination rules, and then position the program relative to the market.

At this point, the committee should review the initial concept, typically including the results from the interviews and benchmark study. This should yield a narrower menu of alternatives. The committee can flesh out the design to be as specific as possible, showing examples of the impact on the individuals involved. The committee will also need to obtain accounting, tax, securities law, ERISA, and shareholder expert opinions. It should also review expected proxy material with an eye toward its potential impact on shareholder relations.

The committee should brief the full board on possible outcomes and then finalize the design and seek board approval. Management will need to develop a communication plan – letters, plan documents, meetings – approved by the compensation committee. After the plan is implemented, the committee should conduct a full review to determine the effectiveness of the executive compensation program.

9 Aligning All Employee Pay to Improve Corporate Performance

> In the past twenty-five years, researchers have done more than seventy empirical studies of these [broad-based employee stock ownership] forms of risk sharing. Taken together, the studies provide compelling evidence for the net gain that the partnership approach can produce for a company's public shareholders.[1]
>
> Joseph Blasi, Douglas Kruse, and Aaron Bernstein,
> *In the Company of Owners: The Truth About Stock Options and Why Every Employee Should Have Them*

All employees perform at higher levels when they are eligible for performance-based short-term and stock-based incentives. This common framework makes it possible to align executive pay with pay for broader employee groups and provide sharply higher pay for top performers at all levels – crucial elements in a company's success.

Unfortunately, most of the controversy surrounding executive pay in recent years has focused on ways to create a false alignment by regulating the compensation process and limiting the amounts of pay that would otherwise be set by market forces.

Critics argue that by lowering executive pay, morale – and therefore productivity – will be higher because employees will believe that they are being treated fairly. There is no empirical evidence to support this position. Studies of internal pay equity and perceptions of fairness show that employees focus on the effectiveness and fairness of the performance measurement and evaluation process rather than the actual amounts of compensation.

In other words, companies should strive to create alignment by making nonexecutive compensation more like executive compensation instead of by restricting executive pay. Restrictions will only remove the market mechanisms that have worked well for the vast majority of companies and for the economy as a whole. Instead of reducing executives' ownership stake, companies should increase the stake for all employees. And instead of capping or cutting the amount that executives can earn, companies should raise the amounts that nonexecutives can earn when they perform at high levels. The point is to put more power behind pay-for-performance, not less.

Elements of Alignment

Aligning pay throughout the organization unifies all employees in a common commitment to corporate objectives. The failure to align pay can result in a basic distrust of management, an indifferent attitude toward the company's goals, or, even worse, people pulling in opposite directions.

An aligned compensation system allows broad participation in the company's reward plans. It also means limiting special incentives and perquisites for top executives. Our experience indicates that employees accept high levels of compensation for executives and high pay differentiation for high and low performers when they have an opportunity to reap proportionate rewards for their own efforts.

Alignment does not require pay equality or a flat pay structure. It also does not mean putting the same amount of pay at risk for executives and employees, who have different levels of risk tolerance. It simply requires similar programs and opportunities to increase pay through higher performance.

Our research shows that in successful companies, even when all employees are eligible for stock options, only half perform well enough to receive them. The top performers at all levels earn substantially more than the lowest performers. Incentive plans for employees should mimic incentive plans for executives by drawing a direct line between the employee's performance, the size of the rewards, and when they pay out.

Alignment has several components. First, as many employees as possible must be included in a pay-for-performance model that sharply distinguishes between different levels of performance. Second, the architecture and performance measures of compensation programs should be aligned at all employee levels.

ALIGNING ARCHITECTURE AND PERFORMANCE MEASURES

Although the amounts paid out will vary considerably, the architecture of the pay programs – namely, the number and nature of the cash and stock incentive plans – must be as similar as possible. Perquisites that emphasize the difference between executives' and employees' compensation packages, such as use of company jets, reduce alignment.

For example, at one company located in a major city, parking was a huge problem. The company gave the top 50 executives premier parking spaces that were in full view of the main entrance. With the typical employee walking a long distance or taking a bus in bad weather, these parking spaces affected employee morale. Although the spaces were a valued benefit for the executives, that value was outweighed by the damage done to employee productivity.

Alignment does not necessarily translate into the same programs for both executives and nonexecutives. The goal is to align behaviors, actions, incentives, and rewards through a direct line of sight between performance and payouts. To recognize each group's risk tolerance and impact on organizational performance, a company might use options, performance shares, and restricted stock for executives; performance shares and restricted stock for managers; and restricted stock for non-managerial employees.

Companies must also align the performance measures used to trigger payouts. At one company, different incentive plans for junior and senior executives led to a situation where the senior executives' plan paid out, while the junior executives' did not. To avoid this problem, the company created an on/off "gate" for the senior plan so that it did not pay out unless the other plan paid out as well. In all cases, the executive plan should pay out only if all other employees receive a payout.

Untenable Forms of Alignment

Some critics have called for companies to band together and cap executive pay as a multiple of employee pay or cap CEO pay as a multiple of the next-highest-paid executive's pay. Others have suggested that companies cap stock grants to executives when they reach a certain multiple of the executive's base salary. But companies that cap pay will quickly see their top talent move on to companies without caps or into fields – such as investment banking, private equity, and consulting – where they can still reap the full rewards of their work. Price and wage caps of this sort almost always fail because of unintended consequences. Examples can be found in the $1 million incentive pay cap issue and the change in severance plans.

The changes in employee compensation now taking place in the United States – cutting back on stock options and reducing the value

FIGURE 9.1

Companies with More Performance Pay Outperform Others

	HIGH STI/LTI	HIGH SALARY
Salary as percentage of total rewards	63%	79%
STI/LTI as percentage of total rewards	13%	8%
Three-year TRS	44%	25%

Note: TRS = total return to shareholders = stock price appreciation + dividends/beginning stock price.

Source: Watson Wyatt.

of employee stock purchase plans – are already creating alignment and morale problems that may produce substantial economic damage. Instead of reducing pay-for-performance levels for executives, the objective must be to raise performance-pay opportunities for all employees.

Performance-Pay Solutions

Effective pay-for-performance for the broad employee population means sharp differences in pay for high and low performers, incentive programs similar to those for executives, and performance measures (also aligned with measures at the top) that trigger payouts when objectives and targets are met.

Watson Wyatt research shows that companies with more pay-for-performance features – including stock incentives plus pay differentiation – outperform companies with fewer features and that companies that put a larger portion of employee pay into incentive programs generate higher returns than companies with lower amounts (see Figure 9.1).

Aligning pay and rewarding top performers is especially critical for managerial employees. Economic theory suggests that stock-based incentive programs are most effective in rewarding executives and senior managers, who have the greatest ability to affect a company's performance. Organizations where nearly all executives and managers are eligible for stock option programs outperform companies where eligibility is more limited (see Figure 9.2).

Successful companies provide greater rewards for high-performing employees. However, in the past, most companies spread stock options evenly across the organization. As more organizations shift to restricted stock for the broad employee population, there is an enormous opportunity to differentiate these rewards for top performers. Unlike stock options, restricted stock conveys an intrinsic value from the grant and

FIGURE 9.2
Stock-Based Incentive Compensation Programs for Executives/Managers and Superior Returns

	STOCK OPTIONS		RESTRICTED STOCK		EMPLOYEE STOCK PURCHASE PLANS (WITH A DISCOUNT)	
	HIGH	LOW	HIGH	LOW	HIGH	LOW
Percentage of executives/ managers eligible	93%	5%	36%	0%	98%	0%
Market premium	31.7%	18.7%	33.6%	26.7%	67.8%	0.8%
Three-year TRS	38%	37%	50%	24%	57%	27%

Source: Watson Wyatt.

thus can be used to reward top performers at higher levels while still providing alignment.

Our research shows that the most successful companies take a portfolio approach to stock-based incentives, using options to supplement actual share ownership. In Figure 9.2, we see that firms with the widest eligibility for restricted stock plans (36 percent of executives and managers eligible) perform better than firms that do not use restricted stock. The same is also true of companies with discounted stock purchase plans.

A 2005 Watson Wyatt study of 265 companies with a minimum of 1,000 employees each and a related survey of 1,100 employees in those organizations found sharp distinctions between the performance-pay programs at high- and low-performing companies. The high performers realized a three-year TRS of 117 percent and the low performers 26 percent. The high-performing companies had a much higher – and therefore better – gap in pay increases between high- and low-performing employees.

In the study, 71 percent of the high-performing companies reported that their reward plans are effective, compared with only 47 percent of the low-performing companies. Additionally, high-performing companies are more likely to report that their reward system is linked to business strategy and encourages desired employee behavior (see Figure 9.3).

To design effective performance-pay plans, companies must factor in employee preferences and tolerance for risk. Companies also must carefully communicate the plans and the performance measures used. Not surprisingly, the study found that top-performing employees have a better understanding of the value of their rewards package. Nearly two-thirds (63 percent) of top performers indicate at least a moderate understanding, compared with 36 percent of poor performers. Unfortunately,

FIGURE 9.3
High-Performing Firms Align Reward Programs

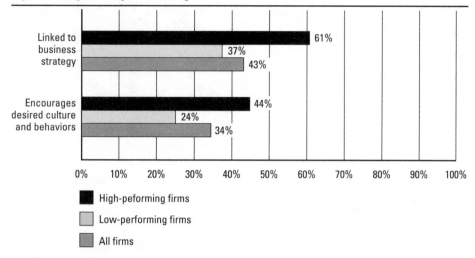

Source: Watson Wyatt Worldwide.

many companies are doing a poor job of executing performance pay for broad employee groups.

MERIT INCREASES

Pay-for-performance programs succeed only if the pay difference for high- and low-performing employees is substantial. The study found that only 10 percent of top performers think they are paid significantly better than poor performers. It is easy to understand why they believe this because the first vehicle for rewarding performance – the annual merit increase – often fails to provide sharply higher amounts for top performers (see Figure 9.4).

Watson Wyatt research shows that the average merit raise for all employees in 2004 was 3.7 percent, with 5.6 percent for top performers, 3.5 percent for average performers, and 2.5 percent for poor performers. These increases do not sufficiently differentiate between high and low performance. Moreover, employers reported that almost half of all employees consider merit increases an annual entitlement, and most of the remaining employees see them as an entitlement to some extent. Instead of the 3-percentage-point spread the study found, a more effective spread would be 8 to 10 points, with poor performers receiving no increase and the best performers receiving 8 percent to 10 percent.

FIGURE 9.4
Merit Increases Do Not Show Sufficient Differentiation

	AVERAGE RAISE LAST YEAR
Top performers	5.6%
Average performers	3.5%
Poor performers	2.5%
All employees	3.7%

Source: Watson Wyatt.

SHORT-TERM INCENTIVES

Companies need short-term and stock-based incentives for the broad employee population, with a structure that is similar to incentives for executives and with performance measures set so that executive plans do not pay out unless employee plans pay out. The study found that companies that put more of their pay into incentive programs instead of higher salaries outperform others (see Figure 9.5).

Short-term incentives provide an effective tool for differentiating individual pay based on performance. Companies with the largest pay distinctions between high and low performers significantly outperform organizations with smaller differentials. The strong correlation between company performance and sharply differentiated rewards is shown in Figure 9.6.

Our research shows that the median payout to employees meeting expectations is 100 percent of the bonus pool, while employees who perform in the top 10 percent receive only 5 percent more. Moreover, 27 percent of companies with STI plans pay bonuses to employees who are poor performers. Companies would benefit from even larger distinctions between pay for high and low performers.

FIGURE 9.5
Companies with More Performance Pay Outperform Others

	HIGH STI/LTI	HIGH SALARY
Salary as percentage of total rewards	63%	79%
STI/LTI as percentage of total rewards	13%	8%
Three-year TRS	44%	25%

Note: TRS = stock price appreciation + dividends/beginning stock price.
Source: Watson Wyatt.

FIGURE 9.6
Sharper Distinctions in Bonuses Generate Higher TRS

	HIGH-DIFFERENTIATION COMPANIES	LOW-DIFFERENTIATION COMPANIES
STI payout to high-performing employees vs. low-performing employees	4.7	2.1
Market premium	30%	6.7%
Three-year TRS	47%	−2%

Source: Watson Wyatt.

STOCK-BASED INCENTIVES

Stock-based incentives are a critical part of pay-for-performance for executives and nonexecutives alike. The Watson Wyatt 2005 study found that 42 percent of companies offer stock options to nonexecutives, and 33 percent offer other long-term incentives. Although stock-based incentives for broad employee groups have a track record of boosting company performance (see Figure 9.7), the use of these long-term incentives for nonexecutives has declined considerably with the new expensing requirement.

Discounted employee stock purchase plans are also valuable tools for providing long-term incentives for broad-based employee groups. But the recent changes in U.S. stock option accounting requirements may reduce the value of the typical program design.

Employee Stock Ownership

A number of studies demonstrate that stock-based pay plans motivate all employees to create higher shareholder value. One of the most extensive

FIGURE 9.7
Broad-Based Employee Stock Purchase Plans (ESPP) and Higher Returns

	HIGH	LOW
Percentage of employees (other than executives) eligible for discounted ESPP	96%	0%
Market premium	63.8%	0.5%
Three-year TRS	57%	24%

Source: Watson Wyatt.

studies in recent years is *In the Company of Owners: The Truth about Stock Options and Why Every Employee Should Have Them*, by Joseph Blasi, Douglas Kruse, and Aaron Bernstein.[2] The authors attribute the soaring success of 100 top high-tech companies during the 1990s largely to the fact that their executives and employees owned a third of the company's stock – top officers holding 14 percent and employees holding 19 percent of outstanding stock – with 17 percentage points of that in stock options. Their research found that companies that offered options to all employees had substantially higher average productivity growth and annual returns than companies that did not.

The study concludes that even limited amounts of employee stock ownership, with employees holding about 8 percent of the company's stock, boost productivity by a one-time (but permanent) 4 percentage points and raise TRS by an average of about 2 percentage points. Profit levels, measured by return on assets, return on equity, and profit margins, increase by 14 percent. These gains remain in place as long as the ownership plans continue. The authors calculated these gains in profits and returns after factoring in dilution for outside shareholders.

The study notes that, for decades, U.S. companies have used a variety of stock-based pay plans – including stock options, Employee Stock Ownership Plans (ESOPs), 401(k) investment options, and stock purchase plans – that reward employees for high performance and create a "partnership" between employees and management in pursuit of the company's strategic objectives. As the quotation at the beginning of this chapter indicates, Blasi, Kruse, and Bernstein believe that these sorts of employee-based programs add tremendous value for shareholders.

A 2005 article in the Harvard Business School's *Working Knowledge* excerpts the book *Equity: Why Employee Ownership Is Good for Business* by Corey Rosen, John Case, and Martin Staubus, which provides substantial evidence of the business benefits of broad equity ownership among employees. The authors find that "Ownership is indispensable because it is what tips the balance of the conventional employment equation."[3] Companies with equity-based plans for broad employee groups report that their employees are committed to corporate strategic objectives and perform at high levels.

The Role of Stock Options

The best-performing companies clearly have vertically aligned pay programs, usually built around stock options. But the new accounting cost

FIGURE 9.8

Decline in Stock Option Grants

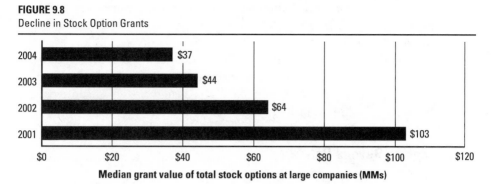

Median grant value of total stock options at large companies (MMs)

Source: Watson Wyatt.

requirement and the discounted value that employees place on stock options have challenged that model and produced dramatic declines in stock option use for alignment.

Throughout the 1990s, incentive programs for broader employee groups increasingly incorporated stock option plans that essentially aligned their pay with executive compensation. But a Watson Wyatt study found that, between 2001 and 2004, the total economic value of stock option grants at the nation's largest corporations shrank by almost 60 percent, from $118 billion to $51 billion, despite a rising stock market. The stock price at the typical S&P 1500 company rose 34 percent from 2001 to 2004 – 18 percent in 2004 alone. Had the companies continued to grant the same number of shares of options under the same terms, the value of grants would have risen by 34 percent rather than decline by 60 percent.

The study also found that the Black–Scholes economic value of stock options granted at the typical company declined 64 percent, from $103 million in 2001 to $37 million in 2004 (see Figure 9.8). In 2004 alone, the value fell 17 percent. The decline occurred in all major industry sectors and reflects a drop in the number of employees receiving stock options as well as shrinking grant sizes at all employee levels. The study is based on public data from companies in the S&P 1500. Data for 2005 showed a further decline.

As the attractiveness of stock options fades, companies are eliminating them for broad employee groups, reducing eligibility, or replacing them with restricted stock and other long-term incentive awards to create a better range of incentives. A 2005 study by Watson Wyatt found that most companies had altered their stock-based rewards. Most of these changes reduced the rewards for nonexecutives more than those for executives (see Figure 9.9).

During this transition, the challenge remains for employers to create strong incentives that will keep executives and employees focused on their companies' future performance. The design of stock incentives may become more important than their dollar amount.

Moving Beyond Options

The majority of S&P 1500 firms we studied reduced the number and percentage of stock options they granted between 2001 and 2005 because of extreme volatility in the market and the new accounting requirement. Many companies have replaced their stock option grants with cash or other equity vehicles. Other companies have simply reduced eligibility to save shares and accounting costs.

In our experience, however, the tension between sustaining executive grants and reducing broad employee stock incentive participation may not have been fully explored before decisions were made. At one recent compensation committee meeting, members discussed the size of the CEO's LTI grant for several hours; the reduction in the discount on the ESPP – which affected 20,000 employees – was discussed for 15 minutes.

As with the reduction in the eligibility for stock options, the reduction in the ESPP discount affects morale. The typical ESPP had a 15 percent discount baked into the stock purchase price combined with a 3- to 12-month option period. In fact, the model plan was structured so that employees could purchase company stock at a 15 percent discount from the lowest price at either the start or the end of the purchase period. The new accounting rules – FAS 123(R) – allow for a zero-cost ESPP if the discount is equal to or less than 5 percent and there is no "lower-of" or "look-back" feature.

These plans have created billions of dollars of value for nonexecutive employees. Historically, they had no accounting cost. Of course, they had a significant economic cost in terms of share use. But these plans, by definition, require a funded employee stock purchase, albeit at very favorable terms – a valuable feature for both employees and shareholders.

About one-third of the companies with ESPPs have already redesigned their plans, mostly by eliminating the lower-of or look-back feature, by reducing the discount to 5 percent, or both. Our research,

FIGURE 9.9
Reductions in Stock-Based Programs for Non-Executive Employees

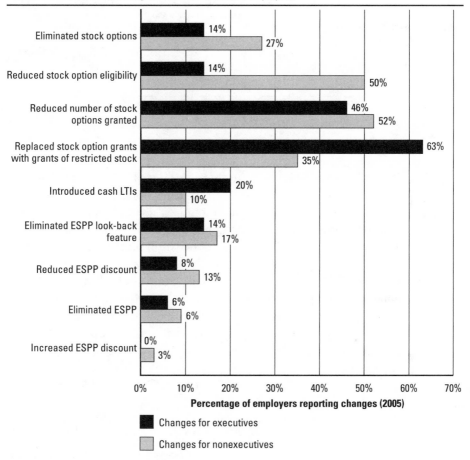

Source: Watson Wyatt.

detailed here, has shown that employees are not happy with these changes. The effects on morale are likely to affect corporate financial and stock market results.

But there is another reason for companies to reduce their use of stock options: Employees greatly undervalue them. This is true for newly granted at-the-money options and for underwater options. Practitioners, consultants, and researchers have known for some time that employees' perceived value of options is less than their actual economic or opportunity cost to the company.

FIGURE 9.10
High and Low Stock Option Expense and Company Performance

2003 EXPENSE (INDUSTRY-ADJUSTED)	CHANGE IN 2004	GRANT VALUE (CENTS PER SHARE)		ONE-YEAR ANNUALIZED TRS (MEDIAN)
		2003	2004	
Low	Increase	3.4	8.6	24.1%
	Cut	4.1	1.2	20.8%
Medium	Increase	12.1	19.4	18.6%
	Cut	13.1	7.2	15.7%
High	Increase	33.5	45.1	9.8%
	Cut	32.4	16.6	15.5%

Source: Watson Wyatt.

However, some employees do not discount stock options. The possible positive reasons include strong recent stock price performance, and the possible negative reasons include a misunderstanding of how options work, lower personal risk aversion, personal wealth, and nonpecuniary factors. Nevertheless, the evidence from some recent programs in which employees could exchange underwater stock options for cash or restricted stock points to a major discount. Thousands of employees have exchanged stock options for cash or stock at a price substantially below the options' already reduced Black–Scholes value, which still represents the best estimate of their actual ongoing cost to the company.

Our research shows that the market has already begun to regard stock option expense like any other expense in the sense that low expense is better than high expense (see Figure 9.10). Presumably, the market assumes that companies know what they are doing regarding their methods to motivate employees and appropriately factor cost pressures into their incentive programs. This is probably not entirely true.

Our research also shows that companies with already high expenses that increased their stock option expense from 2003 to 2004 saw dramatically lower TRS than companies that either reduced their expense or already had a low expense. This implies that all companies should estimate the ROI on stock-based incentive investments before granting them and change their strategy accordingly.

Converting to Restricted Stock

We have documented the value that employees place on stock options compared with options' Black–Scholes cost to the company. Employees value shares of restricted stock much more highly than stock options, with a 10 percent and a 22 percent discount for the first 100 shares and

FIGURE 9.11

Estimated Average Discounts for 100 Shares of Restricted Stock

	VALUE EMPLOYEE	VALUE	DISCOUNT ESTIMATES
All firms	$16.41	$20.00	18%
Large firms	$16.61	$20.00	17%
Small firms	$15.89	$20.00	21%
Positive three-year TRS	$17.26	$20.00	14%
Negative three-year TRS	$16.07	$20.00	20%
Conservative investors	$15.57	$20.00	22%
Aggressive investors	$18.02	$20.00	10%
Never exercised option before	$16.06	$20.00	20%
Exercised option before	$16.79	$20.00	16%
Do you know your company's stock price within $2?			
Yes	$16.25	$20.00	19%
No	$17.28	$20.00	14%
Accurate on TRS?			
Yes	$17.37	$20.00	13%
No	$16.10	$20.00	20%
What is your current annual salary?			
$50,000–$74,999	$15.96	$20.00	20%
$75,000 or greater	$16.63	$20.00	17%
Is the current stock price higher than the average exercise price?			
Yes	$16.25	$20.00	19%
No	$16.82	$20.00	16%
What percentage of shares are in the money?			
75% or more	$18.05	$20.00	10%
Less than 75%	$15.90	$20.00	21%

Source: Watson Wyatt.

an average of 18 percent (see Figure 9.11). For larger grants, employees place a greater discount on the value of those shares but still regard them as having much higher value than stock options. These values imply that organizations could substantially reduce costs – say, 20 percent to 30 percent – by converting their stock option plans to grants of restricted stock for most employees.

The following is an example of a stock option to restricted stock conversion based on employee perception of value. Assume that a company grants 500 options with a $20 strike price and a Black–Scholes value of $10. For the company, that grant has a $5,000 accounting cost. For the employee, however, the value of the stock option grant is approximately $2,500. Instead of options, the company could give the employee approximately 160 restricted shares, which are worth the same $2,500 to the employee. The resulting cost to the company ($3,200) would be 36 percent lower ($5,000 minus $3,200).

This estimate is based on the relatively conservative assumption that the discount increases linearly with the size of the award rather than the more aggressive – and more likely – case in which the discount increases at an increasing rate. Using this method would yield a larger estimate of the potential savings. Whether a given company can or should provide discounts of this magnitude depends on its circumstances. Furthermore, shifting from stock options to restricted stock (or cash) reduces the upside potential and potentially the emphasis on performance.

Some companies have adopted restricted stock for top executives and kept stock options for the broader employee group. However, this creates misalignment; if the stock price is flat, the executives still receive value from their restricted stock but the employees do not, as their options are underwater.

Adjusting Stock-Based Incentives

Stock options may be losing their appeal. But companies can use a combination of stock incentives at the broad employee level, especially restricted stock – which can motivate and engage employees – and stock purchase plans, in addition to or instead of stock options, to create a program that decreases accounting costs, increases the perceived value delivered to employees, and is shareholder-friendly.

In light of this and other research, we urge all companies to consider modifying their stock-based incentives. Companies may find that they can:

- Design alternative programs with higher value to employees and greater motivational value.
- Reduce total expense. Other research has shown that lower accounting expense from stock incentives is associated with higher subsequent TRS (see Figure 9.10).

- Develop programs that are more shareholder-friendly.

In addition, companies can take the following steps to maximize the value of their long-term incentive plans:

- Consider factors other than stock option values and accounting treatment. In designing incentives, the idea is to create motivation, retention, and excitement. Lower turnover costs or higher productivity that can result from a well-designed program may swamp the accounting expense.
- Reduce overhang by lowering future share requests to shareholders and by reducing run rates. Use a portfolio of plans, as opposed to a pure stock option plan, to reduce total share use. Manage to the accounting cost.
- Educate employees. Many employees do not understand how stock options and restricted stock operate.
- Conduct conjoint analysis or estimate the trade-offs between stock options and cash or stock equivalents. Companies can also use focus groups to estimate how much employees discount the value of stock options.
- Tailor any design by considering such factors as culture, performance, levels of stock ownership, future prospects, and dividends.

Alignment in Practice

Some companies have successfully aligned their compensation programs. A major financial institution, for example, designed vertically aligned programs within the context of total rewards. It is issuing equity for the first time with designs that apply to the entire employee population. Plan funding and metrics are consistent throughout the organization.

A pharmaceutical company developed a pay philosophy that aligns every employee from "floor to ceiling" around common strategic objectives, business tactics, and performance measures. It created cascading performance measures for all employees in the company's annual bonus program, with aligned performance measure weightings and a logical pay mix. The company's long-term incentive programs apply the same philosophy. The company uses broad-based option grants.

Most biotechnology firms continue to use broad-based equity plans. They may not offer stock options all the way down to the receptionist level, but such options commonly cover mid-level scientists. High-tech companies with less than $1 billion in annual sales commonly follow a similar model; about half of the senior-level technical contributors receive some type of equity grant, still mostly options but in some cases restricted stock as well.

The idea is that all employees share in the company's success but at different levels, depending on job function. Many of these tech companies are only one management generation away from the company founders, some of whom came from stratified companies where a lack of alignment created performance and morale problems. A majority of high-tech and biotech companies try to avoid executive benefits and perks because they do not want to create a two-class system. They may provide executive car allowances, club dues, and physicals, but these perks are not a big part of executive remuneration.

At UPS, the annual incentive level is the same for the entire organization, including the CEO. Its 2005 compensation committee report contains this statement:

> The Committee exercises its judgment on the level of incentive payments based on considerations including overall responsibilities and the importance of these responsibilities to UPS's success. . . . Criteria for evaluation include financial targets and other important goals such as customer satisfaction, employee engagement, operational performance and shareowner value creation. In addition, we assess each executive in terms of leadership, managerial skills and talent, business knowledge and execution of UPS's overall business strategy, and adherence to our values. Annual incentive grants . . . allow employees to acquire shares of class A common stock. The size of the grants is determined by a formula that takes into consideration profits, monthly salary, the number of participants and the level of participation. The level of participation for the Chief Executive Officer and other executive officers is the same as for approximately 11,000 participating employees at or above the center manager level. Over the past five years, the grants to the top five executives have totaled less than 5 percent of the grants issued to all employees.

Building Better Alignment

Whatever form the plan takes, the point is to keep the broader employee population in the game – motivated, engaged, and performing at ever-higher levels. This means tying pay to performance at all levels of the organization and aligning executive and nonexecutive pay plans. Companies can accomplish this by following these steps:

1. Adopt pay plans that include four common elements for all employees: base salary, short-term incentives, long-term incentives, and benefits. This lays the groundwork for shared opportunity and a performance-pay culture. It also supplies the structure for sharply differentiating rewards for high and low performers and for aligning employee and shareholder interests.
2. Create identical or similar performance measures for executives and the broader employee population. Alignment and performance-based pay rest on objective measures, preferably a combination of company-wide results, such as TRS or earnings per share, and more limited line-of-sight measures based on the specific performance goals of a smaller unit.
3. Establish credible uniform performance management programs and ensure that the best performers are paid better than lower-performing employees at all organizational levels. The board should establish special committees to review the top executives' performance regularly, similar to employees' periodic performance evaluations.
4. Minimize or eliminate executive benefits and perquisites that are not related to specific job requirements. Although some travel and security-related perks may be necessary, and life insurance considerations are different, benefits for executives and the broader employee population should be similar.
5. Ensure that cost-effective and properly valued plans are implemented at all levels. Do not provide pay programs that cost $1 per unit but are valued at $.50.

Aligning pay plans, incentive opportunities, and performance measures throughout an organization is crucial. A top-down regulatory approach to alignment will only damage the entire market-based process. Increasing performance incentives and stock ownership for both executive and nonexecutive employees and rewarding high performers at every level can drive business success.

10 International Executive Pay Comparisons

> International convergence to U.S. pay levels would occur if, and only if, the economic value of foreign executives to their firms increased enough to entitle them to receive higher compensation. This type of change would arise only if foreign CEOs' decision-making powers increased, foreign firms grew larger, or foreign firms' growth opportunities expanded.[1]
>
> Randall S. Thomas, John S. Beasley II Professor of Law and Business, Vanderbilt University Law School

Throughout the world, U.S. compensation ranks at the top in both pay opportunity and amounts received. But other economically successful countries – including the United Kingdom, France, Canada, and many in the Asia-Pacific region – have different economic and business approaches, including their approach to executive pay. These models fit with the unique culture and corporate governance systems of each country, and all exhibit some pay-for-performance sensitivity.

Many critics of the U.S. executive pay system argue that shareholders would benefit from adopting features from other countries, especially those of the United Kingdom: more performance vesting on stock options and shares; shareholder votes on executive pay; separate chairman and CEO positions; and lower levels of pay opportunity and pay earned.

It makes sense that all economies, and the corporations that constitute a large part of them, should be flexible and adopt successful components from other countries. But just as other countries cannot adopt the U.S. approach in toto, neither can the United States fully adopt other systems. The United States has adopted some of the United Kingdom's practices, primarily performance-based vesting.

Legitimate differences – economic, institutional, structural, social, and cultural – must be factored in. America's deep tradition of

FIGURE 10.1
Gross Domestic Product (GDP) Per Capita, 2004

U.S.	$39.9
Canada	$31.9
Japan	$29.8
EU-15	$28.6
France	$29.6
Germany	$28.4
U.K.	$31.5

Source: U.S. Bureau of Labor Statistics.

entrepreneurialism stands in sharp contrast to the historical evolution of capitalism in other countries. U.S. executives clearly receive higher compensation, but there are vast differences in the economic, regulatory, shareholder concentration, and corporate structures and in the CEO's role at U.S. firms and firms abroad. With more alternative employment opportunities and less-concentrated shareholders, U.S. executives have significantly more economic and labor market power than their international counterparts.

U.S. Competitive Advantage

By any number of measures, the U.S. economy is the most productive of the advanced mature economies (see Figures 10.1 and 10.2). In addition, U.S. equity markets have performed extremely well in the last 20 years, consistently outperforming those of its industrialized competitors (see Figure 10.3).

Although the strength of the U.S. economy clearly does not derive solely from its executive pay practices, those practices – with their high potential risks and rewards – are an integral part of a corporate model that has generated the most productive economy in the world. Certainly, it would be difficult to conclude that these pay practices have damaged the U.S. economy or that the economy could have been even more productive without them.

By most measures, productivity growth rates in the United States outstrip those of Canada, Japan, and the major European competitor nations (see Figure 10.4).

U.S. executives are paid for making decisions that keep U.S. companies lean, efficient, and positioned for growth. The relatively unregulated

FIGURE 10.2
Average Annual Growth Rates in
Real GDP Per Capita, 1994–2004

U.S.	2.2%
Canada	2.3%
Japan	1.1%
EU-15	2.0%
France	1.8%
Germany	1.3%
U.K.	2.0%

Source: U.S. Bureau of Labor Statistics.

nature of the U.S. economy, compared with other advanced, mature economies, means that U.S. executives have considerably more freedom and responsibility in pursuing the strategies and policies that will create value for their shareholders. And although U.S. executives are commonly vilified for their decisions to reduce headcount or tightly control spending on wages and benefits, in almost all cases these decisions ultimately protect the economic efficiency, competitive position, and long-term success of the company. That economic efficiency creates a dynamic and robust labor market capable of absorbing virtually all of those laid-off employees.

The United States leads the large advanced economies in job creation (see Figure 10.5) and reported an unemployment rate of less than 5 percent in 2005. One of the characteristics of its economy and corporations is the ability to recover quickly after a downturn, which speaks to the

FIGURE 10.3
U.S. and Other Industrialized Countries Stock Market
Performance (major index)

YEAR	U.S. S&P 500	JAPAN	FRANCE	U.K.
1990	100	100	100	100
1995	188	83	114	170
2000	408	65	369	286
2006	393	72	306	268

Note: All dates November, except for 2006.

Source: Yahoo! Finance.

FIGURE 10.4
Average Annual Growth Rates in Manufacturing
Productivity, 1994–2004

U.S.	5.7%
Canada	2.5%
Japan	4.8%
France	4.2%
Germany	3.1%
U.K.	2.7%

Source: U.S. Bureau of Labor Statistics.

flexibility of the companies, their efficient structure, and the willingness and ability of their executives to make rapid adjustments.

Not only is the unemployment rate in the major European economies almost double that of the United States, but the average duration of unemployment is much longer and the percentage of the unemployed who are jobless for more than one year is more than three times as high for the EU 15 (see Figures 10.6 and 10.7) – a crucial advantage for U.S. workers. The unemployment rates in the United States for 2005 and 2006 were even lower than in previous years.

The International Executive Pay Gap

One of the most useful treatments of the distinctions that underpin the international differences in executive pay is a 2005 study titled "Explaining the International CEO Pay Gap: Board Capture or Market Driven?" by

FIGURE 10.5
Average Annual Growth Rates in Employment,
1994–2004

U.S.	1.2%
Canada	2.0%
Japan	–0.2%
EU-15	1.1%
France	1.1%
Germany	0.0%
U.K.	1.0%

Source: U.S. Bureau of Labor Statistics.

FIGURE 10.6

Comparative Civilian Unemployment Rates, 2002–2004

	U.S.	CANADA	AUSTRALIA	JAPAN	FRANCE	GERMANY	ITALY	U.K.
2002	5.8	7.0	6.4	5.4	9.0	8.7	8.7	5.2
2003	6.0	6.9	6.1	5.3	9.6	9.7	8.5	5.0
2004	5.5	6.4	5.5	4.8	9.8	9.8	8.1	4.8

Source: U.S. Bureau of Labor Statistics.

Randall S. Thomas.[2] Thomas notes that commentators and the media have argued that the differences between U.S. and foreign CEO pay are the result of high agency costs or board capture:

> The international pay gap arises, the story goes, because foreign CEOs don't have the same power over their boards. In most foreign corporations, control shareholders act as strong checks on executive pay. Control shareholders will recoup most of the firm's surplus that is not paid out to the factors of production, such as CEOs, and therefore have strong financial incentives to keep executive pay abroad low. Thus, by comparison to U.S. levels, foreign CEOs are paid less.[3]

But Thomas rejects the argument. Board capture theory does not explain why U.S. executive pay grew so rapidly after the early 1980s. There is no evidence that CEOs' power over their boards grew during this time; in fact, most evidence is to the contrary. Nor does the theory explain why bigger firms pay more than smaller ones or why the supply of executives has not skyrocketed in response to the alleged huge compensation that CEOs have been receiving for the last 20 years. Furthermore, it

FIGURE 10.7

Persons Unemployed One Year or Longer
as a Percentage of Total Unemployment, 2004

U.S.	12.7%
Canada	9.5%
Japan	33.7%
EU-15	42.4%
France	41.6%
Germany	51.8%
U.K.	21.4%

Source: U.S. Bureau of Labor Statistics.

does not explain why boards pay incoming CEOs so much; after all, they have no prior relationship with the directors.[4]

Instead of the managerial power theory, Thomas offers four market-based explanations of the gap between U.S. and foreign pay levels: (1) U.S. executives' contribution to firms' value, (2) decision-making power, (3) opportunity costs, and (4) bargaining power. He concludes that international pay levels are largely determined by underlying economic forces, such as the marginal productivity of executives, the difference in alternative job prospects, and foreign companies' relatively smaller size. These factors are dictated by markets and will adjust as markets adjust.[5]

A 2006 *Wall Street Journal* article presents a balanced argument that the United Kingdom "reins in CEO compensation, as shareholders hold more sway" but wonders whether this is "overrated" and a valid model for the United States to follow.[6] The article further notes:

- There is a "brain drain" of U.K. talent because of its executive pay model.
- The United Kingdom suffers from bureaucratic corporate governance rules.
- Management buyouts are on the rise as a result of these bureaucratic rules.
- The definitions of performance-based compensation are "overly narrow" and possibly too challenging to be motivational.

We now take a closer look at executive pay practices among some major U.S. trading partners and the corporate structures and market conditions that underpin the differences in these practices.

United Kingdom

The typical components of executive pay in the United Kingdom – base salary, annual bonus, long-term incentives, and pension – are similar to those in the United States, but there are important differences: a lower level of overall remuneration; the broader use of whole shares as well as options in LTIPs; the requirement to meet performance conditions before options or whole shares can vest; and the greater influence of institutional investors such as pension funds and insurance companies.

Recent influences on executive pay packages include the requirement to account for share plans under the International Financial Reporting Standard 2 (IFRS 2). This standard – similar to FAS 123(R) – applies to all

U.K. companies listed on the London Stock Exchange, effective January 1, 2005. However, this has not yet had the dramatic effect that might have been expected.

We have not yet seen much innovation in option plan design to minimize the accounting charge, such as reducing the vesting period, indexing the exercise price, or capping the gain. Perhaps the reason for this apparent inertia is that, for many U.K. companies, the accounting charge is not that significant, particularly in the context of the other changes to their financial numbers arising from the adoption of international accounting standards.

The other aspect of share plan design for both options and LTIPs that can influence the accounting charge is the nature of the performance conditions. Market-related conditions, such as relative TRS, result in a lower initial charge, but there is no reversal of the charge even if the test is not passed and no shares vest.

On the other hand, non–market-related conditions, such as EPS targets, are likely to result in a higher initial charge, but this can be reversed if the test is not passed. It is not clear which is considered the better alternative, and many companies seem to have decided that there are more important considerations than accounting issues when determining the nature of the performance targets.

The other major external change relates to rules governing the maximum amount of pension that can be paid from a tax-approved pension plan and, in particular, the introduction of the "lifetime allowance," which sets a maximum amount on the pension that can be built up in a tax-sheltered environment. Initially, this allowance is set so that it equates to a defined-benefit pension of £75,000 per year. While there have previously been limits on the amount of tax-approved pensions that executives can build up, the new rules both simplify and extend the restrictions.

The legislative changes are coming at a time of major change in pension plan design. In particular, traditional final salary benefits are being replaced by defined-contribution plans for new hires, even at the board level. Watson Wyatt research shows that the contributions made to such plans for executives, while often higher than for the broad employee groups, are well below the level that would be necessary to replace fully the traditional two-thirds of final salary pension.

Companies are, however, often prepared to provide an alternative to a pension provision above the lifetime allowance, provided it is cost-neutral. The most common alternative is a cash allowance. The next most popular option, particularly at larger companies, is an unfunded pension promise.

This change in the level of pension provisions will have broad implications for the compensation packages of U.K. executives. Once they no longer have the cushion of knowing that they can retire on a substantial pension, they will need to accumulate wealth through other vehicles to fund a prosperous retirement. This increases the pressure on the LTIPs to deliver. It also forces companies to review the role of the pension provision in the compensation package and the level of pension to provide. Many companies have yet to address this issue.

Although U.K. companies are reducing pensions, at least for new hires, they are still increasing annual bonuses, particularly at larger companies, but in many cases these are delivered in shares that must be held for a number of years rather than as additional cash. Institutional investors are still taking a keen interest in annual bonuses. They usually look for any increase in the maximum bonus level to be accompanied by a commensurate increase in the degree of difficulty of the performance target.

Perhaps the most significant change concerns performance conditions. Historically, the vesting of stock options has been subject to an EPS growth performance test that has been set at a relatively low level, such as inflation plus 3 percent. The rationale has been to avoid rewarding executives unduly if the share price has risen but the company performance has been poor, as might happen in a bull market. But the views of investors are changing, and they are now looking for these tests to be more closely aligned with market expectations for EPS growth.

The primary performance test for LTIPs has usually been based on three-year TRS relative to a peer group rather than earnings per share growth. Relative TRS measures are still popular with institutions, and more of these tests are being applied to option plans, not just LTIPs. However, while such tests deliver alignment with shareholders, Watson Wyatt research shows that they do not provide a particularly good incentive for executives because there are too many external influences that affect the relative TRS positioning. It also could yield payouts for negative TRS, a situation that would make board members uncomfortable.

Also, because of the difficulty of selecting a peer group of a reasonable size, more companies are moving to split their LTIP, with part of the vesting dependent on the result of a relative TRS test and part based on performance against a financial metric related to value creation. These metrics can include return on equity (ROE), return on capital employed (ROCE), or economic value added (EVA). One key issue with the use of such metrics is how to set the appropriate degree of stretch in the target.

According to Watson Wyatt research, compensation for FTSE 100 executive directors declined in 2005 – largely because of increasingly demanding performance conditions imposed on their long-term incentive plans – but the average base salary and bonus continued to rise, by 9.1 percent and 29 percent, respectively.

These bonuses rewarded an average increase in profits of 20 percent in 2004. But chief executives' total compensation fell on average by 7 percent, to £2.1 million, because the value of their long-term incentives had in many cases been reduced. Similarly, the base salaries and bonuses for other FTSE 100 executive directors rose in 2005, by 7.8 percent and 22 percent, respectively, while on average their total remuneration fell by 18 percent, to £980,000.

Institutional investors may have been too tough in trying to ensure that executive pay is aligned with shareholder interests. Shareholders have understandably been keen to make sure that the long-term incentives offered to executives are paid out on their actual performance rather than fortunate market conditions. But the performance measures have in some cases reduced the real value of the incentives to the executives. The question is: Does this leave executives suitably motivated and aligned with shareholders' interests?

In summary, after a number of years marked by considerable convergence in compensation design, particularly in the areas of long-term incentives and pensions, we are now seeing increasing evidence that U.K. companies are tailoring their compensation packages to their own situations rather than simply following standard practice. Shareholders are often prepared to accept this if the rationale is carefully articulated.

In the rest of Western Europe, the pay levels are lower than in the United Kingdom, with less disclosure and fewer performance-related components. This is starting to change as the European Union begins to issue recommendations on corporate governance, including executive compensation. But in some countries, including Germany, there is continuing opposition to certain aspects of the EU's position, such as increased executive pay disclosure. In some quarters, there is concern about a move toward the Anglo-Saxon model of greater shareholder focus rather than the "stakeholder capitalism" now practiced.

But the increasing globalization of companies and their shareholders is a powerful force for change. The real question is not whether these changes will occur but how quickly.

France

The typical components of senior executives' pay in France are base salary, annual bonus, long-term incentives, and pension – similar to those in the United States. But, in France, stock options are almost the only long-term incentive vehicle, and the pay gap between the higher- and lower-level executives is less significant.

Executive compensation is a political issue for both state-owned and private companies for France's largest 40 companies (CAC 40). First, public perception of corporate governance and top executives' pay remains influenced by France's socialist, state-run approach to the economy. Privatization of large companies is a relatively recent phenomenon, and many top executives still have a public sector background. Until recently, there were even debates on whether executive pay in newly privatized companies should be fixed or capped as it was at public sector companies.

Second, France has one of the highest rates of social security contributions and income taxes in the world. The fact that stock options – mostly available to executives – are exempt from social security charges and taxed at lower rates adds political flavor to this already controversial issue.

Stock option plans, introduced in 1970 and modified in 2000 and 2004, remain the only tax-efficient selective compensation vehicle. Because these plans are subject to a compulsory four-year holding period, most companies do not include any other performance vesting conditions.

In the last couple of decades, executive compensation has steadily increased as changes in the economic and political scenes – the privatization of large companies in the 1980s and ongoing globalization – led French companies to reinforce their global presence. Companies in France increasingly compared their executive pay levels with those at other European multinationals, mainly in the United Kingdom and Germany, and even with U.S. multinationals, particularly in the pharmaceutical, luxury, and aircraft industries.

After several strikes in France in 2005, finance minister Thierry Breton introduced the New Economic Regulation Law, further tightening corporate disclosure requirements. The law requires that the board of directors present a report containing the following information: "All elements of remuneration, fixed, variable or extraordinary, paid in the accounting period, as well as any benefits awarded, including the description of the award criteria and appropriate benefit calculations."[7]

With respect to nonexecutive directors, all major companies must disclose in their annual reports the fees paid as well as the names of the beneficiaries. Nonexecutive directors cannot receive both salary and stock options. By law, they must hold shares in their company, with the number of shares set by the company's statutes.

As of 2005, annual reports must contain disclosure on pension accruals, promises for sign-in bonuses, and golden parachutes, as well as other forms of remuneration, such as perquisites.

Companies are assessing how their executive compensation packages compare with those of peer companies. Compensation committees and nonexecutive directors are expected to assume a more important role in remuneration policy. Nonexecutive directors, who propose board members' pay package, must remain independent and unbiased – a major issue for compensation committees.

Total cash compensation for the top positions in France is generally lower than in the United States and the United Kingdom but sometimes higher for the lower executive positions. Annual bonuses, which are based on company results, are roughly 100 percent of base salary for CEOs and 50 percent to 75 percent of base salary for senior executives. CEOs' performance objectives are mainly quantitative, based on the company's strategic objectives, such as acquisitions, or operating profits. Board members' quantitative objectives are linked to group operating profits and/or to business unit profits. There are often additional qualitative objectives, which are mostly managerial.

Traditionally, the focus has been on incentives such as promotion and career advancement. Turnover rates in large French companies are estimated at 1 percent to 2 percent. With the increased globalization of the French economy, top executives have begun paying close attention to their companies' market valuation to satisfy their investors and shareholders. In addition, there is increased competition for skilled employees in industries such as high tech and finance. These factors led to the introduction of performance-related compensation (i.e., variable pay).

In 2004, 80 percent of the companies listed on the CAC 40 had a formal or informal variable pay policy. The level of variable pay is increasingly linked to quantitative criteria, such as turnover, gross profit, cash flow, or decrease in expenditure, and qualitative criteria, such as strategy implementation (for example, mergers and acquisitions or management development).

Performance objectives are usually set annually. Only two CAC 40 groups set their CEO variable-pay objectives for a period of more than one year, and several groups introduced a three-year period for some of their business unit managers.

As with most social programs, ceilings or caps apply to executive pensions, which significantly reduce replacement ratios for the more highly paid individuals. For this reason, many companies use supplementary pension plans as a part of the executive pay package. Typical replacement ratio targets range from 40 percent to 60 percent of gross final salary, which corresponds to net replacement ratios ranging from 50 percent to 70 percent.

Most companies listed in France offer long-term incentive plans to their executives. Stock option plans remain the most common because of their tax efficiency; 34 of the 40 companies on the CAC 40 use them. Most plans are driven by tax rules, and awards are usually annual or regular. In some companies, grant levels are similar to those in the United Kingdom. But the value of options granted by French companies amounts to only one-fifth to one-third of that granted by their U.S. counterparts.

Restricted-share plans or performance shares are rare because of unfavorable tax treatment similar to cash compensation. Performance-linked plans are not widely used now.

We expect to see more performance conditions, new grants, or higher levels of grants linked to ownership and more midterm cash bonuses. In 2004, 5 out of the 34 CAC 40 companies with executive stock option plans reported using performance-vesting conditions.

Shareholders determine the percentage of the company's share capital that may be freely granted, up to a maximum of 10 percent; vesting and holding periods, with a minimum of two years each; and performance conditions. They vote their approval of the plan and delegate the power to implement it to the board of directors for a maximum period of 38 months.

Trends in senior executive compensation could include greater alignment of the longer-term bonuses and incentives with a company's economic cycle; setting clear added-value objectives for communication to shareholders and stakeholders; selection of peer groups/companies for benchmarking, including European, Asian, and U.S. companies, taking into account the differences in purchasing power; and more demand for independent advice from outside directors and experts. The expectations and leadership styles of the new generation of executives will probably lead to new management and compensation models.

Canada

Canada has seen more changes in executive compensation practices during the first half of this decade than in the previous two decades combined. Some of these changes are similar to those occurring in the United States, but there are significant differences:

- Canadian companies have been much more conservative in their use of stock options, even though options provide better tax treatment for executives than other forms of long-term incentives.
- The major institutional investors have formed the Canadian Coalition for Good Governance to pressure companies to improve their governance, especially in the area of executive compensation. The group is committed to ensuring that companies do a better job of linking executive pay and company performance.
- While stock option expensing has been mandatory in Canada since 2004, it has not had a major impact on the design of executive compensation programs.

Similarities with the United States include the following:

- There is significant pay-for-performance. Specifically, highly paid CEOs work for higher-performing companies.
- Compensation committees have become proactive. In the past, they primarily reacted to management's proposals and accepted the tools that management gave them to reach conclusions about compensation. The committees are increasingly retaining compensation consultants.
- The environment in which executive pay decisions are made has become more complex because of new legislative, corporate governance, and accounting requirements.
- Recent corporate scandals have affected institutional investors, who do not want the negative publicity of being associated with companies that are not following best practices in governance. These investors are happy to pay executives well for high performance but are concerned about pay for failure and want full disclosure of all elements of executive compensation. They are pushing to expand the types of

reward elements covered by disclosure rules to include retirement benefits and SERPs as well as severance benefits.

In addition, compensation committees' mandates address a broader section of human resource issues with respect to executives, such as performance appraisals, HR policies and programs, and succession planning.

The Canadian stock market represents only 3 percent of the total equity market worldwide and is dominated by the resource and financial sectors. Given the economic differences between Canada and the United States, a mid-cap company in the United States would likely be a large-cap company in Canada. At the same time, Canadian companies frequently have to compete with the U.S. market for senior executive talent.

Publicly traded Canadian organizations have come under the microscope as they face mounting shareholder and media scrutiny about their executive compensation practices. Shareholders want a more complete picture of how companies pay their executives, particularly variable pay and long-term incentives. They also want evidence that what companies pay their executives is aligned with company performance and shareholder returns.

Watson Wyatt Canada's 2005 study of the compensation of CEOs from more than 200 Toronto Stock Exchange (TSX)–listed companies shows strong links between CEO pay and company performance. The study's findings include the following:

- CEOs of high-performing companies received 31 percent more total cash compensation in 2004 than in 2003; CEOs of poor-performing companies received no increase.
- CEOs of high-performing companies received almost four times as much total actual compensation in 2004 as CEOs of poor-performing companies ($3.1 million versus $0.8 million).
- CEOs of high-performing companies in 2004 had an average 97 percent year-over-year gain in the in-the-money value of their exercisable stock options, whereas CEOs of poor-performing companies had 45 percent losses.
- Poor-performing companies are less likely than high-performing companies to pay their CEOs annual bonuses.
- Companies whose CEOs have high stock ownership outperform companies with low CEO ownership.

- Large-cap companies are responding more quickly to the pressure from major investors to use full-value share plans rather than rely solely on options for their long-term incentives.
- Large-cap companies are moving more quickly than small- and mid-cap companies to improve disclosure of their executive compensation.

All of the companies in the study have a stock option plan. But the use of stock option grants, although still prevalent, has been decreasing steadily in the last few years, and only two-thirds of the companies granted stock options to their CEOs in 2004. Nevertheless, the total value of CEOs' year-over-year long-term incentive grants has remained unchanged as restricted share units, performance share units, and stock appreciation rights grow in popularity.

Concerns about potential dilution and the relative size of stock option pools can probably explain the limited use of stock options in executive compensation in Canada in spite of their advantageous tax treatment. Option gains when realized are taxable at a rate similar to that of capital gains, whereas the share units (restricted or performance) are taxed at their fair market value.

The role of the compensation consultant has come to the fore in Canadian governance circles in the last year. For example, the Canadian Securities Administrators, a national body representing the provincial securities commissions, now requires all proxy circulars to disclose the name of the consultant used by the board of directors, together with brief descriptions of the consultant's mandate and any other services provided, in the annual report on executive compensation.

Asia

Pay for executives in Asia is highly correlated with business performance, but in a manner that is different from both the North American and the European corporate models.

Economic power in Asia is quite concentrated. Asian corporations are to a large extent controlled by families, governments, and – through interlocking networks – other corporations. Figure 10.8 shows the extent to which companies in many Asian countries are held by controlling shareholders.

Families continue to hold large controlling stakes in many Asian countries, especially Indonesia, Malaysia, Hong Kong, and Thailand. In Singapore, the state holds a substantial stake in many companies. The

FIGURE 10.8

Controlling Shareholders in Asia

COUNTRY	WIDELY HELD	CONTROLLING SHAREHOLDER			
		FAMILY	STATE	WIDELY HELD FINANCIAL	WIDELY HELD CORPORATION
Taiwan	26.2%	48.2%	2.8%	5.3%	17.4%
Hong Kong	7.0%	66.7%	1.4%	5.2%	19.8%
Indonesia	5.1%	71.5%	8.2%	2.0%	13.2%
Korea	43.2%	48.5%	1.6%	0.7%	6.1%
Malaysia	10.3%	67.2%	13.4%	2.3%	6.7%
Philippines	19.2%	44.6%	2.1%	7.5%	26.7%
Singapore	5.4%	55.4%	23.5%	4.1%	11.5%
Thailand	6.6%	61.6%	8.0%	8.6%	15.3%

Source: OECD (2003); Claessens et al. (2000); and La Porta et al. (1999).

same is true in China, where more than two-thirds of the shares listed on the Shanghai and Shenzhen stock exchanges are, in one way or another, in the hands of various organs of the state. In the Philippines, interlocking networks of corporations hold stakes in each other.

Consequently, only a small portion of company stock is widely held in Asia. These ownership structures affect how executive pay is set, with family, government, and corporate representatives on Asian boards aiming to extract excessive pay for themselves rather than for the senior management team.

A second characteristic of the Asian corporate model that influences executive pay is that central governments tend to play an important role in the economy. Unlike in Europe, where governments issue detailed regulations that provide for a social safety net, the role of governments in Asia is more supportive than regulatory, especially in the protection of national industries and the good of society.

Savings and capital accumulation are encouraged. Prices, interest rates, and currencies are kept relatively low. In Asia, the labor income disparity tends to be lower than in the U.S. corporate model. Jobs are provided for most. The unemployed are protected through elaborate social welfare plans and intricate family networks. Given the large populations, the economy is driven mainly by an increase in workers (with the notable exception of Japan) and much less by increases in productivity and efficiency.

The economies of Asia can be described as somewhat mercantilist, in contrast with the U.S. economy, which is based on entrepreneurialism,

FIGURE 10.9
Unitary and Dual Boards

Unitary Board	Separate Management Board
Hong Kong, India, Korea, Philippines, Singapore, Thailand, United Kingdom, United States	Indonesia, Germany, The Netherlands
Separate Audit Board	**Separate Audit and Management Boards**
Taiwan, China, Japan, Italy, Argentina, Brazil, Mexico	Russia, Ukraine

Source: OECD (2003).

and the European economies, which are managed according to the principles of a social contract. As a result, executive pay levels reflect an emphasis on internal equity and harmony rather than external market competitiveness.

Asian economies are dependent on the banking sector. Capital markets are not well developed, except in Hong Kong, Singapore, and, to some extent, Malaysia. Asian companies depend on bank-based financing, even though banks are not direct equity stakeholders in the companies to which they lend. Consequently, the equity markets do not have the same impact on executive performance and compensation that they do in the United States. Managerial decisions are less influenced by a diverse base of equity investors. Instead, they are co-determined by a broad but closely knit web of stakeholders.

Boards in many Asian countries show vestiges of the colonial past. Indonesia, for example, has the same dual board structure as the Netherlands, with a supervisory board and a board of management. Boards in China, Japan, and Taiwan also have a separate supervisory board, although its role is more limited and restricted to auditing.

The Chinese corporate governance model is taking on characteristics of both the Anglo-Saxon unitary board and the continental European dual-board structures, with nonexecutive directors serving on the board and representatives from both capital and labor serving on supervisory boards, similar to the supervisory boards in many European countries.

Companies in countries with legal systems rooted in Anglo-Saxon common law – Singapore, Hong Kong, Malaysia, the Philippines, and Thailand – are governed through a unitary board structure, with a large number, although not necessarily a majority, of independent directors (see Figure 10.9).

Because company structure and executive compensation vary widely in Asia, it is important to note differences in specific nations.

JAPAN

The Japanese governance structure consists of a board of directors and a board of supervisors. Shareholders have the power to appoint members to both boards at shareholder meetings. The board of directors is in charge of the daily operation of the firm. Corporate shareholders hold each other's shares, and directors are their representatives.

However, Japanese companies are facing pressure from international investors for external independent directors. A few firms, especially those with foreign investment, have adopted a more Anglo-Saxon–based system of corporate governance. The boards of these companies have outside directors and operate with a committee structure.

Nevertheless, the vast majority of companies have boards composed of inside directors. Given the large stake held by corporate shareholders, there is little need for disclosure of pay information because it is assumed that those who need such information already know it. There is limited use of stock compensation in Japan. Pay is driven more by seniority and position than by target-based performance metrics.

SINGAPORE

Even though the state is a significant shareholder in many Singaporean companies, creating long-term shareholder value is the key performance objective for many of them, including government-linked corporations.

Companies operate a unitary board, with compensation committees reviewing and approving executive compensation against market benchmarks. Many companies use a stock-based compensation program consisting not only of stock options but also restricted stock and performance shares. Executive stock ownership is encouraged.

Singapore has adopted IFRS 2, which mandates the expensing of share-based payments. The compensation committee regularly assesses the performance of executives on the basis of total returns to shareholders. Singapore leads the rest of Asia in boards with separate chairs and CEOs. The mix of pay at the median for CEOs is shown in Figure 10.10.

CHINA

China is undergoing major reform of its state-owned sector. At the same time, many entrepreneurial companies are forming, often with shareholder interests from other corporations. Companies that have listed on

FIGURE 10.10
CEO Pay Mix in Singapore

	PERCENTAGE OF TOTAL PACKAGE
Annual guaranteed cash compensation	49%
Annual incentive	18%
Fair value of stock award	33%

Source: Watson Wyatt.

overseas stock exchanges, such as the Hong Kong or New York exchanges, have adopted international market- and performance-based executive pay packages.

In the state-owned sector, pay is set administratively, not by the market. The differentials in base pay between senior and lower-level employees are small. Bonuses are often determined by complex formulas based on the company's asset size, revenue, and number of employees and bear little relation to objective performance metrics, such as profit or shareholder returns. These formulas differ from city to city. They are open to manipulation and abuse and give managers an interest in collusion with other managers.

While actual base pay may constitute only 5 percent to 10 percent of the total package, the bonuses are very large. But because these bonuses are typically based on the size of the organization and do not fluctuate widely based on performance, they could be considered part of guaranteed cash compensation. Some companies have adopted bonus programs tied to real performance, often based on incremental profits over the prior year.

Many companies have listed their shares on the Hong Kong stock exchange, either as "red chips" or as "H-shares." Red chips are companies incorporated outside of the People's Republic of China (PRC) and not governed by Chinese company law. H-share companies are incorporated in China and are held to Chinese company law.

The typical mix of pay among the five highest-paid executives at red-chip companies that grant stock options is shown in Figure 10.11.

Red-chip companies can grant stock-based compensation, typically in the form of stock options, to their PRC national employees. In fact, 83 percent of these companies grant stock options to their employees. Figure 10.12 shows the annual run rates for stock option use at these companies for reporting periods ending on June 30, 2005.

FIGURE 10.11
Executive Pay Mix at Chinese Companies

FIGURE 10.11
Executive Pay Mix at Chinese Companies

	RED CHIPS	H-SHARES
Guaranteed cash	46%	68%
Annual bonus	19%	32%
LTI value	35%	N/A

Source: Watson Wyatt.

Figures 10.13, 10.14, and 10.15 show the results of Watson Wyatt's pay and performance correlation analysis for chief executives at red-chip companies. As shown in Figure 10.13, Chinese companies listed on the Hong Kong exchange that pay high bonuses show higher two-year top-line growth. There was no correlation with ROE. Chinese companies that grant high stock awards show much better one-year TRS and a better return on equity (see Figure 10.14). Watson Wyatt research also looked at the correlation between total direct compensation (base pay, annual bonuses, and value of the long-term incentive awards) and TRS and ROE. Again there is a strong correlation between pay and performance at Chinese red-chip companies (see Figure 10.15).

HONG KONG

In the last three years, Hong Kong has introduced sweeping changes in its corporate governance regime. Many Hong Kong companies are owned by families and widely held corporations. Consequently, the regulatory regime focuses to a large extent on so-called connected transactions. The roles of chair and CEO are typically not separated.

Boards may operate with only three independent nonexecutive directors. Compensation committees, which became mandatory in fiscal year 2005, require only a majority of independent nonexecutive directors. Reporting periods and pay for directors, including executive directors, must now be disclosed on an individual, named basis, with breakdowns

FIGURE 10.12
Annual Run Rate for Red-Chip Companies

	25TH PERCENTILE	50TH PERCENTILE	75TH PERCENTILE	AVERAGE
Annual stock option run rate	0.79%	1.48%	2.19%	1.87%

Source: Watson Wyatt.

FIGURE 10.13
High Bonuses and Top-Line Growth

	BONUS (US$'000)	TWO-YEAR CAGR IN REVENUES	ONE-YEAR ROE
High	$82.1	22.33%	9.19%
Low	$0.0	19.43%	12.44%
All	$56.8	19.43%	11.50%

Source: Watson Wyatt.

for guaranteed compensation, annual bonuses, and the value of the stock awards. Stock compensation must be expensed in the profit-and-loss (P&L) statement.

The mix of pay among the five highest paid executives is shown in Figure 10.16.

Fifty-three percent of Hong Kong–listed companies grant options or other forms of stock-based compensation. Hence, employee stock awards are, in fact, somewhat less common among Hong Kong companies than among the Chinese red chips. Figure 10.17 shows the annual run rates at these Hong Kong companies for reporting periods ending June 30, 2005.

Watson Wyatt research on CEO pay and company performance at Hong Kong listed companies shows a high correlation between performance pay and company performance. Companies that pay high bonuses tend to have substantially higher top-line revenue growth and better ROE ratios than companies that pay low bonuses (see Figure 10.18). High–stock-paying companies tend to have substantially better one-year total returns to shareholders than low–stock-paying companies; they also tend to have a better ROE (see Figure 10.19).

FIGURE 10.14
High Stock Awards and TRS

	OPTION FAIR VALUE (US$'000)	ONE-YEAR TRS	ONE-YEAR ROE
High	$379.2	20.9%	14.8%
Low	$91.2	–3.3%	11.4%
All	$217.6	16.0%	12.2%

Source: Watson Wyatt.

FIGURE 10.15
Total Direct Compensation (TDC) and TRS

	TDC (US$'000)	ONE-YEAR TRS	ONE-YEAR ROE
High	$653.3	18.7%	12.1%
Low	$267.4	−1.73%	11.2%
All	$449.9	10.9%	11.5%

Source: Watson Wyatt.

FIGURE 10.16
Pay Mix for Hong Kong Executives

	COMPANIES GRANTING STOCK	COMPANIES NOT GRANTING STOCK
Annual guaranteed cash compensation	48%	69%
Annual incentive	27%	31%
Fair value of stock award	25%	

Source: Watson Wyatt.

FIGURE 10.17
Run Rates at Hong Kong Companies

	25TH PERCENTILE	50TH PERCENTILE	75TH PERCENTILE	AVERAGE
Annual stock option run rate	0.25%	1.03%	2.59%	2.13%

Source: Watson Wyatt.

FIGURE 10.18
Bonuses and Performance at Hong Kong Companies

	BONUS (US$'000)	TWO-YEAR CAGR IN REVENUES	ONE-YEAR ROE
High	$737.4	11.2%	15.3%
Low	$0.0	5.8%	10.7%
All	$271.7	9.7%	11.7%

Source: Watson Wyatt.

FIGURE 10.19
Stock Awards and Performance at Hong Kong Companies

	OPTION FAIR VALUE (US$'000)	ONE-YEAR TRS	ONE-YEAR ROE
High	$777.2	42.5%	19.6%
Low	$91.8	21.7%	12.9%
All	$290.6	23.1%	15.3%

Source: Watson Wyatt.

Throughout Asia, company ownership, the strong influence of the state and families, underdeveloped capital markets, and dual board structures in many countries affect the way executive pay is set. Pay is not set or even heavily influenced by the executives, except possibly when the CEO is also a key shareholder. Rather, pay is set by boards made up of controlling shareholders and correlates strongly with company performance.

Summary

There are many different executive pay models in the developed countries of the world. As Figure 10.20 shows, the United States has the

FIGURE 10.20
Summary Table of International Executive Pay Situations

EXECUTIVE PAY ISSUE/CONTEXT	COUNTRY					
	U.S.	CANADA	U.K.	FRANCE	JAPAN	HONG KONG
1 Shareholder power	Fragmented but growing	Strong	Strong	Medium	Weak	Medium
2 Board independence	High but controversial	High	High	High	Low	Medium
3 Executive labor market "power"	High	Medium	Medium	Low	Very low	Medium
4 Use of stock incentives	High	Medium	Medium	Low	Very low	Medium
5 Overall pay levels	Very High	Medium	Medium	Medium	Low	Low
6 Benefits perquisites	Medium/High	Medium	Medium/High	High	High	Medium
7 Regulation	Medium	High	High	High	High	High
8 Pay-for-performance	High but controversial	Medium	Medium	Medium	Medium/Low	Medium/Low

Source: Watson Wyatt.

highest pay, arguably the greatest correlation of pay with performance, and certainly the most controversial pay system. As each of these countries has a successful economy, it is difficult to be overly prescriptive about what changes they should make. However, it remains imperative that market-based economies continue to experiment with new executive compensation programs.

CONCLUSION

The Future of Executive Compensation

In the mythology that surrounds executive compensation, unchecked executives collect unearned rewards and grow rich at the expense of shareholders, employees, and the broader community. The media's fascination with renegade executives and their boards has overshadowed evidence that realizable executive pay is highly sensitive to corporate performance and that boards act decisively when financial results are unacceptable. We hope the account provided will reset the terms of the debate so that constructive discussions about executive compensation and the U.S. corporate model can flourish.

The process for setting executive pay at the vast majority of companies follows the principles of pay-for-performance and complies with the extensive set of laws and regulations governing executive pay practices and the role of the board of directors. The same force that sets pay opportunity for all Americans determines CEO pay: relatively free, if imperfect, labor markets, in which companies offer the levels of compensation necessary to attract and retain the employees who generate value for shareholders. The problem is not that CEOs receive too much performance-driven stock-based compensation but that nonexecutives receive too little.

The issue should not be the dollar amount paid to U.S. CEOs – or how that amount compares with pay levels in other countries or whether it represents high or low multiples of pay for the average worker. The first and last question must be whether the CEO creates an adequate return on the company's investment. In virtually all areas of business, boards routinely evaluate and adjust the amounts that companies invest in all resources, and shareholders directly or indirectly endorse or challenge those decisions. Executive pay is no different.

The relative scarcity of top talent is apparent to any board that has had to replace a CEO. In most pay negotiations, these vital assets use their legitimate, market-driven bargaining power to obtain pay commensurate with their skills. Boards are willing to risk millions of dollars for the right talent because properly designed pay opportunities drive superior corporate performance. And most important, numerous economists believe that the U.S. pay model is a significant source of competitive advantage for the U.S. economy, driving higher productivity, profits, and stock prices.

Companies design executive pay programs to accomplish the classic goals of any human capital program: attracting, retaining, and motivating people to perform at the highest levels. The motivational factor is crucial: It addresses the question of how a company achieves the greatest return on its human capital investment and rewards executives for making the right decisions to drive shareholder value. U.S. incentive pay and pay-at-risk programs are particularly effective, especially with high-level executives, in achieving this motivational goal.

Not every aspect of compensation links to motivation. Base salaries, pensions, and other benefits are more closely tied to basic attraction and retention and are an essential part of a portfolio that balances the need for income and security with the opportunity to create significant asset appreciation.

Pressures, including institutional investor resistance, accounting changes, SEC investigations, and scrutiny from labor unions and the media, are forcing companies to rethink their executive compensation programs, especially stock-based incentives. The key is to tackle the real problems without sacrificing the performance-based model and the huge returns it has generated. Boards are struggling to achieve greater transparency and more rigorous execution of their pay practices – a positive move for all parties. Pensions and severance plans are also under pressure and will likely decline in value over the coming years.

The real threat to economic growth, job creation, and higher living standards now comes from regulatory overreach as proponents of the executive pay mythology continue to push for government and institutional control over executive pay. To the extent that the mythology leads to a rejection of the pay-for-performance model and imposition of restrictions on the risk-and-reward structure for setting executive compensation, U.S. corporate performance will suffer.

As new regulations make it more difficult to execute the stock-based elements of the pay-for-performance model – for example, by reducing broad-based stock options – we will see less alignment between executive and rank-and-file compensation. We are already witnessing the unintended consequences of the new expensing requirement as companies cut the broad-based stock option plans that have benefited millions of workers and given them a direct stake in the financial success of the companies for which they work.

Instead of changing executive pay plans to make them more like pay plans for employees, we should be reshaping employee pay to infuse it with the same incentives that drive performance at higher levels in the company. A top-down regulatory approach to alignment will only damage the entire market-based pay setting and performance management process that has worked so well. Instead of placing artificial limits on executive pay, we should focus squarely on increasing performance incentives and stock ownership for both executive and nonexecutive employees and rewarding high performers throughout the organization.

In some ways, the negative attention focused on executive pay has increased the pressure that executives, board members, human resources staffs, and compensation consultants feel when they enter into discussions about the best methods for tying pay to performance and ensuring the success of the company. The managerial power argument has contributed to meaningful discussions about corporate governance and raised the level of dialogue in boardrooms. These are positive developments.

Nonetheless, companies must now adjust their pay practices to address new pressures and genuine problems without sacrificing their ability to reward performance and maximize value. Throughout this book, we have presented plan designs for short- and long-term incentives that are tightly tied to performance and value creation. We have also discussed the detailed metrics needed to monitor and modify these plans as the regulatory environment evolves.

In this new era of stock option expensing, the goal is to maximize value delivery – perceived and actual – for a given level of expense. This transformation from an option-centric long-term incentive strategy to a portfolio approach is well under way. The portfolio approach allows companies to accomplish multiple objectives. At a high level, a balanced program might include restricted stock to promote retention in a cost- and share-efficient manner, stock options to ensure shareholder alignment, and leveraged incentive opportunities for exceptional stock price performance, while a long-term performance plan can focus attention and rewards on key underlying drivers of shareholder value. Additionally, unlike stock options, the expense associated with a long-term performance plan can be reversed if certain performance goals are not attained.

Although stock option expensing and concerns over dilution are leading more companies to move to full-value share programs, stock options will remain a core long-term incentive for senior executives and continue to create shareholder alignment. Performance shares and vehicles that promote stock ownership will continue to increase in prevalence, as will share retention requirements.

And because increasingly aggressive actions by institutional investors and their advisers are making it more difficult for companies to get share plans approved by shareholders, we may see some companies increase their use of cash-based long-term incentive plans. Additionally, the use of share-based plans for nonmanagement employees will continue to decline. The unfortunate and unintended outcome of stock option expensing is that efforts to curtail dilution and reduce expense will reduce incentives for broad-based employee groups more than for top executives.

Amid these changes, however, aligning executive and shareholder interests remains paramount. High levels of direct executive stock ownership, especially if the executives purchase the stock, align executive and shareholder needs, and drive higher levels of stock market and financial performance. With ownership, agency costs and moral hazards decline – and company performance rises.

The market for director talent will continue to be tight, and the burden placed on boards will continue to grow. Consequently, director pay will also increase, with the transition to full-value shares accelerating. Promoting director stock ownership will be at the forefront of program design, with stock ownership guidelines and net share holding requirements becoming more common. Director pay will continue to evolve under a market-based system to ensure that top directors continue to carry out their duties in monitoring executive performance.

The compensation committee is uniquely positioned to balance executive and shareholder interests. In both new and existing executive compensation programs, the committee must design and implement executive pay in a way that balances the interests of executives and shareholders by creating excellence in corporate governance, setting the CEO's pay as rigorously as possible, and building a pay-for-performance environment.

Good governance produces pay that is commensurate with performance, provides significant stock ownership for management and the board, and protects against excessive dilution. It begins with a compensation philosophy that minimizes fixed costs and perquisites and maximizes pay-for-performance.

Setting executive compensation as rigorously as possible means collecting data from the right peer group, reviewing the pay and performance histories of the company and the CEO, determining the risk and cost of losing the CEO, and examining the strategic needs of the company. In addition, the committee must create a pay-for-performance environment that facilitates high levels of performance and ties executive compensation closely to that performance. This entails putting at least half of the executive's pay opportunity at risk. It also means generating high levels of stock ownership, with a fixed date for grants, a requirement for preannounced trading plans, limited time vesting, and no hedging. The committee must eliminate or restrict perquisites and set severance payments no higher than industry standards.

The compensation committee must also align executive pay with broader employee compensation and create superior proxy disclosure to preserve the company's reputation and meet the SEC's new requirements. Building good governance and creating a rigorous, performance-based executive compensation system is a complex and time-consuming challenge for committees in the post-Enron world. Filling boards and their compensation committees with the best talent available will help ensure success.

Resolving the real issues that surround some aspects of executive compensation will require informed discussion and a rational, market-based approach. Without this discussion, the performance-based model – and the value it has created – is in jeopardy. Those who will suffer most are the shareholders and employees who rely on the U.S. corporate model and the executives who execute it to generate investment returns and employment opportunities. The ability to move forward in a competitive global landscape is best done by those who are rewarded for the risks and challenges they undertake.

EPILOGUE

Back in the Boardroom

September 1, 2006

As the chair of the compensation committee walked into the room for the committee meeting, she felt confident that the right decisions were being made with respect to the two key compensation issues on the agenda.

Back in May, she had wondered whether the committee would ever reach agreement on changes to the stock incentive plan. At the time, senior management recommended moving away from options, which they argued had low perceived value relative to the expense and dilution they incurred. The concern of the chair was that a shift to restricted stock vesting based solely on time would subvert the committee's pay-for-performance philosophy.

She also struggled to reconcile the desire to have vertical alignment throughout the organization with the recognition that employees have various risk profiles that could warrant assorted long-term incentive-vehicle strategies. On top of that, market trends were showing that many companies were reducing participation in equity plans at lower employee levels. This was counter to the desire of the committee and senior management to promote broad-based ownership.

The other challenging issue was the new employment agreement for the CEO. The CEO was instrumental to the company's turnaround and current success, which in turn led to outside offers, so something had to be done to lock him in for the long term. But his initial suggestions – enhanced SERP benefits and restricted stock – were inconsistent with the committee's desire to align pay with performance.

Moreover, the chair wondered whether it would be appropriate to revisit provisions in the original agreement that had been necessary to induce the CEO to join the company but were perhaps less necessary going forward. Of particular concern, and a target of a shareholder proxy proposal, were severance benefits that provided three times salary and a bonus if the CEO was terminated for reasons other than cause, or in connection with a change in control, and an additional payment to compensate him for excise taxes incurred to the extent that such termination payments constituted a golden parachute under the tax code.

The chair knew that one of the keys to resolving these issues was the constructive and collaborative process that took place after the May meeting. Senior management and the committee first had to agree on guiding principles and top priorities. With the stock incentive plan, the priority was to continue to promote broad-based ownership, achieve vertical alignment throughout the organization by adhering to a common incentive platform, and differentiate awards on the basis of employee line-of-sight performance.

Based on the first objective of promoting broad-based ownership, the committee agreed to retain the broad-based employee stock purchase plan with a 15 percent discount but eliminate the look-back period and institute a three-month holding requirement. Although the holding requirement was not overly long, it communicated an ownership message to participants. The look-back period was eliminated in response to surveys showing that most employees did not perceive the value of the look-back; by eliminating it, the company reduced the plan's expense without detracting from its perceived attractiveness.

To further the ownership objective, the compensation consultant helped design a management stock purchase plan in which management could defer earned bonuses into company stock (restricted stock units) on a pretax basis. In exchange for giving up current compensation, any shares purchased by way of deferral would be matched on a one-to-two basis, providing one share for every two purchased. To promote a long-term perspective and retention, the matched shares (also restricted stock) carried sale restrictions that lapsed only if the executive remained with the company for an additional three years.

On the long-term incentive front, the committee discussed employee choice, where, up to a certain limit, employees could decide whether they would receive options or full-value shares. Ultimately, management suggested adopting a consistent platform using performance-contingent stock at all employee levels. But to meet the goal of aligning pay with line-of-sight performance, the performance conditions would be based on employee level. The more senior the employee level – and thus the greater the magnitude of impact and span of influence – the greater the weight would be on company performance.

After much exploration, the committee decided that the number of shares awarded rather than the vesting of shares should be contingent on performance. They established one-year performance goals that will determine the number of shares earned but provide that any earned awards will then be subject to a two-year vest to promote shareholder alignment and long-term retention.

Negotiating the new CEO employment agreement required more finesse. Although retaining the CEO was critical, particularly given the overtures being made by other companies, the chair did not want to sacrifice the alignment of pay with performance. Accordingly, she instructed the compensation consultant to revisit the CEO's entire employment and compensation arrangement and to think broadly when developing recommendations for the new agreement.

The consultant outlined an employment deal independent of the current arrangement. In thinking about the types of pay implicit in an employment arrangement, the consultant established three buckets. The first was characterized as service-based pay – fixed pay and benefits guaranteed as long as the CEO was employed by the company – and included base salary, full-value share awards vesting solely on the passage of time, health and welfare benefits, and perquisites.

The second bucket, event-based pay, included pay and benefits triggered by certain events. In the event of the CEO's retirement, the pay would take the form of retirement benefits, both normal and supplemental. In the event of his termination for reasons other than cause, the pay would take the form of severance benefits equal to a multiple of three times the CEO's salary and annual bonus. Finally, in the event of his termination in connection with a change in control, the pay would take the form of severance benefits equal to three times his salary and bonus, accelerated equity vesting, and an excise tax gross-up provision.

The third bucket – performance-based pay – included the annual incentive opportunity and the new performance-based stock program.

Under the committee's direction, the consultant was tasked with minimizing the size of the service- and event-based buckets and maximizing the proportion of pay in the performance-based bucket. To accomplish that and still provide a competitive package, it was necessary to restructure some of the existing service- and event-based pay arrangements so that they could flow into the performance-based bucket.

In the service-based bucket, base pay and health and welfare benefits would remain as they were, with the salary reflecting market norms and benefits consistent with those provided to all other employees. The opportunity for greater performance alignment could be accomplished by revisiting the final service-based element: restricted stock. The challenge was to adapt time-vested restricted stock to a performance-based program.

The proposed solution was to align the amount of restricted stock with performance. To do so, the consultant recommended both leveraging the recently adopted management stock purchase plan and increasing the CEO's annual bonus opportunity but requiring that the increased portion be subject to a mandatory pretax deferral into restricted stock units. In exchange, the CEO would receive a match of time-vested restricted share units, whose number would vary based on performance in the annual incentive program. The better the performance, the higher the share match. To promote a long-term perspective, any shares acquired upon vesting net of payment of taxes would be subject to a holding requirement until retirement.

In the event-based bucket, the first element to be addressed was the SERP. The committee discussed whether to freeze the current benefit accrual of the SERP and, going forward, provide annual contributions to a capital accumulation account for the CEO that would vary based on company performance. Although this has merit, the committee decided instead to replace the accrued SERP obligation with a performance-oriented vehicle with a high level of security. The committee's solution was to "buy" the CEO out of his SERP benefit obligation using restricted stock. The number of shares awarded was based on the actuarially determined present value of the obligation. The shares would vest at the time of the CEO's retirement.

Finally, the committee addressed the issue of the CEO's severance benefits with the goal of eliminating pay for failure and aligning change-in-control benefits with shareholder value. The challenge was to reconcile shareholders and institutional investors' desire to limit severance pay to a one times pay multiple with the fact that the market supported a two or three times multiple.

Although the committee considered linking the severance multiple to historical shareholder returns, in order to stay within competitive norms, it decided to retain the severance benefits as currently constituted.

On the change-in-control front, the committee was aware that shareholder advocacy groups were claiming that senior executives would be unduly enriched at the time of a change in control − primarily because of the acceleration of outstanding, unvested equity incentives. The proposed solution was to adjust the percentage of equity awards that will vest based on the premium that shareholders receive in the event of a transaction. If the premium is less than 5 percent, zero shares will have their vesting accelerate. If the premium is greater than 5 percent but less than 10 percent, 50 percent of the outstanding shares will vest. If the premium is more than 10 percent but less than 15 percent, 75 percent of the shares will vest. And if the premium is greater than 15 percent, 100 percent of the shares will vest.

After the committee's deliberation, the chair discussed the proposed arrangements with the CEO, and the CEO appreciated the challenge the committee faced in trying to balance the interests of shareholders with the retention and performance alignment of senior management. The CEO suggested implementing a share ownership guideline to allow him some flexibility in diversifying his holdings so long as the guideline is attained. The chair agreed that was a reasonable approach given how much of the CEO's wealth would now be tied up in company stock. The CEO also asked that the compensation arrangements of senior management be reviewed with respect to market competitiveness and appropriate internal equity. Knowing that the committee's job is ongoing, the chair agreed to take that up at the next meeting.

APPENDIX A

Legal and Regulatory Requirements for Executive Compensation Plans

This appendix provides an overview of the legal and regulatory requirements that apply to the executive compensation programs discussed throughout this book.

Nonqualified Stock Options

- **Overview.** Nonqualified stock options (NQSOs) can be a highly motivating employee compensation program that provides unlimited upside potential based on future stock appreciation without a company cash expenditure. NQSOs can be highly dilutive, however, and require the grantor to incur a compensation expense that may not have a corresponding tax deduction if stock does not appreciate as forecast or if options expire out-of-the-money.
- **Design.** Nonqualified stock options provide an employee or other service provider with the opportunity to buy company stock, typically at the grant-date fair market value, for a specified period of years. Ten-year terms have been typical over the years, as a legacy from the incentive stock option (ISO) rules, although companies have been considering reducing this term to seven or eight years in light of the potential expense reduction that can be realized under FAS 123(R).

Options most often include a time-based vesting schedule that requires the recipient to render continued services over a period of years. Vesting can also be based on the attainment of performance goals, although these plans are less prevalent than those with time-based vesting. Vesting schedules can be graded (e.g., 25 percent vesting per year over four years) or cliff (e.g., 100 percent vesting after four years). Other forms of vesting are allowed.

With the enactment of Internal Revenue Code Section 409A, effective January 1, 2005, NQSOs cannot be issued with an exercise (strike) price that could be less than the grant-date fair market value. Options with exercise prices that vary based on company performance are likely to become rare. Premium-priced stock options, where the exercise price is set above the grant-date strike price, are still permissible and have been granted by a few Fortune 100 companies. Section 409A permits NQSOs to be issued by private companies, but the proposed regulations have a strict set of rules to help ensure that valuations of grants are based on true indicators of fair market value.

Nonqualified stock options are typically granted so that the recipient can cover the exercise price from one of three sources: paying cash from personal holdings; turning in existing stock holdings whose fair market value at the exercise date covers the exercise price; or by a cashless (net) exercise. In a cashless exercise, either the company or a third-party broker lends the participant the exercise price, which is immediately or soon thereafter paid back through a sale of shares received via the exercise. Under this transaction, the recipient receives the net proceeds of the transaction in stock after shares are sold to cover the exercise price and tax withholding.

- **Payment timing**. The employee can exercise at any time after vesting and before expiration.
- **Accounting treatment under FAS 123(R)**. The grant-date fair value is charged to earnings over the service (vesting) period for time-vested options. The initial expense calculation can be made using any reasonable methodology, the two most common being Black–Scholes and a lattice-based approach. Anticipated forfeitures can be factored into the initial calculation, with future forfeitures taken into account as adjustments in later reporting periods.

The anticipated tax deduction will be taken into account based on forecast stock appreciation until the exercise date. For performance-vested options, an expense is recorded during the reporting period only if the attainment of goals is forecast as "probable" by the end of the service period. If it is not probable, the expense would be reversed in that reporting period. However, if the performance condition is tied to the market performance of the company's stock, the expense first determined at the grant date cannot be reversed in a later reporting period, even though the goal will not be attained.

- **Dilutive impact**. Options are relatively more consumptive of issued shares than other types of grants because more shares are necessary to deliver desired value through appreciation. Performance-vested options can be even more consumptive, as more options are granted to cover the risk that goals may not be attained. They also have a relatively high impact in determining dilutive earnings per share (EPS) under the treasury stock method because all options, rather than the forecast net settlement after payment of taxes and exercise price, are considered outstanding. Institutional Shareholder Services (ISS) will calculate a company's "burn rate" as the total number of equity awards (in the form of stock awards and stock options) granted in any given year divided by the number of common shares outstanding. The gross number of equity awards is considered in the burn rate calculation and is not discounted by tendered shares in payment of an option, shares withheld for taxes, or added back shares repurchased by the company using the option proceeds.
- **Employee tax impact**. At exercise, the employee incurs ordinary income tax for the difference between the exercise-date fair market value and the strike price (the spread). Future share sales will be at favorable long-term capital gains rates if sold more than one year after the date of exercise.
- **Company tax impact**. A tax deduction is available for the spread at exercise. The $1 million pay cap of IRC Section 162(m) ought not to apply to option grants, which are inherently performance-based, assuming the shareholder approval and compensation committee composition requirements of Section 162(m) have been met. The company must report the amount includible in the employee's income on a Form W-2 to sustain the tax deduction. There will be a mismatch between the tax deduction and accounting expense.
- **Shareholder approval**. Stock option plans generally must be approved by shareholders, with the number of shares to be issued under the plan, under both NYSE and NASDAQ rules. Most often, the plan authorizes the board or the compensation committee to have the discretion to issue options to designated employees with an appropriate exercise price, vesting schedule, option term, and exercise mechanism. Only future changes made to the plan that would rise to the level of a material revision (NYSE) or material amendment (NASDAQ) need be resubmitted for shareholder vote.
- **Proxy disclosures**. Beginning with the 2007 proxy statement, option and stock appreciation right (SAR) grants to the company's named

executive officers (NEOs) – the three highest-paid executives, the CEO, and the CFO – must be disclosed in several places on the company proxy. Option grants appear in the Summary Compensation table based on their FAS 123(R) value. Thus, for example, a time-vested option that would be expensed over the vesting period for financial statement purposes would be disclosed over the vesting schedule, although forfeitures are not factored in until they actually occur. All option and SAR grants also appear in a new Grant of Plan-Based Awards table that provides backup details on the number of grants, exercise price, and vesting schedule. Outstanding and unexercised options and SARs are shown in a new Outstanding Equity Awards at Fiscal Year-End table, while options and SARs exercised are shown in the Option Exercises and Stock Vested table.

- **Retentive power**. The retentive power is strong during the vesting period as the value of the company's stock is rising but is weak in a declining price environment. Underwater options, where the strike price is above the market value, are a demotivator.
- **Performance focus**. The plans have a strong focus with time-vested options based on stock price appreciation and a very strong focus with the addition of performance goals for vesting.
- **Alignment with shareholder interests**. There is strong alignment as the value of the company's stock is rising but a disconnect when the stock price is falling. Overall dilution/overhang levels must be within industry norms to retain the perception of alignment.

Incentive Stock Options

- **Overview**. Incentive stock options (ISOs) have the same attributes as NQSOs but can provide favorable tax treatment to the recipients. By providing ISOs to participants, the company will forgo a tax deduction on the portion of the ISO that qualifies for favorable employee tax treatment.
- **Design**. Same as with NQSOs.
- **Payment timing**. Same as with NQSOs.
- **Accounting treatment under FAS 123(R)**. Same as with NQSOs.
- **Dilutive impact**. Same as with NQSOs.
- **Employee tax impact**. Incentive stock options permit favorable tax treatment to employees on the first $100,000 in stock value (measured at the grant date) on underlying grants that vest in any year. Favorable tax treatment means that there is no tax at the date of exercise and capital gains treatment at the sale of the stock if it is held at least

two years from when the option was granted and at least one year after the option was exercised. Where the holding requirements are not met, the gain is treated as ordinary income. Alternative Minimum Tax (AMT) treatment may apply, however, for certain ISO option exercises. Incentive stock option treatment is available only if the exercise price is no less than fair market value.

- **Company tax impact**. The company receives no tax deduction at option exercise. A tax deduction is available if the holding period requirements are not met, but only to the extent the company reports this amount on an employee's Form W-2.
- **Shareholder approval**. In addition to the requirements under the NYSE and NASDAQ rules for approval of stock plans applicable to NQSOs, ISO plans must also be approved by shareholders within 12 months of an initial grant under the plan to receive favorable tax treatment.
- **Proxy disclosures**. Same as with NQSOs.
- **Retentive power**. Same as with NQSOs.
- **Performance focus**. Same as with NQSOs.
- **Alignment with shareholder interests**. Same as with NQSOs.

Stock Appreciation Rights

- **Overview**. Stock appreciation rights (SARs) are similar to NQSOs in providing unlimited upside potential on future stock price appreciation but differ in that they are most often settled in cash. Traditionally, cash-settled SARs have been used by companies that wish to avoid additional dilution or are not willing to share equity grants with their employees, even though a variable liability must be recorded for the cash obligation. With the advent of FAS 123(R), we expect that more companies will use stock-settled SARs in lieu of stock option grants. Both grants would require that an expense be recorded; however, stock-settled SARs would be less dilutive than option grants.
- **Design**. Traditionally, SARs have been designed to provide an employee or other service provider with the opportunity to receive a cash equivalent of the increase in value of a company's stock, based on the difference between the fair market value at exercise and the grant-date fair market value, net of taxes. They are unusual in the cash-based compensation world because they are the only vehicle where the employee can decide when to exercise his or her right to receive cash. All other cash-based compensation forms are paid based on preset distribution timing schedules.

Stock appreciation rights typically include a vesting schedule and often are issued for a specified period of years. Ten-year terms have been typical over the years, although companies have been considering reducing this term with the advent of FAS 123(R). Vesting can also be based on attainment of performance goals, although these plans are less prevalent than those with time-based vesting. As with options, vesting schedules can be graded (e.g., 25 percent vesting per year over four years) or cliff (e.g., 100 percent vesting after four years).

With the enactment of IRC Section 409A, effective January 1, 2005, SARs cannot be issued at a discount, so their value cannot be measured at less than the grant-date fair market value. Section 409A permits SARs to be issued by private companies, but the proposed regulations have a strict set of rules to help ensure that valuations of SAR grants are based on true indicators of fair market value.

Stock appreciation rights are typically granted so that the recipient receives the net proceeds of the underlying stock appreciation at exercise, after the company withholds the appropriate taxes from the proceeds. They are sometimes issued in tandem with NQSOs as an instrument to help cover the cash needs for a participant to exercise the options and cover any applicable taxes. Increasing in popularity are stock-settled SARs, whereby the net settlement proceeds are converted to shares. Although this program incurs the same accounting expense as an option program, it can be less dilutive because only the net shares delivered are considered outstanding under the Treasury method of counting outstanding shares.

- **Payment timing**. The employee can exercise at any time after vesting and before expiration.
- **Accounting treatment under FAS 123(R)**. Stock-settled SARs with time vesting are treated the same as options. The grant-date fair value is charged to earnings over the service (vesting) period. The initial expense calculation can be made using any reasonable methodology, the two most common being Black–Scholes and a lattice-based approach. Anticipated forfeitures can be factored into the initial calculation, with future forfeitures taken into account as adjustments in later reporting periods. The anticipated tax deduction will be taken into account based on forecast stock appreciation until the exercise date.

For performance-vested, stock-settled SARs, an expense is recorded during the reporting period only if the attainment of goals by the end of the service period is forecast as probable. If it is not probable, the expense would be reversed in that reporting period. However, if the performance condition is tied to the market performance of the company's stock, the expense first determined at the grant date cannot be reversed in a later reporting period, even though the goal will not be attained.

Cash-settled SARs are recorded as a liability on a mark-to-market basis, amortized over the vesting period. This means the liability will increase or decrease based on periodic fluctuations in the stock price, a concept traditionally referred to as variable accounting. This treatment contrasts with that of stock-settled SARs, where the expense is fixed based on the grant-date fair value and will not vary once the initial expense is determined over the service period.

- **Dilutive impact**. Stock-settled SARs are less consumptive than equivalent options, as only the forecast net-settled shares are used in determining dilutive EPS. Cash-settled SARs are nonconsumptive. Unless a plan requires SARs to be settled in cash, ISS will value SARs where there is discretion to settle in cash or stock as full-value awards when calculating the burn rate.
- **Employee tax impact**. At exercise, the employee is taxed at ordinary income rates on the difference between the exercise-date fair market value and the grant-date price. For stock-settled SARs, future share sales will be at favorable long-term capital gains rates if sold more than one year after the date of exercise.
- **Company tax impact**. The company receives a tax deduction for the income recognized by the employee at exercise. The $1 million pay cap under Section 162(m) ought not to apply to SAR grants, which are inherently performance-based, assuming that the shareholder approval and compensation committee composition requirements of Section 162(m) have been met. There will be a mismatch between the tax deduction and accounting expense.
- **Shareholder approval**. Cash-settled SARs are not required to be approved by shareholders. However, because SARs are often granted under broader equity plans that authorize the grant of options or SARs, these programs are often approved by shareholders. A stock-settled SAR program requires approval by shareholders, with the number of shares to be issued under the plan, under both NYSE and NASDAQ rules.

Most often, the plan authorizes the board or the compensation committee to have the discretion to issue options or SARs to designated employees, with an appropriate exercise price, vesting schedule, term, and exercise mechanism. Only future changes made to the plan that would rise to the level of a material revision (NYSE) or material amendment (NASDAQ) need be resubmitted for shareholder vote.

- **Proxy disclosures**. Proxy disclosure for SARs is the same as for stock options.
- **Retentive power**, Retentive power is strong during the vesting period as the value of the company's stock is rising but is weak in a declining price environment. Underwater SARs, where the grant price is above the market value, are a demotivator.
- **Performance focus**. Stock appreciation rights have a strong performance focus, regardless of whether they are stock- or cash-settled.
- **Alignment with shareholder interests**. Stock appreciation rights provide strong alignment as the value of the company's stock is rising but a disconnect when the stock price is falling. Overall dilution/overhang levels for stock-settled SARs are less of a concern than with options but still must be within industry norms to retain the perception of alignment.

Restricted Stock Units

- **Overview**. Restricted stock units (RSUs) are similar to restricted stock in providing the full value of employer stock to the employee but are more flexible in providing the opportunity for continued tax deferral beyond the initial vesting date. They can be settled in cash or stock, depending on how the company views their dilutive effect and the company's desire to share equity grants with employees. If settled in cash, the company must record a liability for the variable cost of the cash obligation.
- **Design**. Historically, RSUs were created to provide an employee or other service provider with the opportunity to receive a cash equivalent in company stock at a future vesting date. As RSUs became more commonplace, and companies better understood that they were subject to the tax rules governing deferred compensation, many companies adopted them in lieu of restricted stock to give their employees more flexibility as to when they would recognize taxable income, with the same fixed accounting treatment as restricted stock. Most equity programs now are drafted to permit issuance of RSUs or restricted stock, although we are seeing far more companies issuing stock-settled RSUs.

Cash-settled RSUs provide less favorable variable accounting treatment for public companies and for this reason tend not to be used by them. Restricted stock units are typically granted so that the recipient receives the net proceeds of the underlying stock value at the payment date, after the company withholds the appropriate taxes from the proceeds. They can provide the employee with dividend equivalent units (DEUs) that can be paid in cash currently or paid at the distribution date of the underlying RSUs. Like RSUs themselves, DEUs can be paid in cash or settled in stock.

As with restricted stock, vesting can be time-based or based on the attainment of performance goals. As with options, vesting schedules can be graded (e.g., 25 percent vesting per year over four years) or cliff (e.g., 100 percent vesting after four years).

As noted earlier, the real advantage of RSUs is the ability of employees to defer delivery and taxation beyond the original vesting date. With the enactment of IRC Section 409A, effective January 1, 2005, deferral elections for RSUs must be made on a timely basis to properly defer taxation. For time-vested RSUs, a delayed distribution date must be elected at least 12 months before the date when the RSU would otherwise vest. For performance-vested RSUs, a delayed distribution date must be elected at least six months before the end of the performance period. The distribution can be delayed until any future date, depending on the employee's desire and the plan's design.

- **Payment timing**. Proceeds (stock or cash) from RSUs are paid at the vesting date. Those that include a deferral feature are paid at the previously elected distribution date.
- **Accounting treatment under FAS 123(R)**. Stock-settled RSUs with time vesting are treated in the same way as restricted stock. Grant-date fair value (based on the quoted market price on the grant date for public companies) is charged to earnings over the service (vesting) period. No additional expense is recorded if the payment date is delayed; only the vesting schedule is relevant in determining the period during which the expense is amortized. Anticipated forfeitures can be factored into the initial calculation, with future forfeitures taken into account as adjustments in later reporting periods. The anticipated tax deduction will be taken into account based on forecast stock appreciation until the exercise date.

For performance-vested, stock-settled RSUs, an expense is recorded during the reporting period only if the attainment of goals is forecast as probable by the end of the service period. If it is not probable, the expense would be reversed in that reporting period. However, if the performance condition is tied to the market performance of the company's stock, the expense first determined at the grant date cannot be reversed in a later reporting period, even though the goal will not be attained.

Cash-settled RSUs are recorded as a liability on a mark-to-market basis, amortized over the vesting period. This means the liability will increase or decrease based on periodic fluctuations in the stock price, a concept traditionally referred to as variable accounting. This treatment contrasts with that of stock-settled RSUs with time vesting, where the expense is fixed based on the grant-date fair value and will not vary once the initial expense is determined over the service period.

- **Dilutive impact**. Stock-settled RSUs are less consumptive than options or SARs because fewer full-value shares are needed to deliver the desired expected value. Cash-settled RSUs are nonconsumptive. In calculating the burn rate, ISS will apply a premium on stock-settled RSUs to equalize their value against stock options based on the different annual stock volatilities of companies. The premium ranges from 1 RSU as equivalent to 1.5 option shares for high-volatility companies to 1 RSU as equivalent to 4 option shares for low-volatility companies.
- **Employee tax impact**. Despite the added complexity brought forth by IRC Section 409A, the tax consequences upon payout of RSUs are fairly straightforward. The participant will have ordinary income on the fair market value of the stock at the date of payment. For RSUs with a deferred payment date, FICA taxation will take place at the date of vesting.

Restricted stock units are considered nonqualified deferred compensation under Section 409A. If RSUs are paid out immediately at vesting, the plan automatically meets Section 409A requirements. If the plan delays payment until a fixed date in the future, the plan also will automatically meet Section 409A requirements. If the employee can elect his or her payment date beyond the vesting date, generally this election must be in place before the date the RSU is granted, with limited exceptions for performance-based compensation. However, Section 409A would be violated if an employee could make a deferred-payment election after the RSU was granted.

It must be noted that if the Section 409A rules are not met, participants may be taxed as of the earlier of the date when the compensation otherwise would have been paid or the date when the RSUs become fully vested. There is also a penalty for this failure of an additional 20 percent tax on top of the early-income inclusion.

Dividend equivalent units will typically be retained under the plan and either reinvested in additional RSUs or paid in cash at the RSU distribution date. Under either alternative, there will be no current tax consequences from DEUs credited until paid. Whether paid in additional RSUs or cash, these amounts are taxed as ordinary compensation income when distributed. To meet the requirements of Section 409A, DEUs must be distributed at the same time and in the same manner as the underlying RSUs.

- **Company tax impact**. The company receives a tax deduction for the income recognized by the employee at payment. The $1 million pay cap of IRC Section 162(m) would apply to time-vested RSUs at the payment date. Performance-vested RSUs are not to be subject to Section 162(m), assuming the shareholder approval and compensation committee composition requirements of Section 162(m) have been met. There will be a mismatch between the tax deduction and accounting expense.
- **Shareholder approval**. Cash-settled RSU plans are not required to be approved by shareholders. However, because RSUs are often granted under broader equity plans that authorize the granting of restricted stock or RSUs, these programs are often approved by shareholders. A stock-settled RSU program will be required to be approved by shareholders, with the number of shares to be issued under the plan, under both NYSE and NASDAQ rules.

Most often, the plan authorizes the board or the compensation committee to have the discretion to issue restricted stock or RSUs to designated employees, with an appropriate vesting schedule and term and subject to payment deferrals. Only future changes made to the plan that would rise to the level of a material revision (NYSE) or material amendment (NASDAQ) need be resubmitted for a shareholder vote.

- **Proxy disclosures**. Beginning with the 2007 proxy statement, restricted stock and RSUs granted to NEOs, the CEO, and the CFO must be disclosed in several places on the company proxy. Grants appear on the Summary Compensation table based on their grant-date fair market value over the vesting schedule, although forfeitures are not factored in until they actually occur. For example, a time-vested RSU expensed over the vesting period for financial statement purposes would be disclosed the same way on the proxy. All restricted stock and RSUs also appear on a new Grant of Plan-Based Awards table that provides backup details on the number of grants, grant-date value, vesting schedule, and estimated future payouts for performance-vested grants. Unvested restricted stock and RSUs are shown on a new Outstanding Equity Awards at Fiscal Year-End table, while restricted stock and RSUs that vest during the year are shown in the Option Exercises and Stock Vested table. Restricted stock units whose settlement date is delayed until the future will be disclosed on the Non-qualified Deferred Compensation table along with all other deferred compensation.

- **Retentive power**. For time-vested RSUs, the retentive power is strong during the vesting period. For performance-vested RSUs, it is strong during the restriction period if goals are being achieved but substantially weaker if goals are unlikely to be achieved.
- **Performance focus**. The performance focus is weak if RSUs are time-vested but is strong if the plan calls for performance-based vesting.
- **Alignment with shareholder interests**. For stock-settled RSUs, there is strong alignment when the stock price is rising but a disconnect when the stock price is falling. For cash-settled RSUs, alignment is relatively weaker. Overall dilution/overhang levels for stock-settled RSUs are usually of minimal concern.

Restricted Stock

- **Overview**. Restricted stock (RS) is a grant of stock to the employee that includes a substantial risk of forfeiture until service- and/or performance-vesting criteria are met. Actual stock certificates are often issued at grant, although the certificate includes a legend that details the conditions under which the share will be forfeited. Most companies hold the shares in escrow until vesting to make it easier to administer the program. Employees can make what is known as an 83(b) election, whereby they agree to take into income the value of the RS at grant-date fair market value, even though they risk forfeiting the share. Employees may choose to make an 83(b) election in a rising stock price environment, thereby avoiding a higher tax hit at the later vesting date.
- **Design**. Restricted stock provides employees with the right to earn company stock at a future vesting date. It is typically granted so the recipient receives the net proceeds of the underlying stock value at

the vesting date, after the company withholds the appropriate taxes from the proceeds. Restricted stock can provide the employee with dividends and voting rights prior to vesting, or it can retain dividends to be paid at the vesting date. Vesting can be time-based or based on attainment of performance goals. As with options, vesting schedules can be graded (e.g., 25 percent vesting per year over four years) or cliff (e.g., 100 percent vesting after four years).

- **Payment timing**. Although RS is considered to be transferred to the employee at the grant date, true payment does not occur until the vesting date, at which time the employee can transfer or sell the share.
- **Accounting treatment under FAS 123(R)**. Restricted stock is treated in the same manner as stock-settled RSUs.
- **Dilutive impact**. Restricted stock is less consumptive than options or SARs because fewer full-value shares are needed to deliver the desired expected value. In calculating the burn rate, ISS will apply a premium on stock-settled RSUs to equalize their value against stock options based on the different annual stock volatilities of companies. The premium ranges from 1 RSU as equivalent to 1.5 option shares for high-volatility companies to 1 RSU as equivalent to 4 option shares for low-volatility companies.
- **Employee tax impact**. Restricted stock is taxed at the date of vesting – the date when restrictions lapse – or the date it becomes freely transferable, whichever is earlier. The full value of the RS is includible in income on this date unless a prior 83(b) election has been made. If an 83(b) election is made, the value of the RS at grant-date fair market value is taken into income, even though the risk of forfeiting the share remains.

If dividends are paid on RS before vesting, they are taxed as ordinary compensation income. Dividends retained and paid at the vesting of the underlying stock also are taxed as ordinary income.

- **Company tax impact**. The company receives a tax deduction for the income recognized by the employee at vesting. The $1 million pay cap of IRC Section 162(m) would apply to time-vested RSUs at the payment date. Performance-vested RS is not to be subject to Section 162(m), assuming that the shareholder approval and compensation committee composition requirements of Section 162(m) have been met. There will be a mismatch between the tax deduction and accounting expense.

- **Shareholder approval**. Restricted stock programs, with the number of shares to be issued under the plan, must be approved under both NYSE and NASDAQ rules. Most often, the plan gives the board or the compensation committee the discretion to issue the equity instruments it deems appropriate to the employees it determines, with an appropriate vesting schedule and term and subject to payment deferrals. Only future changes made to the plan that would rise to the level of a material revision (NYSE) or material amendment (NASDAQ) need be resubmitted for a shareholder vote.
- **Proxy disclosures**. Restricted stock is disclosed on the proxy in the same manner as stock-settled RSUs.
- **Retentive power**. For time-vested RS, the retentive power is strong during the vesting period. For performance-vested RS, it is strong during the restriction period if goals are being achieved but is substantially weaker if goals are unlikely to be achieved.
- **Performance focus**. The performance focus is weak if shares are time-vested but strong if the plan calls for performance-based vesting.
- **Alignment with shareholder interests**. There is strong alignment when the stock price is rising but a disconnect when the stock price is falling. Overall dilution/overhang levels for RS are usually of minimal concern.

Summary of the Regulatory and Institutional Mandates and Recommendations

This appendix summarizes the corporate governance mandates and recommendations of large institutional investors and the organizations that advise these investors. The items, drawn from the organizations' Web sites, are restricted to issues pertaining to executive compensation.

CalPERS

The California Public Employees' Retirement System (CalPERS) manages pension and health benefits for more than 1.4 million California public employees, retirees, and their families. CalPERS has embarked on a sweeping executive compensation reform initiative, the principal elements of which include the following:

- Submitting to the SEC a comprehensive proposal for increased disclosure related to executive compensation in 2005;
- Advocating the enhancement of exchange listing standards that incorporate compensation philosophy and practice to better align boards and management of listed companies with shareowners;
- Engaging and communicating investors' compensation program preferences to the compensation consulting industry;
- Waging a visible shareowner campaign against the largest companies that refuse to implement CalPERS' executive compensation model, focusing on directors sitting on compensation committees that can be reasonably linked to approving poor executive compensation packages and policies.

CalPERS also evaluates these criteria:

- Compensation committee members who sit on multiple boards that exhibit a weak link between executive compensation and economic performance.
- Egregious use of severance packages related to mergers, acquisitions, and spin-offs, including the use of single-trigger accelerated equity vesting and the use of excise tax gross-ups.
- High percentages of negative votes for equity plan approval in recent years. Low levels of support may be an indication of investor concern over the compensation practices.
- Companies with the highest levels of total equity dilution and the highest run rates (equity granted per year divided by total shares outstanding).
- Companies that use broad-based plans with grant patterns that indicate excessive distribution of equity grants to the top five executives.
- Compensation committees with the greatest percentage of sitting and retired CEOs to determine if there is a correlation with poor pay-for-performance characteristics.

The CalPERS plan also includes a provision for recognizing "pay-for-performance leaders." This entails compiling examples of superior pay-for-performance practices and significant improvements in compensation plans.

TIAA–CREF

The Teachers Insurance and Annuity Association–College Retirement Equities Fund (TIAA–CREF) is a long-term investor in the U.S. and international equity markets. Its statement on executive compensation includes many points, the most notable of which are the following:

- Equity-based plans should emphasize restricted stock awards. Restricted stock (as opposed to option grants) more closely aligns the interests of executives and shareholders, and the value to the recipient and cost to the corporation can be determined easily and tracked continuously.
- When stock options are awarded, a company should develop plans for performance-based options, which set performance hurdles to achieve vesting; premium options, with vesting dependent on attainment of a predetermined appreciation of stock; and/or indexed options, with a strike price tied to an index.

- Companies should also require that stock obtained through the exercise of options be held for substantial periods of time, apart from sales permitted to meet tax liabilities produced by such exercise.
- Executive pension plans should provide retirement income formulas that are comparable (as a percentage of final average pay) with those of employees throughout the organization. Supplemental executive retirement plans (SERPs) may be used to supplement a "qualified" pension entitlement to allow this total to be achieved; however, SERPs should not be used to enhance retirement benefits beyond what is reasonable.

Fidelity

Fidelity Investments is the largest mutual fund company in the United States, with approximately 360 funds and 19 million shareholders. While it evaluates plans on a case-by-case basis, the guidelines generally call for withholding its vote for plans or plan amendments that do not meet the following conditions:

- The dilution effect of new shares authorized, plus the shares reserved for issuance in connection with all other stock-related plans, should not exceed 10 percent. However, for companies with a smaller market capitalization, the dilution effect should not exceed 15 percent. If the plan does not meet this test, the dilution effect is also evaluated in light of any unusual factors involving the company.
- The minimum exercise price of stock options should be no less than 100 percent of fair market value on the date of grant.
- Neither the board of directors nor its compensation committee should be authorized to materially amend a plan without shareholder approval.
- The plan should not authorize the repricing of stock options (including the cancellation and exchange of options) without shareholder approval.
- The restriction period for restricted stock awards (RSAs) normally should be at least three years. Restricted stock awards with a restriction period of less than three years, but at least one year, might be acceptable if the RSA is performance-based.

Fidelity's guidelines also oppose the use of employment contracts that will result in cash grants of more than three times annual compensation (salary and bonus) in the event of termination of employment following a change in control of a company. In general, the guidelines call for voting against such golden parachute plans "because they impede potential takeovers that shareholders should be free to consider." Adoption of such golden parachutes generally will result in withholding of the Fidelity funds' votes for directors who approve such contracts and stand for reelection at the next shareholder meeting.

Vanguard

Vanguard Group had total assets of $750 billion in U.S. mutual funds as of September 13, 2004, with 18 million institutional and individual shareholder accounts. Vanguard's proxy voting guidelines with respect to stock-based compensation plans regard the following favorably:

- stock ownership guidelines and/or net share retention requirements;
- stock awards that vest based on performance; and
- broad-based stock option plans.

Factors that could result in nonapproval include:

- total potential dilution (including all stock-based plans) exceeds 15 percent of shares outstanding;
- annual option grants have exceeded 2 percent of shares outstanding; and/or
- plans that permit repricing without shareholder approval, provide for the issuance of reload options, and/or contain an automatic share replenishment ("evergreen") feature.

Vanguard also maintains voting guidelines for executive severance agreements. Severance benefits triggered by a change in control that do not exceed three times an executive's salary and bonus may generally be approved by the compensation committee of the board without submission to shareholders. Any such arrangement under which the beneficiary receives more than three times salary and bonus – or where severance is guaranteed absent a change in control – should be submitted for shareholder approval.

Union-Sponsored Funds

According to the AFL-CIO, union-sponsored funds submitted 43 percent of the corporate governance proposals voted on in 2004; 40 percent of these focused on executive compensation. The AFL-CIO's proxy voting guidelines include the following elements:

- Long-term incentive compensation should constitute more than 50 percent of an executive's total compensation.
- Executive compensation policies and plans should be created by fully independent directors – with the assistance of independent compensation consultants – and approved by shareholders.
- Use of fixed-price stock options to compensate executives is detrimental to the corporation and its shareholders. The trustees support performance-based alternatives to stock options, such as long-term incentive plans and performance-vesting restricted stock.
- Stock option plans dilute the earnings and voting power of shares outstanding. A vote should be cast against any proposal if total dilution of either outstanding voting power or outstanding shareholder equity is more than 10 percent.
- Equity compensation plans should not exceed an annual stock option grant rate of one percent of shares outstanding to senior executives. The voting fiduciary should also oppose plans that reserve a specified percentage of outstanding shares for award each year (an evergreen plan) instead of having a termination date.
- The voting fiduciary should generally oppose plans if a significant proportion (e.g., more than 10 percent) of option shares granted the previous year were issued to the top five executives.
- Executives should be required to hold a substantial portion of their equity compensation awards, including shares received from option exercises (e.g., 75 percent of their after-tax stock option proceeds), while they remain at a company.
- The voting fiduciary should support the use of performance-vesting restricted stock so long as the absolute amount of restricted stock being granted is a reasonable proportion of an executive's overall compensation.

Examples of union-sponsored shareholder proposals abound. The AFL-CIO Reserve Fund proposed that Wal-Mart adopt a policy that a significant portion of future equity compensation grants to senior executives would not vest until performance goals were achieved. The American Federation of State, County and Municipal Employees Fund proposed that Amgen, Inc., adopt a policy requiring that senior executives retain a significant percentage of shares acquired through equity compensation programs during their employment and that the committee not adopt a percentage lower than 75 percent of net after-tax shares. In another shareholder action, the International Brotherhood of Teamsters proposed that Coca-Cola seek shareholder approval for future severance agreements that provide benefits exceeding 2.99 times the sum of the executive's base salary and bonus.

Other Organizations

Executive compensation is also the focus of other organizations that have the potential to influence shareholders and policymakers. These organizations have stepped up their efforts to monitor and influence executive compensation policies in recent years. Descriptions of the major organizations follow.

THE COUNCIL OF INSTITUTIONAL INVESTORS

The Council of Institutional Investors is an organization of large public, labor, and corporate pension funds. Its stated goal is to encourage member funds, as major shareholders, to take an active role in protecting plan assets and to help members increase the return on their investments as part of their fiduciary obligations. Founded in 1985 in response to controversial takeover activities, the group now has more than 140 pension fund members, whose combined assets exceed $3 trillion, and more than 130 educational sustainers. It is recognized as a significant voice for institutional shareholder interests.

The council's corporate governance policies include a detailed policy statement on all aspects of executive compensation. The policy endorses pay-for-performance but with an explicit warning about excessive pay:

> While the Council believes that executives should be well paid for superior performance, it also believes that executives should not be excessively paid. It is the job of the board of directors and the compensation committee to ensure that executive compensation programs are effective, reasonable and rational with respect to critical factors such as company performance, industry considerations and compensation paid to other employees inside the company.

The council's specific policies on executive compensation include the following:

- Compensation programs should not be driven by competitive surveys, which have become excessive and subject to abuse.
- Compensation of the executive oversight group should be driven predominantly by performance. Performance measures applicable to all performance-based awards (including annual and long-term incentive compensation) should reward superior performance – based

predominantly on total stock return measures and key operational measures – at minimum reasonable cost and should reflect downside risk.

- The compensation committee should understand all components of executive compensation and annually review total compensation potentially payable to the oversight group under all possible scenarios, including death/disability, retirement, voluntary termination, termination with and without cause and changes of control.

- The compensation committee should retain and fire outside experts, including consultants, legal advisers and any other advisers when it deems appropriate, including when negotiating contracts with executives. Compensation advisers should be independent of the company, its executives and directors and should report solely to the committee. Use of outside compensation consulting firms retained by the compensation committee should be disclosed, along with the compensation committee's assessment of the advisers' independence and a description of other business performed for the company.

- Since salary is one of the few components of executive compensation that is not "at risk," it should be set at a level that yields the highest value for the company at the least cost. In general, salary should be set to reflect responsibilities, tenure and past performance, and to be tax-efficient – meaning no more than $1 million.

- Meaningful performance periods and/or cliff vesting requirements – consistent with a company's investment horizon, but no less than three years – should attach to all long-term incentive awards, followed by pro rata vesting over at least two subsequent years for senior executives.

- Except in extraordinary circumstances, such as a permanent change in performance cycles, long-term incentive awards should be granted at the same time each year.

- Stock option prices should be indexed to peer groups, performance vesting and/or premium-priced to reward superior performance based on the attainment of challenging quantitative goals.

- Dividend equivalents: To ensure that executives are neutral between dividends and stock price appreciation, dividend equivalents should be granted with stock options, but distributed only upon exercise of the option.

- Stock awards should be linked to the attainment of specified performance goals and in some cases to additional time-vesting requirements. Stock awards should not be payable based solely on the attainment of tenure requirements.

- Executives, not companies, should be responsible for paying personal expenses – particularly those that average employees routinely shoulder, such as family and personal travel, financial planning, club memberships and other dues. The compensation committee should consider capping all perquisites at a de minimis level.

- Companies should provide employment contracts to executives only in limited circumstances, such as to provide modest, short-term employment security to a newly hired or recently promoted executive. Such contracts should have a specified termination date (not to exceed three years).
- Executives should be entitled to severance payments in non–change-in-control situations only in the event of wrongful termination, death or disability. Termination for poor performance, resignation under pressure or failure to renew the contract should not qualify as wrongful termination.
- Any provisions providing for compensation following a change-in-control event should be "double-triggered," stipulating that compensation is payable only (1) after a control change actually takes place and (2) if a covered executive's job is terminated because of the control change.
- Companies should not compensate executives for any excise or additional taxes payable upon the receipt of severance, change-in-control or similar payments.
- SERPs should be an extension of the retirement program covering other employees. They should not include special provisions, such as above-market interest rates and excess service credits, not offered under plans covering other employees.
- Investment alternatives offered under deferred compensation plans for executives should mirror those offered to employees in broad-based deferral plans.
- Executives and directors should own, after a reasonable period of time, a meaningful position in the company's common stock. Executives should be required to own stock – excluding unexercised options and unvested stock awards – equal to a multiple of salary, scaled based on position, such as two times salary for lower-level executives and up to six times salary for the CEO.
- Executives should be required to sell stock through preannounced program sales or by providing a minimum 30-day advance notice of any stock sales.

INSTITUTIONAL SHAREHOLDER SERVICES

Institutional Shareholder Services (ISS) is the largest provider of proxy voting and corporate governance services. It serves more than 1,200 institutional and corporate clients worldwide by analyzing proxies, issuing research, and making voting recommendations for more than 28,000 companies. It is the most established, influential – and some would say notorious – proxy voting advisory service.

ISS implemented a new policy in 2004 to examine any disparity between CEO pay and company performance as measured by total direct compensation and negative one- and three-year total shareholder returns. A disparity between pay and performance will generally warrant a "withhold" vote from the compensation committee members, who are responsible for overseeing the company's compensation programs. In 2004, nearly two dozen firms triggered the policy, while 230 others drew a "cautionary note" that ISS would monitor their CEO compensation practices.

ISS is applying a new burn rate override approach to stock-based plans. Even if the aggregate plan cost is within the allowable cap, ISS will recommend against new plans or amendments if the three-year average burn rate exceeds the standard. The standard is based on the Global Industry Classification System (GICS) assignment and Russell 3000 index membership, and the limit is one standard deviation above the relevant GICS mean. Full-value awards "count" the same as either 1.5, 2, or 4 stock option grants based on the company's 200-day volatility.

ISS has also updated its pay-for-performance policies, which affect vote recommendations for compensation committee members. The policies apply if CEO total direct compensation (as calculated by Equilar) increases in the last year and one-year and three-year TRS are both negative. The main problem with this approach is that TDC is often determined long before TRS as of year-end is known.

The organization has also implemented a new "liberal share counting" policy that reflects its policy of measuring the economic cost of a plan. Plan designs that replenish share reserves using certain methods (e.g., count only net shares issued, add back shares tendered to exercise awards, add open market stock purchases) will have all awards valued as full-value shares. The new policy also applies to plans authorizing SARs and only counting net shares issued against plan reserve (or not specifying). This has diminished the attractiveness of SARs relative to stock options.

The organization has also made some positive policy changes. Amendments that improve a plan and do not add to its cost will get favorable recommendations, even if the cost of all plans exceeds the allowable cap. In addition, stock plans exclusive for board members may receive approval, even if the cost of all plans exceeds the allowable cap. Also, pay-for-performance and burn rate overrides may not necessarily result in a negative vote recommendation from ISS. For the burn rate, the company must commit to maintaining its future burn rate below the industry average and disclose this commitment publicly.

The ISS proxy voting guidelines include its methods for equity plan analysis. Equity incentive plan cost cannot exceed an allowable value transfer/dilution cap. ISS uses 95 percent weighting for shareholder value transfer, which measures the cost of options or shares as a percentage of market value, and 5 percent weighting for voting power dilution, which is shares awarded plus those available for award as a percentage of fully diluted shares outstanding. The company's results are compared with an industry group of peers and a "primary index" group of peers. ISS states that comparative burn rates should be reasonable compared with the industry and primary index groups of peers.

ISS's qualitative assessment of equity compensation plans includes executive stock ownership guidelines. The organization considers establishing guidelines to be a positive impact. It prefers that plans specify minimum vesting provisions and that performance goals be disclosed to shareholders. ISS recommends that guidelines be established to require executives to hold all or some of the net proceeds of option exercises. The organization believes that a meaningful retention ratio (net proceeds basis) is at least 50 percent for full tenure.

GLASS, LEWIS & COMPANY

Glass Lewis is an independent research firm with a focus on governance. It advises its investor clients, which include a number of institutional investors. Glass Lewis clients include 7 of the top 10 mutual funds and 9 of the top 15 pension funds.

Glass Lewis employs about 30 analysts, who follow 6,200 companies worldwide. Glass Lewis is different from ISS, which also provides services to issuers, but several institutional investors subscribe to both. Unlike ISS, Glass Lewis does not provide governance advice. Many companies have discovered that it is difficult to overcome "against" recommendations from both proxy advisory services. The Glass Lewis stock plan evaluation focuses on economic cost. ISS has incorporated many features introduced by Glass Lewis, but the Glass Lewis evaluation of stock plans is less rigid than the ISS approach.

Glass Lewis provides voting recommendations on all proposals, with a particular emphasis on equity-based compensation plans, mergers and acquisitions, employee stock purchase plans, option repricing, and deferred compensation programs. Glass Lewis estimates the future costs of annual grants and overall plans and compares plans based on a number of peer-based standards. It uses standards that are similar to the ISS standards – one standard deviation from the mean. Its overall recommendation reflects qualitative issues as well.

The standards that Glass Lewis applies include the estimated annual cost as a percentage of revenues, income, and cash flow; the estimated annual cost as a percentage of market capitalization; the estimated annual cost per employee; the historical annual cost as a percentage of net income; and the historical burn rate. Unlike ISS, Glass Lewis does not offer a product to "test run" stock plan proposals using its models.

The firm's recommendations for equity compensation plans include the following:

- Companies should seek more shares for their programs only when they need them.
- Programs should be small enough that companies need approval from shareholders on a regular basis.
- Annual net share count and voting power dilution should be limited.
- The annual cost of the program should be reasonable as a percentage of financial results and in line with the peer group.
- The expected annual cost of the program should be reasonable in comparison with the value of the business.
- The intrinsic value received by those granted options in the past should be reasonable compared with the financial results of the business.
- The program should deliver reasonable value on a per-employee basis when compared with programs at peer companies.
- If an options program is relatively expensive, the company should not be granting options just to senior executives and board members.
- Programs should not permit repricing of stock options.
- Programs should not contain excessively liberal administrative or payment terms.

NATIONAL ASSOCIATION OF CORPORATE DIRECTORS

The National Association of Corporate Directors (NACD) is a national nonprofit membership organization designed to serve the corporate governance needs of corporate boards and individual board members. Its 15,500 members and customers represent companies ranging from Fortune 100 public companies to small, "over-the-counter," closely held, and private firms.

The 2003 Report of the NACD Blue Ribbon Commission provides a specific set of principles and practices to guide boards and compensation committees in their deliberations over executive pay. That report, titled *Executive Compensation and the Role of the Compensation Committee*, recommends that boards universally adopt the principle of "fairness," discouraging unexplainable gaps between the CEO's pay and the pay of other senior managers – or between executives and other employees – unless these are justified and explained. The report also recommends that compensation committee members be diverse and fully independent and willing to challenge the appropriateness of past practices. The committee should consider engaging an independent compensation consultant to assist in the development of both a compensation philosophy and specific pay packages. Consultants employed by management and the committee should be approved by the board and disclosed to shareholders.

The NACD's report recommends that executives be rewarded for meeting short-term targets, but companies also should award additional variable compensation based on achieving key metrics over an extended period of time using company performance measures, rather than stock price, as a criterion.

Pay plans should give managers a long-term stake in the company through ownership requirements and stringent holding periods for that ownership. Performance objectives should be established with full engagement and approval of the board, not delegated to the compensation committee. Pay should be linked to performance as reported, and performance metrics should not be changed after the fact to compensate for a failure to meet stated objectives.

The NACD report also states that executives should purchase stock with their own funds, and the company should adopt minimum holding periods on shares from company plans. It recommends 30-day advance notice of stock sales and a six-month holding period after the termination of employment. The report also states that the compensation committee should monitor overhang levels and understand the value of options granted, both exercised and unexercised. Companies should consider public announcements of all important compensation developments.

THE CONFERENCE BOARD

The Conference Board is a global, independent, not-for-profit membership organization that conducts research, issues forecasts, assesses trends, and publishes information and analyses for corporate executives and the public. It stresses the importance of performance-based executive compensation that reinforces strategic goals. It also suggests that a company recapture incentive pay in the event of malfeasance. It recommends that companies strive for the accumulation of meaningful amounts of equity by executives and that directors own and retain substantial amounts of stock. The Conference Board also recommends that companies specify minimum holding periods for equity received by executives and directors.

Equity compensation should be approved by shareholders, including material modifications to existing awards. Disclosure should highlight EPS after dilution and the portion of future shareholder value that will go to executives and employees. The Conference Board endorses advance notice of executives' intent to directly or indirectly dispose of stock and public disclosure of executive officer employment agreements promptly following their execution.

Academic Articles on Pay-for-Performance and the Effectiveness of the Executive Labor Market

Adams, Renee B., Heitor Almeida, and Daniel Ferreira. "Powerful CEOs and Their Impact on Corporate Performance." *Review of Financial Studies* (Winter 2005), vol. 18 (4): 1403–1432.

Aggarwal, Rajesh K., and Andrew A. Samwick. "The Other Side of the Trade-off: The Impact of Risk on Executive Compensation." *Journal of Political Economy* (February 1999), vol. 107 (1): 65–105.

Anderson, Mark C., Rajiv D. Banker, and Sury Ravindran. "Executive Compensation in the Information Technology Industry." *Management Science* (April 2000), vol. 46 (4): 530–547.

Anderson, Ronald C., and John M. Bizjak. "An Empirical Examination of the Role of the CEO and the Compensation Committee in Structuring Executive Pay." *Journal of Banking and Finance* (July 2003), vol. 27 (7): 1323–1348.

Baber, William R., Surya N. Janakiraman, and Sok-Hyon Kang. "Investment Opportunities and the Structure of Executive Compensation." *Journal of Accounting and Economics* (June 1996), vol. 21 (3): 297–318.

Bainbridge, Stephen M. "Executive Compensation: Who Decides?" *Texas Law Review* (May 2005), vol. 83 (6): 1615–1662.

Bloom, Nick, and John Van Reenen. "Measuring and Explaining Management Practices across Firms and Countries." Center for Economic Performance, London School of Economics, mimeo (2006).

Boschen, John F., and Kimberly J. Smith. "You Can Pay Me Now and You Can Pay Me Later: The Dynamic Response of Executive Compensation to Firm Performance." *Journal of Business* (October 1995), vol. 68 (4): 577–608.

Bryan, Stephen, LeeSeok Hwang, and Steven Lilien. "CEO Stock-Based Compensation: An Empirical Analysis of Incentive-Intensity, Relative Mix, and Economic Determinants." *Journal of Business* (October 2000), vol. 73 (4): 661–693.

Carpenter, Mason A., and W. M. Gerard Sanders. "Top Management Team Compensation: The Missing Link between CEO Pay and Firm

Performance?" *Strategic Management Journal* (April 2002), vol. 23 (4): 367–375.

Conyon, Martin J., and Lerong He. "Compensation Committees and CEO Compensation Incentives in U.S. Entrepreneurial Firms." *Journal of Management Accounting Research, American Accounting Association* (2004), vol. 16: 35–57.

Conyon, Martin J., and Kevin J. Murphy. "The Prince and the Pauper? CEO Pay in the United States and United Kingdom." *Economic Journal* (November 2000), vol. 110: F640–671.

Conyon, Martin J., and Joachim Schwalbach. "Executive Compensation: Evidence from the UK and Germany." *Long Range Planning* (August 2000), vol. 33 (4): 504–526.

Core, John E., and Wayne Guay. "The Use of Equity Grants to Manage Optimal Equity Incentive Levels." *Journal of Accounting and Economics* (December 1999), vol. 28 (2): 151–184.

Core, John E., Wayne R. Guay, and David F. Larcker. "Executive Equity Compensation and Incentives: A Survey." *Federal Reserve Bank of New York Economic Policy Review* (April 2003), vol. 9 (1): 27–50.

Core, John E., Wayne R. Guay, and Randall S. Thomas. "Is U.S. CEO Compensation Inefficient Pay without Performance?" Vanderbilt Law and Economics Research Paper No. 05–05; University of Pennsylvania Institute for Law & Economic Research Paper 05–13 (January 2004).

Core, John E., Wayne R. Guay, and Randall S. Thomas. "Is U.S. CEO Compensation Broken?" *Journal of Applied Corporate Finance* (Fall 2005), vol. 17 (4): 97–104.

Core, John E., and David F. Larcker. "Performance Consequences of Mandatory Increases in Executive Stock Ownership." *Journal of Financial Economics* (June 2002), vol. 64 (3): 317–340.

Cyert, Richard M., Sok-Hyon Kang, and Praveen Kumar. "Corporate Governance, Takeovers and Top Management Compensation: Theory and Evidence." *Management Science* (April 2002), vol. 48 (4): 453–469.

Feldstein, Martin S. "Why Is Productivity Growing Faster?" *Journal of Policy Modeling* (July 2003), vol. 25 (5): 445–451.

Frydman, Carola. "Rising Through the Ranks: The Evolution of the Market for Corporate Executives, 1936–2003." Harvard University Working Paper (November 2005).

Frydman, Carola, and Raven E. Saks. "Historical Trends in Executive Compensation: 1936–2003." Harvard University (November 2005).

Gabaix, Xavier, and Augustin Landier. "Why Has CEO Pay Increased So Much?" MIT Department of Economics Working Paper No. 06–13 (May 2006).

Gayle, George-Levi, and Robert A. Miller. "Has Moral Hazard Become a More Important Factor in Managerial Compensation?" Tepper School of Business, Carnegie Mellon University Working Paper (November 2005).

Gordon, Jeffrey N. "Executive Compensation: If There's a Problem, What's the Remedy? The Case for Compensation Discussion and Analysis." *Journal of Corporation Law* (Summer 2006), vol. 30: 695.

Habib, Michel A., and Alexander Ljungqvist. "Firm Value and Managerial Incentives: A Stochastic Frontier Approach." *Journal of Business* (November 2005), vol. 78 (6): 2053–2094.

Hall, Brian J., and Jeffrey B. Liebman. "Are CEOs Really Paid Like Bureaucrats?" *Quarterly Journal of Economics* (August 1998), vol. 113 (3): 653–691.

Hanlon, Michelle, Shivaram Rajgopal, and Terry Shevlin. "Are Executive Stock Options Associated with Future Earnings?" *Journal of Accounting and Economics* (February 2004), vol. 36 (1–3): 3–43.

Harris, Richard, Donald S. Siegal, and Mike Wright. "Assessing the Impact of Management Buyouts on Economic Efficiency: Plant-Level Evidence from the United Kingdom." *Review of Economics and Statistics* (February 2005), vol. 87 (1): 148–153.

Hayes, Rachel M., and Scott Schaefer. "Implicit Contracts and the Explanatory Power of Top Executive Compensation for Future Performance." *RAND Journal of Economics* (Summer 2000), vol. 31 (2): 273–293.

Hermalin, Benjamin E., and Nancy E. Wallace. "Firm Performance and Executive Compensation in the Savings and Loan Industry." *Journal of Financial Economics* (July 2001), vol. 61 (1): 139–170.

Himmelberg, Charles P., and R. Glenn Hubbard. "Incentive Pay and the Market for CEOs: An Analysis of Pay-for-Performance Sensitivity." Columbia University Working Paper (2000).

Himmelberg, Charles P., R. Glenn Hubbard, and Darius Palia. "Understanding the Determinants of Managerial Ownership and the Link between Ownership and Performance." *Journal of Financial Economics* (September 1999), vol. 53 (3): 353–384.

Holmström, Bengt R., and Steven N. Kaplan. "Corporate Governance and Merger Activity in the U.S.: Making Sense of the 1980s and 1990s." *Journal of Economic Perspectives* (Spring 2001), vol. 15 (2): 121–144.

Holmström, Bengt R., and Steven N. Kaplan. "The State of U.S. Corporate Governance: What's Right and What's Wrong?" National Bureau of Economic Research Working Paper No. 9613 (Cambridge, MA: National Bureau of Economic Research, 2003).

Hubbard, R. Glenn, and Darius Palia. "Executive Pay and Performance: Evidence from the U.S. Banking Industry." *Journal of Financial Economics* (September 1995), vol. 39 (1): 105–130.

Ittner, Christopher D., Richard A. Lambert, and David F. Larcker. "The Structure and Performance Consequences of Equity Grants to Employees of New Economy Firms." *Journal of Accounting and Economics* (January 2003), vol. 34 (1): 89–127.

Kaplan, Steven N. "The Evolution of U.S. Corporate Governance: We Are All Henry Kravis Now." *Journal of Private Equity* (Fall 1997): 7–14.

Murphy, Kevin J. "Executive Compensation." In *Handbook of Labor Economics*, Ed. O. Ashenfelter and D. Card (North Holland: Elsevier: 1999), vol. 3, chap. 28, pp. 2485–2563.

Murphy, Kevin J. "Explaining Executive Compensation: Managerial Power versus the Perceived Cost of Stock Options." *University of Chicago Law Review* (Summer 2002), vol. 69 (3): 847–870.

Murphy, Kevin J., and Ján Zábojník. "Managerial Capital and the Market for CEOs." Marshall School of Business, University of Southern California (September 2004).

O'Byrne, Stephen F., and David S. Young. "Top Management Incentives and Corporate Performance." *Journal of Applied Corporate Finance* (Fall 2005), vol. 17 (4): 105–114.

Perry, Tod, and Marc Zenner. "CEO Compensation in the 1990s: Shareholder Alignment or Shareholder Expropriation." *Wake Forest Law Review* (2000), vol. 35 (1): 123–152.

Perry, Tod, and Marc Zenner. "Pay for Performance? Government Regulation and the Structure of Compensation Contracts." *Journal of Financial Economics* (December 2001), vol. 62 (3): 453–488.

Rajan, Raghuram G., and Julie M. Wulf. "Are Perks Purely Managerial Excess?" National Bureau of Economic Research Working Paper No. W10494 (Cambridge, MA: National Bureau of Economic Research, May 2004).

Rees, Lynn L., and David M. Stott. "The Value-Relevance of Stock-Based Employee Compensation Disclosures." *Journal of Applied Business Research* (Spring 2001), vol. 17 (2): 105–116.

Roe, Mark J. "The Shareholder Wealth Maximization Norm and Industrial Organization." *University of Pennsylvania Law Review* (June 2001), vol. 149 (6): 2063–2082.

Sanders, W. M. Gerard. "Behavioral Responses of CEOs to Stock Ownership and Stock Option Pay." *Academy of Management Journal* (June 2001), vol. 44 (3): 477–492.

Snyder, Franklin G. "More Pieces of the CEO Compensation Puzzle." *Delaware Journal of Corporate Law* (2003), vol. 28 (1): 129–211.

Thomas, Randall S. "Explaining the International CEO Pay Gap: Board Capture or Market Driven?" *Vanderbilt Law Review* (May 2004), vol. 57 (4): 1171–1268.

Notes

1. THE MYTHS AND REALITIES OF PAY-FOR-PERFORMANCE

1. www.afl-cio.org, May 2, 2005.
2. Louis Lavelle, "A Payday for Performance," *BusinessWeek*, April 18, 2005, p. 78.
3. Brian J. Hall and Jeffrey B. Liebman, "Are CEOs Really Paid Like Bureaucrats?" *Quarterly Journal of Economics*, vol. 113, no. 3 (August 1998), pp. 653–691.
4. Peter Drucker, "The American CEO," *Wall Street Journal*, December 30, 2004.
5. Xavier Gabaix and Augustin Landier, "Why Has CEO Pay Increased So Much?" May 8, 2006. MIT Department of Economics Working Paper No. 06–13.
6. Alan Reynolds, *Income and Wealth* (Westport, CT: Greenwood Press, 2006).
7. Brian J. Hall and Kevin J. Murphy, "The Trouble with Stock Options," *Journal of Economic Perspectives*, vol. 17 (Summer 2003), pp. 49–70.
8. Geoffrey Colvin, "Catch a Rising Star," *Fortune*, February 6, 2006, p. 50.
9. Landon Thomas, Jr., "Up, Up and Away from Wall Street," *New York Times*, February 4, 2006, pp. C1, C13.
10. Emily Thornton, "Going Private," *BusinessWeek*, February 27, 2006, pp. 53–62.
11. Kathryn Kranhold and Joann Lublin, "$100 Million Helps Lure Away General Electric Veteran," *Wall Street Journal*, August 24, 2006, p. B1.
12. Booz Allen Hamilton, "CEO Succession in 2004: The World's Most Prominent Temp Workers" (New York: Booz Allen Hamilton, May 2005).
13. Russell Reynolds Associates, "The CFO Turnover Study" (New York: Russell Reynolds Associates, May 2005).
14. World Economic Forum, "Global Competitiveness Report," September 28, 2005.
15. David Yermack, "Good Timing: CEO Stock Option Awards and Company News Announcements," *Journal of Finance*, vol. 52, no. 2 (1997), pp. 449–477.

2. MANAGERIAL POWER

1. Kevin Murphy, "Explaining Executive Compensation: Managerial Power versus the Perceived Cost of Stock Options," *University of Chicago Law Review*, vol. 69, no. 3 (Summer 2002), p. 850.
2. Lucien Bebchuk and Jesse Fried, *Pay without Performance: The Unfulfilled Promise of Executive Compensation* (Cambridge, MA: Harvard University Press, 2004).

3. Bengt Holmström and Steven Kaplan, "The State of U.S. Corporate Governance: What's Right and What's Wrong?" *Journal of Applied Corporate Finance*, vol. 15, no. 3 (2001), pp. 8–20.
4. John E. Core, Wayne R. Guay, and Randall S. Thomas, "Is U.S. CEO Compensation Inefficient Pay without Performance?" *Michigan Law Review*, vol. 103 (2005), pp. 1142–1185.
5. Randall S. Thomas, "Explaining the International CEO Pay Gap: Board Capture or Market Driven?" Vanderbilt University Law School, Law & Economics Working Paper No. 03–05.
6. Ibid., p. 132.
7. Iman Anabtawi, "Overlooked Alternatives in the Pay without Performance Debate," January 2005, unpublished manuscript available at http://www.law.ucla.edu/docs/213253232005anabtawi.pdf.
8. Stephen Bainbridge, "Executive Compensation: Who Decides," *Texas Law Review*, vol. 83 (2005), pp. 1616–1662.
9. Murphy, "Explaining Executive Compensation: Managerial Power versus the Perceived Cost of Stock Options."
10. Holmström and Kaplan, "The State of U.S. Corporate Governance.
11. Martin Conyon and Lerong He, "Compensation Committees and CEO Compensation Incentives in US Entrepreneurial Firms," *Journal of Management Accounting Research*, vol. 16, no. 1 (2004), pp. 16, 35–56.
12. Franklin Snyder, "More Pieces of the CEO Compensation Puzzle," *Delaware Journal of Corporate Law*, vol. 27 (2003), p. 129.
13. Tod Perry and Marc Zenner, "CEO Compensation in the 1990s: Shareholder Alignment or Shareholder Expropriation," *Wake Forest Law Review*, vol. 35, no. 1 (Spring 2000), pp. 123–152; and "Pay for Performance? Government Regulation and the Structure of Compensation Contracts," unpublished manuscript, 1999.
14. Murphy, "Explaining Executive Compensation."
15. Adolf Berle and Gardiner Means, *The Modern Corporation and Private Property* (Macmillan, 1932).
16. "Grace's Large Pay Stirs Bonus Debate," *New York Times*, July 27, 1930, p. 33.
17. "Bethlehem Bonuses Are Cut by New Plan, Salaries Increased," *New York Times*, July 3, 1931, p. 1.

3. EXTERNAL PRESSURES: THE NEW CONTEXT FOR EXECUTIVE COMPENSATION

1. Rogers v. Hill, 289 U.S. 582 (1933).
2. As noted Robert Creamer's book *Babe: The Legend Comes to Life* (New York: Simon & Schuster, 1974), a source has never been identified for this quotation.
3. See Carola Frydman and Raven E. Saks, "Historical Trends in Executive Compensation," Harvard University, mimeo, November 14, 2004.
4. Joseph Nocero, "Disclosure Won't Tame CEO Pay," *New York Times*, January 14, 2006, p. C1.
5. Thomas McCarroll, "Executive Pay: The Shareholders Strike Back," *Time*, May 4, 1992, p. 46.
6. Dan K. Webb, "A Report to the New York Stock Exchange on Investigation Relating to the Compensation of Richard A. Grasso" (Chicago: Winston & Strawn, December 15, 2003).
7. Kimberley Strassel, "Behind the Spitzer Curtain," *Wall Street Journal*, June 14, 2005.

8. Ibid.
9. Ibid.
10. Meredith Burbank, "SEC Settlement with GE Shows Increased Scrutiny of Executive Compensation Disclosure," *Southwest Tech Wire*, September 28, 2004.
11. Ibid.
12. Ibid.
13. Anne Moran, "IRS Audits of Executive Compensation Suggest the Need to Review Executive Pay Practices and Procedures," *Employee Relations Law Journal*, vol. 30, no. 2 (2004), pp. 100–114.
14. NYSE Corporate Accountability and Listing Standards Committee, June 6, 2002.
15. From SEC Release No. 34–48745, November 4, 2003, and NYSE Section 303A Corporate Governance Rules, November 3, 2003.
16. This quotation and related information in this section are from H.R. 3764, The Sarbanes-Oxley Act of 2002.
17. Tim Beason, "Feeling the Pain," *CFO*, May 2005.
18. Monarch Casinos 2004 Form 10-K, as reported in the *Wall Street Journal*, April 4, 2005.
19. The Conference Board, "U.S. Institutional Investors Continue to Boost Ownership of U.S. Corporations," press release, January 22, 2007.
20. Phyllis Plitch and Kaja Whitehouse, "Executives' Pay Faces New Tactics," *Wall Street Journal*, February 27, 2006, p. B3; "2006 US Proxy Season Review," *ISS Governance Weekly*; Shabina S. Khafri, "Who's Winning?" *Wall Street Journal*, April 11, 2005, p. R3.
21. For more information on the results of this survey, visit Watson Wyatt's Web site at wwww.watsonwyatt.com.
22. Roger Parloff, "HP Shareholders Want Part of Fiorina's Severance Returned," *Fortune*, March 8, 2006.
23. Randall S. Thomas, "Explaining the International CEO Pay Gap: Board Capture or Market Driven?" Vanderbilt University Law School, Law & Economics Working Paper No. 03–05, p. 132.
24. Steven N. Kaplan, "The Staying Power of Leveraged Buyouts," *Journal of Financial Economics*, vol. 29, October 1991, pp. 287–313.
25. Thomas, "Explaining the International CEO Pay Gap," p. 76.
26. Ira T. Kay, *Value at the Top: Solutions to the Executive Compensation Crisis* (New York: Harper Business, 1992), pp. 187–188.
27. Sara B. Moeller, Frederik P. Schlingemann, and Rene M. Stulz, "Wealth Destruction on a Massive Scale? A Study of Acquiring-Firm Returns in the Recent Merger Wave," *Journal of Finance*, vol. 60, no. 2 (April 2005), pp. 757–782.
28. Henry Sendor, "Hedge Funds: The New Corporate Activists," *Wall Street Journal*, May 13, 2005, p. C1.
29. Ibid.
30. Martin Peers and Ann Zimmerman, "Dissident Investor Icahn Wins Board Seats at Blockbuster," *Wall Street Journal*, May 12, 2005.
31. Jeremy York, "General Motors at a Fork in the Road . . . and a Possible Solution for a Robust Resurgence," *Wall Street Journal*, January 10, 2006, p. A1.
32. Matthew Budman, "How Much Should a CEO Make? The Conference Board, *Across the Board*, November/December 2002.
33. "Executive Envy," *Wall Street Journal*, January 21, 2006.

4. END OF AN ERA: THE DECLINE OF THE STOCK OPTION

1. "Calculating Sustainable Cash Flow," Georgia Institute of Technology, DuPree Financial Analysis Lab, October 2003.
2. Brian J. Hall and Kevin J. Murphy, "The Trouble with Stock Options," *Journal of Economic Perspectives*, vol. 17 (Summer 2003), pp. 49–70.
3. Watson Wyatt Worldwide, Managing Stock Option Overhang in Today's Economy (Arlington, VA: Watson Wyatt Worldwide, 2002).
4. Lucien Bebchuk and Jesse Fried, *Pay without Performance: The Unfulfilled Promise of Executive Compensation* (Cambridge, MA: Harvard University Press, 2004), p. 137.
5. Ibid., p. 67.
6. Brian J. Hall, Michael C. Jensen, and Kevin J. Murphy, "Remuneration: Where We've Been, How We Got Here, What the Problems Are, and How to Fix Them," European Corporate Governance Institute Working Paper No. 44/2004, July 2004; and Hall and Murphy, "The Trouble with Stock Options.
7. Watson Wyatt Worldwide, *Stock Incentives: Moving to a Portfolio Approach*, 2004–05 Report on Executive Pay (Arlington, VA: Watson Wyatt Worldwide, 2005).
8. Watson Wyatt Worldwide, *How Do Employees Value Stock Options?* Results from a Special Watson Wyatt Survey (Arlington, VA: Watson Wyatt Worldwide, 2004).
9. Brian J. Hall and Kevin J. Murphy, "Optimal Exercise Prices for Executive Stock Options," *American Economic Review*, vol. 9, no. 2 (May 2000), pp. 209–214.
10. Lisa K. Meulbroek with Li Jin, "Do Underwater Executive Stock Options Still Work? The Effect of Stock Price Movements on Managerial Incentive-Alignment," Harvard Business School Working Paper 02–002.
11. Watson Wyatt Worldwide, *How Do Employees Value Stock Options?*
12. Samuel J. Palmisano, "Final Remarks." Presented at the 2004 IBM annual meeting of stockholders, Providence, Rhode Island, April 27, 2004.

5. THE FUTURE OF LONG-TERM INCENTIVES

1. This presumes the metrics used are not based on share price. As discussed in more detail in Appendix A, share-price–based metrics, whether measured on an absolute or relative basis, require the determination of a fixed fair-value expense that may not be reversed if the company fails to meet the performance objectives.

6. EXECUTIVE STOCK OWNERSHIP: THE SOLUTION TO THE EXECUTIVE COMPENSATION CRISIS

1. John Core and David Larcker, "Performance Consequences of Mandatory Increases in Executive Stock Ownership," *Journal of Financial Economics*, vol. 64, no. 3 (June 2002), pp. 317–340.
2. Aldolf Berle and Gardiner Means, *The Modern Corporation and Private Property* (New York: Macmillan, 1932).
3. Core and Larcker, "Performance Consequences of Mandatory Increases in Executive Stock Ownership.
4. Ibid.
5. Bruce Ellig, "The Evolution of Executive Pay in the United States," *Compensation and Benefits Review*, vol. 38, no. 1 (January/February 2006), pp. 55–61, at p. 59.

7. DIRECTOR COMPENSATION IN THE NEW ENVIRONMENT

1. Anita Raghavan, "More CEOs Say 'No Thanks' to Board Seats," *Wall Street Journal*, January 28, 2005, p. B1.
2. Ibid.
3. Korn/Ferry International, *31st Annual Board of Directors Study* (Los Angeles: Korn/Ferry International, 2004).
4. Watson Wyatt S&P 500 study.
5. Raghavan, "More CEOs Say 'No Thanks' to Board Seats," p. B4.
6. This and other statistics in this section are from Korn/Ferry International, *31st Annual Board of Directors Study*, 2004.
7. Sanjai Bhagat, Dennis C. Carey, and Charles M. Elson, "Director Ownership, Corporate Performance, and Management Turnover," *Business Lawyer*, vol. 54, no. 3 (1999), pp. 885–919.
8. As referenced in several academic articles, notably Michael C. Jensen and William H. Meckling, "Theory of the Firm: Managerial Behavior, Agency Costs and Ownership Structure," *Journal of Financial Economics*, vol. 3, no. 4 (1976), pp. 305–360; and Eugene F. Fama, "Agency Problems and the Theory of the Firm," *Journal of Political Economy*, vol. 88, no. 2 (1980), pp. 288–307.
9. "The Innovative Boards," *Dun's Review*, October 1977.
10. Dana Wechster Linden, Robert Lenzner, and Frank Walfe, "The Cosseted Director," *Fortune*, May 22, 1995, p. 168.
11. Ibid.
12. Korn/Ferry International, 31st Annual Board of Directors Study.
13. Frederick W. Cook & Co., "Director Compensation: NASDAQ 100 vs. NYSE 100" (New York: Frederick W. Cook & Co., October 2006).
14. This section draws from the research outlined in Bhagat, Carey, and Elson, "Director Ownership, Corporate Performance, and Management Turnover.
15. Ibid., pp. 913–917, 919.
16. Ibid., p. 917.
17. Ibid., p. 919.
18. Paula Silva, "Do Motivation and Equity Ownership Matter in Board of Directors' Evaluation of CEO Performance," *Journal of Managerial Issues*, vol. 17, no. 3 (October 2005), pp. 346–362.
19. Benjamin E. Hermalin and Michael S. Weisbach, "The Effects of Board Composition and Direct Incentives on Firm Performance," *Financial Management*, vol. 20, no. 4 (Winter 1991), pp. 297–309.
20. Cynthia J. Campbell, Mark L. Power, and Roger D. Stover, "Quid-pro-quo Exchanges of Outside Director Defined Benefit Pension Plans for Equity-Based Compensation," *Journal of Pension Economics and Finance*, vol. 5, no. 2 (July 2006), pp. 155–174.

8. THE COMPENSATION COMMITTEE: CREATING A BALANCE BETWEEN SHAREHOLDERS AND EXECUTIVES

1. Joann Lublin, "The Serial CEO," Wall Street Journal, September 19, 2005.
2. *In re The Walt Disney Company Derivative Litigation*, 825 A. 2d 275 (Del. Chan. 2003).
3. Shabina Khatri, "Who's Winning?" Wall Street Journal, April 11, 2005, p. R3.

4. John Bogle, *The Battle for the Soul of Capitalism* (New Haven, CT: Yale University Press, 2005), p. 16.

5. Mark Gimein, "You Bought, They Sold," *Fortune*, September 2, 2002, p. 64.

9. ALIGNING ALL EMPLOYEE PAY TO IMPROVE CORPORATE PERFORMANCE

1. Joseph Blasi, Douglas Kruse, and Aaron Bernstein, *In the Company of Owners: The Truth about Stock Options and Why Every Employee Should Have Them* (New York: Basic Books, 2003), p. 154.

2. Ibid.

3. Corey Rosen, John Case, and Martin Staubus, "When Employees Have Equity Attitude," *Working Knowledge*, Harvard Business School, May 16, 2005.

10. INTERNATIONAL EXECUTIVE PAY COMPARISONS

1. Randall S. Thomas, "Explaining the International CEO Pay Gap: Board Capture or Market Driven?" Vanderbilt University Law School, Law & Economics Working Paper No. 03–05, p. 132.

2. Ibid.

3. Ibid., pp. 7–8.

4. Ibid., pp. 8–9.

5. Ibid., p. 134.

6. Jesse Eisinger, "No Excessive Pay, We're British," *Wall Street Journal*, February 8, 2006, p. C1.

7. New Economic Regulation Law, France, 2005.

Index

actual pay, 1, 42
Adelphia, 109
AFL-CIO, 9, 232
agency costs, 108, 109, 118, 184, 207
agency theory, 107
alignment, executive/employee, 5, 179
  stock plans in, 169–179
Altria Group, 133
Amalgamated Bank, 59
American Express, 19
American Federation of State, County
  and Municipal Employees Fund,
  233
American Jobs Creation Act of 2004, 208
American Tobacco, 48
Amgen, Inc., 233
Anabtawi, Iman, 31, 248
APB 25 accounting rule, xvi, 36
Apple, 68
Araskog, Rand, 49
at-the-money stock options, 29, 30, 36
audit committees, 44, 124, 128, 130, 137,
  138

Bainbridge, Stephen, 32, 248
base pay, 5, 154
base salary, xiv, 116, 164, 179, 185, 189,
  190, 205, 211, 234
Bebchuk, Lucien A., 28–30, 31, 32, 34,
  36, 37, 38, 72, 73, 247, 250
BellSouth, 19
Berle, Adolf, 34, 107, 108, 248, 250
Bernstein, Aaron, 162, 170, 252
Bethlehem Steel Corporation, 34
Bhagat, Sanjai, 135, 251
Biggs, John, 141

binomial lattice valuation, 85, 216
Black–Scholes valuation, 78, 79, 80, 87,
  216, 220
Blackstone Group, 20
Blasi, Joseph, 162, 170, 252
Blockbuster, 67, 249
board capture, 31, 184
board of directors, 1, 28, 34, 42, 56, 66,
  123, 125, 136, 142, 161, 190, 191,
  194, 197, 231, 234
Boeing, 12, 41, 135, 141
Bogle, John, 144, 252
bonus plans, 198
Booz Allen Hamilton, 20, 247
Bressler, Richard, 20
Breton, Thierry, 189
Buffett, Warren, 54, 66, 68, 145
burn rates, 237, 238, 239
Bush, George W., 55, 57, 58, 76
business judgment rule, 40, 42, 125, 143,
  144, 146
BusinessWeek, 10, 20, 68, 247

California Public Employees' Retirement
  System (CalPERS), 9, 229, 230
camouflaged compensation, 35–36, 73
Canada, 83, 93, 180, 181, 192–194
Canadian Coalition of Good Governance,
  192
Canadian Securities Administrators, 194
Capellas, Michael, 124
Carey, Dennis C., 135
Carnegie, Andrew, 48
Case, John, 170, 252
cash-based long-term incentive plans,
  119

Center for Corporate & Public
Governance, 68
CEO
  bureaucrat model of, 146
  as caretaker, 63, 248, 251
  termination of, 4
CFO, 20, 53
Chambers, John, 82
change-in-control agreements, 53, 59,
  63, 64, 66, 147, 149, 150, 210, 211,
  212, 231, 232, 236
China, 158, 195, 196, 197, 198
  Hong Kong, 194, 196, 198, 199, 200
Chrysler, 49
Cisco Systems, 71, 82, 130
Clinton, Bill, 50
Coca-Cola, 49, 69, 145, 233
Cohen, Steven A., 20
committee chairs, 128, 129, 137
Compaq, 124
compensation committees, 4, 13, 18, 26,
  40, 41, 42, 43, 44, 45, 53, 56, 68, 90,
  104, 119, 122, 128, 129, 130, 131,
  137, 138, 143, 150, 172, 178, 190,
  192, 193, 197, 199, 207, 208, 209,
  210, 217, 221, 225, 227, 228, 229,
  230, 231, 232, 234, 235, 236, 237,
  240
  10b5-1 plans and, 141–160
  best practices for, 147–151, 154
  consultants and, 150–151
  governance issues and, 147–150
  legal context for, 141–144, 146
  performance pay enforced by, 154–159
Conference Board, The, 59, 69, 240, 249
conflicts of interest, 44
Congress, U.S., 34, 35, 48, 75
constant-dollar technique, 43
consultants, compensation, 29, 33, 39,
  44, 45, 56, 57, 68, 69, 71, 79, 137,
  146, 148, 150, 151, 161, 173, 192,
  194, 206, 210, 211, 212, 233, 235,
  240
  compensation committees and,
  150–151
Conyon, Martin, 32, 248
Core, John E., 30, 107, 114, 248, 250
corporate governance, xvi, 6, 7, 9, 21, 28,
  29, 30, 32, 34, 40, 57, 115, 123, 130,
  137, 140, 143, 144, 146, 147, 148,
  185, 192, 194, 197, 207, 208, 238

corporate model, 3, 4
  Asian, 195
  U.S., 13, 143, 195; cyclical swings, 3;
    executive compensation in, 3–4;
    executives' role in, 4, 21;
    international comparisons and, 185;
    success of, 3, 40
corporate structures, 181, 185
Council of Institutional Investors, 234
Cox, Christopher, 49
Crystal, Graef, 49, 69

Daft, Donald, 69
deferred compensation, 156
  plans, 5, 6
Delaware courts, 42, 143, 144
Dell, 68
Dell, Michael, 68
differentiation, pay, 163, 167
dilution, stock, 50, 57, 72, 77, 82, 84,
  103, 104, 105, 106, 147, 170, 194,
  207, 208, 209, 217, 218, 219, 222,
  226, 228, 230, 231, 232, 233, 238,
  239, 241
director compensation, 56, 123–140
  activity based, 128–130
  for committee chairs and members,
    201–204
  evolution of, 193–201
  optimal structure for, 137–140
  share ownership in, 136
director independence, 55, 56
disclosure, 5, 6, 9, 32, 35, 36, 48, 50, 51,
  52, 53, 55, 57, 138, 142, 147, 150,
  157, 160, 188, 189, 190, 192, 194,
  197, 208, 218, 225, 229, 241
divestitures, 38
dividend equivalent units (DEUs), 223
Donohue, Thomas J., 57
Dow Chemical, 129
Dow Jones Industrial Average, 4
Drucker, Peter, 11, 247
Duke Energy, 130
Dunlap, Albert, 127
Dynegy, 124

eBay, 134
Economist, The, 33
Eisner, Michael, 142
Ellig, Bruce, 115, 250
Ellison, Larry, 68

Elson, Charles M., 135, 251
employee stock ownership plans
    (ESOPs), 170
employee stock purchase plans (ESPPs),
    xvi, 165, 169, 170, 172
employment contracts, 231, 236
Enron, 35, 51, 52, 54, 55, 68, 75, 109,
    124, 126, 142, 208
entrepreneurialism, 181, 195
Equilar, 237
Europe, 15, 30, 195
European Union (EU), 183, 188
executive compensation
    competing views of, 1–5
    cyclical criticism of, 50
    decision-making role and, 3
    downward movement in, 15, 17
    external forces on, 46
    goals of, 4–6
    regulatory and institutional mandates
        for, 241
    risk in, 38
Executive Compensation Resources, 129,
    132
expensing rule, 54
expensing, stock option, 37, 54, 59, 72,
    83, 84, 85, 86, 87, 104, 106, 169,
    174, 192, 197, 206, 207
Exxon Mobil, 133

Feldstein, Martin, 14, 15
Fidelity, 58, 231, 232
Finance Act of 2005, France, 11, 54, 77,
    119, 121, 172, 215, 216, 218, 219,
    220, 223, 227
Financial Accounting Standard 123
    (FAS 123), 11, 54, 78
Financial Accounting Standards Board
    (FASB), 54, 72, 76
Financial Times, 68
Finland, 21
Finlay, J. Richard, 68
Fiorina, Carly, 63, 249
fixed-shares technique, 43
Ford Motor Company, 108
Fortune, 19, 68, 126, 247, 249, 251, 252
401(k) plans, 58, 170
France, 93, 180, 189, 190–192
Frederick W. Cook & Co., 128, 133, 251
Fried, Jesse, 28–30, 31, 32, 34, 36, 37, 38,
    72, 73, 247, 250

full-value shares, 62, 94, 104, 127, 131,
    138, 139, 207, 210, 224, 227

GAAP accounting, 97
Gates, Bill, 71
General Electric, 19, 51, 52, 130, 131
General Motors, 67
Germany, 93, 188, 189
Gillette, 66, 69, 145
Glass, Lewis & Company, 238, 239
Global Crossing, 75
goal setting, 101
Goizueta, Robert, 49, 69
golden parachutes, 59, 210, 232
Goldman Sachs, 133
governance, corporate, 13, 21, 28, 30, 32,
    34, 37, 45, 46, 48, 51, 55, 60, 125,
    146, 147, 150, 158, 180, 188, 189,
    192, 196, 197, 199, 206, 207, 229,
    232, 234, 236, 239
    compensation committee's role in,
        147–150
Grace, Eugene G., 34
Grasso, Richard, 44, 51, 248
Great Depression, 48
Greenspan, Alan, 54
gross-ups, 158
Guay, Wayne R., 30, 248

haircuts, 80
Hall, Brian, 11, 17, 73, 80, 247, 250
Hawley, Michael, 69
He, Lerong, 32, 248
hedge funds, 19, 20, 67, 125, 146
hedging, 38, 39, 158, 208
Hermalin, Benjamin E., 136, 251
Hewlett Packard, 12, 19, 41, 63
high-performing companies, 13, 41, 166,
    193
Hill, George Washington, 48
Holmström, Bengt, 30, 32, 248
Hoover, Herbert, 48
hostile takeovers, 31, 41, 64, 66
human resources, 13, 29, 39, 44, 45, 89,
    148, 151, 193, 206

IBM, 20, 82
Icahn, Carl, 67, 249
*In re The Walt Disney Co. Derivative
    Litigation*, 142
incentive stock options (ISOs), 218

income tax rates, 49, 55, 76, 217
Indonesia, 194, 196
insider trading, 159, 160
institutional investors, xv, 2, 5, 9, 16, 21,
    33, 34, 50, 58, 59, 60, 61, 62, 63, 97,
    98, 106, 144, 148, 152, 156, 157,
    185, 192, 205, 207, 212
  concerns of, 6, 64
Institutional Shareholder Partners, 49
Institutional Shareholder Services (ISS),
    59, 142, 236, 237, 238, 236, 239,
    249
institutional shareholders, 146
Intel, 128
internal promotions, 152
Internal Revenue Code Section 162(m),
    50, 69, 75, 83, 91, 150, 217, 221,
    225, 227
Internal Revenue Code Section 409A,
    55, 58, 120, 216, 220, 223, 224,
    225
Internal Revenue Code Section 83(b), 55
Internal Reveue Service (IRS), 35, 54, 55
International Brotherhood of Electrical
    Workers, 59
International Brotherhood of Teamsters,
    233
international comparisons, 31
  executive pay differences in, 180–185
International Financial Reporting
    Standard 2 (IFRS2), 185, 197
investment firms, 64
Investor Responsibility Research Center,
    59
ITT, 49

Japan, 15, 21, 30, 181, 196, 197
Jensen, Michael, 73, 250, 251
job creation, 3, 182, 205
Jobs, Steve, 68
Jones, Alan, 17, 67
Joyce, John, 20

Kaplan, Steven, 30, 32, 248, 249
Kerkorian, Kirk, 67
Kerr, Jeffrey L., 136
Kilts, James, 66, 145
Komansky, David, 51
Korn/Ferry, 132, 133, 251
Kren, Leslie, 136
Kruse, Donald, 162, 170, 252

labor markets, 3, 4, 5, 9, 18, 30, 31, 49,
    54, 65, 143, 145, 152, 154, 156, 181,
    182, 204
  executive, 3
Larcker, David, 107, 114, 115, 250
lattice model, 105, 220
law firms, 71, 146
leveraged buyouts (LBOs), 31, 64, 65, 66,
    67, 125, 146
Levitt, Arthur, 33
Liebman, Jeffrey, 11, 17, 247
loans, executive, 57
Loewenstein, Mark J., 8
long-term incentive plans, 6, 16, 87–88,
    89, 104, 106, 114, 119, 147, 149,
    169, 172, 179, 185, 188, 189, 191,
    192, 193, 194, 206
  future of, 105
  share award size in, 103, 104

Malaysia, 194, 196
management buyouts
  (MBOs), 64
management stock purchase plans
  (MSPPs), 86, 119–121, 153
managerial capitalism, 144
managerial power, 28–46, 144, 184, 185,
    206
  mythological touchstones for, 34–46
  realities of, 34
Matthews, Jay, 59
MCI, 133
Means, Gardiner, 34, 107, 108, 248, 250
media coverage, 5, 9, 16, 33, 34, 47, 48,
    50, 52, 62, 68, 145, 184, 193, 204,
    205
  anecdotal reporting in, 1
meeting fees, 126, 128, 131, 138, 139
merit increases, 167
Merrill Lynch, 51
metrics, 10, 24, 61, 62, 91, 95, 96, 97, 98,
    99, 100, 105, 156, 157, 158, 177,
    188, 197, 206, 240, 250
Meulbroek, Lisa, 80, 250
Microsoft Corporation, 71, 89, 133
Moeller, Sara B., 66, 249
Monarch Casinos, 57, 249
Monks, Robert, 49
moral hazard, 109, 110, 118, 119, 207
Morgan Stanley, 67
Motorola, 19

Murphy, Kevin, 17, 28, 32, 34, 37, 73, 74, 80, 247, 248, 250
mutual funds, 58, 144, 158, 231, 232, 238

NASDAQ, 55, 71, 72, 217, 219, 221, 222, 225, 228
National Association of Corporate Directors (NACD), 126, 131, 239, 240
NCR Corporation, 19
New Economic Regulation Law of 2001, France, 189, 208, 252
new hires, 19, 45, 82, 186, 187
New York Stock Exchange, 44, 51, 52, 55, 142, 217, 219, 221, 222, 225, 228, 248, 249
New York Times, 33, 34, 48, 247, 248
nonqualified stock options (NQSOs), 215, 216, 218, 219, 220

Omnibus Budget and Reconciliation Act, 69
opportunity costs, 65, 143
Oracle, 68
organizational flexibility, 3
outliers, corporate, 2, 54
overhang, stock option, 72, 177, 218, 222, 226, 228, 240
Ovitz, Michael, 125, 142, 143

Paine Webber Group, 20
Palmisano, Sam, 82
Paul, Vivek, 20
pay equality, 163
pay for failure, 57, 63, 212
pay-for-performance, 10, 17, 35, 83, 163, 165, 167, 204, 230, 237
  case studies of, 23
  compensation committee's role in, 154–159
  for nonexecutive employees, 165–169
pay opportunity, 31, 42, 145, 153, 155, 180
peer group companies, 24, 39, 40, 41, 42, 45, 52, 73, 99, 100, 101, 104, 156, 158, 187, 208, 239
pension funds, 9, 58, 59, 63, 185, 234, 238
pension plans, executive, 147
pensions, directors, 126
pensions, executive, 5

performance-lapse restricted stock, 93
performance share plans, 24, 54, 86, 93, 105, 119, 145, 164, 191, 197, 207
performance vesting, 37, 61, 62, 145, 180, 189, 191, 226, 228
perquisites, 23, 35, 52, 53, 126, 138, 147, 148, 149, 155, 163, 164, 179, 190, 208, 236
Perry, Tod, 33, 248
portfolio approach, 87, 88, 118, 119, 121, 155, 166, 177, 205, 206, 250
Procter & Gamble, 66, 145
productivity growth, 14, 170, 181
proxy statements, 50, 147

ratchet effect, 40, 42, 43, 44, 145
recessions, 3, 44, 48, 49, 50, 51
reformers, 58, 60
regulation, 52, 57, 241
  unintended consequences of, 48, 49, 50, 52, 54, 69, 106, 125, 164, 206, 207
reload options, 232
rents, 18, 184, 195
repricings, 29, 38, 56, 231, 232, 239
reputational risk, 124
restricted stock plans, xiv, xv, xvi, xvii, 16, 19, 41, 49, 54, 57, 58, 62, 69, 76, 83, 86, 87, 88, 89, 91, 93, 94, 95, 104, 117, 118, 119, 126, 132, 133, 134, 144, 153, 155, 157, 164, 165, 166, 171, 174, 175, 176, 178, 197, 206, 209, 212, 222, 223, 225, 226, 227, 228, 230, 231, 233
restricted stock units (RSUs), 120, 121, 222, 223, 224, 225, 226, 227, 228
retainers, 126, 127, 128, 129, 130, 131, 133, 134, 135, 137, 138, 139
retention, 5, 7, 37, 41, 88, 90, 153, 154, 156, 205, 206, 210, 211, 213
Revenue Act of 1950, 205
rising-tide theory, 1, 36, 144
risk aversion, 38, 80, 174
robber barons, 48
Rockefeller, John D., 48
Rogers v. Hill, 48, 248
Rosen, Corey, 170, 252
Ross, Steven J., 49
run rates, 104, 198, 200
Russell Reynolds Associates, 20, 247
Ruth, Babe, 48

SAC Capital, 20
Sarbanes-Oxley Act, 20, 51, 57, 123, 124, 128, 249
scandals, corporate, 28, 44, 51, 57, 68, 70, 75, 126, 142, 189, 192
Schlumberger, 85
Schwarzman, Steven A., 20
Securities and Exchange Commission (SEC), 33, 34, 35, 36, 40, 49, 50, 52, 55, 59, 138, 149, 205, 208, 229, 249
disclosure rules of, 6, 49, 142, 157, 158
Securities and Exchange Commission (SEC) Rule 10b5–1, 58, 159, 160
severance plans, xiv, xv, 2, 5, 10, 53, 57, 63, 141, 142, 143, 145, 147, 150, 156, 158, 164, 193, 208, 210, 211, 212, 230, 232, 233, 236, 249
share holding requirements, 39, 105, 207
share retention requirements, 134, 139, 140, 207
shareholder approval, xv, 2, 56, 83, 150, 217, 219, 221, 225, 227, 228, 231, 232, 233
shareholder lawsuits, 48, 125
shareholder resolutions, 59
shareholders, xv, 1, 2, 3, 4, 5, 6, 9, 10, 17, 18, 20, 22, 23, 28, 29, 32, 33, 34, 35, 37, 48, 49, 50, 53, 54, 56, 57, 58, 59, 62, 63, 65, 66, 67, 68, 70, 79, 82, 84, 99, 104, 105, 106, 107, 108, 109, 110, 111, 112, 116, 118, 119, 122, 125, 127, 132, 136, 139, 142, 143, 145, 146, 147, 149, 152, 154, 155, 157, 158, 159, 162, 166, 170, 172, 174, 177, 179, 180, 181, 182, 184, 185, 187, 188, 189, 190, 191, 193, 194, 197, 202, 204, 205, 207, 208, 212, 213, 217, 219, 221, 225, 230, 231, 232, 233, 234, 238, 239, 240, 241
executive alignment with, 3
short-term incentives (STIs), 95
Silva, Paula, 136, 251
Singapore, 194, 196, 197
Snyder, Franklin, 32, 248
Spencer Stuart, 135
Spitzer, Elliot, 51, 52, 248
Sprint, 19
Staubus, Martin, 170, 252
stock appreciation rights (SARs), 54, 58, 194, 219, 220, 221, 222, 237
stock-based plans, broad employee, 5

stock holding requirements, 133
stock market, 3, 4, 16, 17, 19, 21, 32, 34, 43, 44, 48, 50, 52, 69, 70, 84, 99, 103, 157, 207
stock options, 71–86
decline of, 75–86
for directors, 127
fixed grant dates for, 156
nonexecutive employee, 179
perceived value of, 79–81, 86
stock ownership, executive, 5, 17, 23, 38, 39, 41, 61, 81, 122, 142, 148, 153, 155, 156, 158, 160, 162, 179, 193, 197, 206, 207, 208, 232, 238
agency costs and, 107–109
alternative vehicles for, 118–119
guidelines for, 114–117
holding requirements for, 115–117
MSPPs and, 118–121
superior returns driven by, 192
stock ownership guidelines, 114, 115, 133, 134, 139, 140, 207
stock purchase plans, 166, 176, 238
stock sales, 27, 118, 159, 236, 240
strike prices, 36
supplemental executive retirement plans (SERPs), xiv, xv, xvii, 5, 6, 23, 27, 36, 142, 148, 153, 193, 209, 212, 231
supplemental holding requirements, 116
Sweden, 93
Switzerland, 93

Taiwan, 196
takeovers, 63, 66, 126, 147, 234
talent shortage, executive, 19, 65
tally sheets, 53, 141, 142, 147
Target Corp., 20
Teachers Insurance and Annuity Association–College Retirement Equities Fund. *See* TIAA–CREF
Tech Data Corp., 85
tenure, 40, 41, 235, 238
Texas Instruments, 126
Thailand, 194, 196
Thain, John, 123
Thomas, Randall S., 30, 31, 65, 180, 184, 185, 247, 248, 249, 252
3M, 12, 19, 41, 134, 141
TIAA–CREF, 21, 141, 230
Time, 49, 155, 248

time-vested restricted stock plans, 91, 155
time-vested stock options, 61
timing issues, 38, 39, 55, 120, 159, 219
Tobin's Q, 112, 113
trading restrictions, 57
turnarounds, xv, 24, 41, 209
turnover, 2, 20, 37, 41, 136, 154, 156
Twain, Mark, 48
Tyco, 12, 19, 109, 142
Tyson, Don, 52
Tyson Foods, 52

U.S. Steel Corporation, 108, 135
U.S. Supreme Court, 48
underperforming companies, 41, 65, 136
underwater stock options, 38, 79, 173, 174, 218
unemployment, 3, 38, 65, 182, 183, 195
unions, 2, 9, 59, 205, 232, 233
United Brotherhood of Carpenters and Joiners of America, 59
United Kingdom, 180, 185–189, 191
United Technologies, 134
UPS, 178
upward bias, 41, 44

Vanguard, 58, 144, 232
venture capital firms, 64, 65, 146

vesting, 61, 62, 63, 78, 91, 95, 117, 118, 119, 120, 121, 155, 160, 161, 186, 187, 191, 208, 209, 211, 212, 213, 215, 216, 217, 218, 220, 222, 223, 224, 225, 226, 227, 228, 230, 233, 235, 238
Viacom, 20
volatility, 51, 78, 85, 105, 116, 172, 237

Wall Street Journal, 11, 48, 67, 70, 124, 142, 143, 185, 247, 248, 249, 251, 252
Wal-Mart, 233
Walt Disney Company, 52
Warner Lambert, 115
Washington Post, 59
Watson Wyatt, 10, 16, 17, 23, 60, 72, 76, 80, 83, 98, 110, 111, 124, 127, 132, 165, 166, 167, 169, 171, 186, 187, 193, 199, 200, 249, 250, 251
Webb, Dan, 52, 248
Weisbach, Michael S., 136, 251
Welch, Jack, 51, 52
Wipro, 20
World Economic Forum, 21, 247
WorldCom, 52, 109, 124, 126, 142

Yermack, David, 22

Zenner, Marc, 33, 248